THE POLITICS OF NATIONAL DEVELOPMENT

Chandler Publications in Political Science
Victor Jones, *Editor*

THE POLITICS OF NATIONAL DEVELOPMENT

Political Leadership in Transitional Societies

TAKETSUGU TSURUTANI
Washington State University

CHANDLER PUBLISHING COMPANY
An Intext Publisher
NEW YORK • LONDON

Copyright © 1973 by Intext, Inc.
All Rights Reserved
International Standard Book Number 0-8102-0465-7
Library of Congress Catalog Card No. 70-37749
Printed in the United States of America

To my parents

Contents

Introduction ix
Acknowledgments xiii

I. An Overview: Politics and Political Leadership — 1
The Politics of National Development — 5
The Resistance to National Development — 9
A Meaning of National Development — 17
Politics as Leadership Control — 21
The Difficulty of Inquiry — 22
The Meaning of Political Leadership — 24

II. National Development and Governmental Capability — 32
An Approach to Inquiry — 33
The Categories of Analysis — 37
The Three Components of Governmental Capability — 40
The Regulation of Behavior/The Extraction of Resources/ The Distribution of Resources
The Relationship among the Three Components — 70
The Routinization of Governmental Capability — 75

III. Political Leadership and Governmental Capability — 82
The Leadership Increment and Instability — 83
The Case of Argentina — 87
The Three Requirements of Political Leadership — 91
Commitment/Intelligence and Skill/Dominance
A Typology of Political Leadership — 96
The Problems of Measurement — 101
Anticipation and Manipulation of Change — 109

IV. The Strategy of Compensatory Mobilization — **115**
Curative versus Palliative Policies — 115
Charisma/Crisis/Scapegoat and Repression/Ideology and Myth/Selective Bribery/Traditional Symbols and Values
The Pluralistic Development of Affect — 131
The Need for Genuine Mutuality of Interest — 140

V. The Dangers of Compensatory Mobilization — **148**
The Inherence of Danger — 149
Charisma/Crisis/Scapegoat and Repression/Ideology and Myth/Selective Bribery/Traditional Symbols and Values
Short-Term Adequacy and Long-Term Inadequacy — 154
Compensatory Mobilization and National Development — 157
The Differential Impact of Developmental Policies — 160
On Rates and Stages of Development — 165

VI. Conclusion: Political Leadership, Tradition, and Modernity — **173**
Selected Bibliography — 181
Index — 189

Introduction

Numerous books have been written on the nature and process of modernization and development. To write another, then, would call for some justification. The justification for this book is twofold—substantive and methodological—and will be presented in the first two chapters.

This book essays a look, exploratory in design, into one significant, indeed crucial, dimension of the process of national development and modernization that awaits systematic inquiry: the role of political leadership.

Since the study of modernization and development began to add a new and dynamic dimension to comparative politics two decades ago, categories of concern that had traditionally fallen outside the purview of political science have come to occupy the center of attention. Indeed, the traditional juridical and institutional approaches seem well-nigh passé. We now talk of "political systems" instead of "constitutions." We examine "political cultures" instead of "laws and statutes." We speak of "inputs and outputs" rather than "obedience and authority." We argue about "integration and alienation" rather than "justice and injustice." There is a whole vocabulary of new terms as well as a whole storehouse of new tools designed for description, analysis, and explication; and whatever their quality may be, they are both steadily increasing in size and complexity. In the process of this dynamic, often fascinating development of comparative politics, however, one crucial factor of consideration has been consistently neglected or deliberately deemphasized. I refer to the role of political leadership as a conceptual and analytical category, as distinct from the structure and personnel composition of political leadership. (The latter has been subjected to numerous and extensive studies, and I shall comment on it later.) The student of comparative politics, in some important and not necessarily derogatory sense, has become a part-time sociologist-anthropologist-economist-psychologist. To be sure, there is nothing wrong about this trend as such, though there is much in it that calls for criticism. Furthermore, this is not simply a matter of vogue. No study of politics and political phenomena is really meaningful without critical consideration of what lies outside the so-called political system proper, that is, "the ecology of politics,"[1] which, in more senses than one, makes it tick and renders it dynamic. It is for this reason that political science, as a scholarly discipline, shares a large area of convergence with other social-science disciplines. At the same time, however, we must bear in mind that political science has its central focus and that political phenomena also have their common central component which is essentially and inescapably political. To forget this is to depoliticize politics and to denature the political universe.

Winston Churchill once observed that to govern is to choose. I have noted elsewhere that the proper business of politics consists in choosing from a number of actual *and* potential alternatives a policy or program of action to solve a given problem under a given set of circumstances.[2] The focal property of politics, then, consists in the role its leadership plays "in ordering and directing human behavior and in determining the character of events."[3] Political leadership, in my view, possesses the unique qualities of creativity, independence, and salience of which many contemporary political scientists, nurtured on a behaviorist diet, have all but deprived it. The role of political leadership in this sense clearly suggests manipulative capacity in the same sense as does the role of the artist. By manipulating elements of the political process and ingredients of the political universe, in much the same way that the artist manipulates his materials for esthetic endeavors, political leadership is capable of producing from a given situation an outcome which is not only not germane to or inherent in it but also fundamentally different from what would naturally or indiscreetly come of it. It is for this reason that "the great leaders have [the] ability to turn situational incompatibilities into assets. Situations can be shaped by the force of the great leaders to the same extent that the weak leaders can be shaped by the force of situation."[4] Hence, the choice as essence of governance that Churchill referred to is not necessarily nor usually a matter of *a priori* existence; it can and often should be created by political leadership. In an important sense, therefore, circumstances for action by political leadership are valuationally neutral and intrinsically plastic.

Such, then, is the central hypothesis of the present inquiry: that political leadership is the ultimate determinant of whether and how a nation succeeds in developing and modernizing itself. To elucidate the point of this hypothesis: The case of early Meiji Japan, for example, is generally regarded as a great success story in the annals of modern national development. Furthermore, it is regarded as unique just because Japan is a non-Western nation. At any rate, scholars, especially non-Japanese scholars, have tirelessly pointed out what they consider to have been the factors favorable to the development of Japan and have argued that these factors are woefully lacking in many contemporary developing nations. The "favorable" or positive factors imputed to Meiji Japan include, among others, ethnic homogeneity, the absence of religious and communal cleavages, a tradition of social and political discipline, the presence of a unifying symbol in the person of the emperor, geographical isolation or insulation from potentially hostile powers, the existence of certain technical and entrepreneurial bases for modern commerce and industry, the native diligence and ingenuity of the people, and an eclectic cultural heritage. Not only the presumed existence of these factors but also their efficacy are generally taken for granted by those who regard Meiji Japan's development as a unique success. This prevailing view of Japan's modern development elicits an impression that the success of that country was naturally to have been expected as a foregone conclusion. It is of more than passing interest, however, to note that from these same viewpoints, the prospects for the rapid development of Japan at the very time when she was about to undertake the task of modernization and development would most likely have been judged very poor in comparison to those of China, for example.[5]

Now, regardless of whether or not such an unfavorable forecast would really have been significant, there is no plausible reason to believe that Japan would have succeeded in modernization and development. Apart from the question of whether or not those putative favorable and positive factors that scholars find in hindsight in fact existed to the extent it is now assumed they did and/or the question of the extent to which they, if they in fact existed, were so crucial to the successful national development of Meiji Japan, we can still ask a very relevant question. We should ask the question especially since the study of modernization and development is a growing discipline, so that nothing that passes for knowledge should yet be taken for granted. The qestion is this: Was Japan's predicament within the context of her spatial and temporal circumstances really so kind to her smooth development in contrast to, say, Indonesia, Ghana, Bolivia, or Burma today? The question is valid unless we insist on imputing a constant value to each of those putative factors regardless of differences in time and circumstances. Moreover, one can argue that contemporary developing nations enjoy many positive factors, internal as well as external, which Japan certainly did not enjoy. For example, there are the "lessons" of other nations to study in order to maximize development and minimize disruption; an access to, if not possession of, highly developed scientific and organizational technology; modern communications technology and media; and modern methods of scientific and political control, to mention but a few. Now we can reasonably assume that there are many differences in the degree of difficulty of national development from one situation to another, from one nation to another. We can, however, just as reasonably assume that the task of national development is difficult in any case and that there are certain underlying fundamental principles for the job of overcoming the difficulty, namely, the task of national development, that are applicable in all cases. There is a sense in which we may say that nation-building is to political leadership what building is to the architect. Nation-building warrants skillful uses of materials; there are basic rules or principles as to how the materials are to be manipulated and combined to produce a desired outcome. Search for such principles for the conduct of political leadership, then, is an important part of the present inquiry.

NOTES

1. Alexander J. Groth, *Comparative Politics: A Distributive Approach* (New York: Macmillan, 1971), p. 1.

2. Taketsugu Tsurutani, "Machiavelli and the Problem of Political Development," *Review of Politics*, XXX (July 1968).

3. Sheldon Wolin, *Politics and Vision* (Boston: Little, Brown, 1961), p. 6. Another theorist compares governance with the steering of a ship. To govern, then, is to steer, to guide the behavior, present and future, of society. See Karl W. Deutsch, *The Nerves of Government* (New York: Free Press of Glencoe, 1963), Chap. 11.

4. Eugene E. Jennings, *An Anatomy of Leadership* (New York: Harper & Row, 1960), p. 15.

5. See William W. Lockwood, "Japan's Response to the West: The Contrast with China," *World Politics*, IX (July 1956), 38–41.

Acknowledgments

Were it not for the many debts I have incurred in the process of writing this book, it would display more shortcomings than it does. I owe much to my colleague Terrence Cook for reading the entire manuscript and offering several typewritten (single-spaced) pages of frequently caustic and unfailingly succinct criticism. I suspect he still thinks me incorrigible. Special thanks go to David L. Pflug, my graduate assistant, for his skillful help in collecting many of the empirical data and other research materials and for his quite unselfconscious yet apposite comments and observations. I am also grateful to Donald Baker, Jack Dowell, Jack Gabbert, Patrick Morgan, John Powell, Evan Rogers, Charles Sheldon, and Dennis Walker for reading portions of an earlier draft of the manuscript.

Initial thoughts on the strategy of compensatory mobilization (Chapter IV) were stimulated by a Faculty Research Grant I received while at the University of Maine, but their subsequent development and expansion into the present volume owe much to the atmosphere, colleagues, and students in the Department of Political Science at Washington State University.

Finally, to Joyce Lynd, who typed the two drafts of the manuscript, I offer my appreciation for her cheerful work and quiet competence.

I

An Overview: Politics and Political Leadership

The politics of national development is a very complex phenomenon. In order to understand it clearly, it is necessary first to be clear about the nature of politics, for the role of political leadership in the political process in general and the process of national development in particular hinges on the way we view politics itself.[1]

Politics, we may argue, is at once the condition, the process, and the result of the resolution of conflict. It is the *condition* because it provides the context, the universe, of conflict in society for the satisfaction of want in terms of the allocation of goods, services, and statuses, of which there is never an ample supply. The political universe is both logically and empirically predicated upon the ineradicability of conflict. Politics, at the same time, is also the *process* of the resolution of conflict. It is the process through which the allocation of limited supplies of goods, services, and statuses is authoritatively made or at least attempted and adjustments of various needs and claims in society temporarily achieved. Without this process, society would be (and often has been in the past) reduced to a Hobbesian state of nature. It is the process through which the resolution of conflict is attempted according to both written and unwritten rules to which at least a majority, hopefully, of participants in conflict adhere in order to avoid a state of war of every man against every other man. Politics as process succeeds or fails according as it can or cannot elicit a widespread adherence to those rules, which alone can maintain order in the political universe. In an important sense, therefore, politics is the process of debarbarizing the otherwise barbarous struggle among men and among groups of men competing for those scarce values. It must be stressed, however, that politics does not and cannot eliminate the struggle, Utopian and messianic ideologies notwithstanding. It is only the process through which this debarbarized struggle is constantly engaged in. For this reason, its efficacy is most precarious. It is in perpetual danger of reverting to barbarism as, in fact, it has for countless times throughout history. The ready availability of modern scientific and organizational techniques, moreover, can indeed render such reversion to barbarism appallingly methodical, as the case of Nazi bestiality clearly demonstrates. Finally, politics is also the *result* of the resolution of conflict in that, by resolving conflict, it provides the condition for new conflict arising out of the pattern of allocating values just made. Since the goods, services, and statuses which are coveted are always relatively scarce, the resolution of conflict means at best only partial and temporary adjustment. Some people are satisfied, some only partially satisfied, and others remain unsatisfied. The desires of the unsatisfied may intensify; the partially satisfied want complete satisfaction; even the satisfied will soon find new needs and higher levels of gratification. Hence, the resolution of conflict at one point in time constitutes the condition for conflict at another point in time. There is indeed something of a dialectic dynamic in the relationship among those three aspects of politics. And it is precisely for this reason that political scientists describe politics as the process of conflict "management" rather than "resolution."

Politics in the developing nations, however, requires a view that is capable of illuminating the special problems and considerations that, while not intrinsically disparate from the politics as viewed above, give a unique complexion to it. One such problem or consideration is the tension that pervades the politics of nations in the process of development and modernization. The fundamental cause of the tension is the wide gap between what is desired and what in fact is. Even in the last third of the twentieth century, poverty, both material and human, is by far the most pervasive feature of mankind. The predicament of man and society in its essence has not really changed much since antiquity, despite the veneer of progress and islands of affluence. And it has always been reflected in the interestingly uniform cast of mind of political thinkers from Plato onward. They have invariably built their theories and doctrines on the basis of this poverty of man and society, the nastiness of man's existential universe. Human mentality, as a generic category, has throughout history been unalterably affected by it, and has in turn affected it. Much of the world even in this age of technological revolution and mass political participation is still plagued by disease, malnutrition, hunger, premature death, violence of man against man, prejudice, cupidity, and ignorance. In more senses than one, the world has changed very little. There is, however, one crucial change that has taken place in modern times, a change that has seriously upset the traditional equilibrium in the unchanged man and society. While the human universe existed in a more or less secure balance between the poverty of its condition and the poverty of expectations, as before the Age of Enlightenment, the former mattered not very much. There was, in short, a catholic equilibrium between what was desired and what in fact was. This premodern phenomenon was further augmented by the universal religiosity. Religion taught man to accept poverty, that which had always been and always would be. So when man looked to his tomorrow and his children's future, he expected nothing more than what had been and was. This unquestioning acceptance was the foundation of both solace and bliss. Religion effectively anesthetized man in the condition of otherwise painful poverty. There was, therefore, little compelling problem of society being able to satisfy rising needs and demands of man. The authoritative allocation of values was a relatively easy and routine matter for the political system to dispose, at least as far as masses of people were concerned, for they were outside the political arena, outside the political universe; they were not participants in politics.

Thus, while the teachings of religion camouflaged and abetted the greed and avarice of the few (that is, of the participants in the political arena), such as kings, aristocrats, and bishops, they effectively forestalled the emergence of earthly expectations on the part of the masses. Expectations and aspirations that appeared during the universal preponderance of religiosity were themselves religious ones. There were undoubtedly occasional instances of social movements arising out of secular aspirations, but they were little more than "a series of episodes, punctuating the general story of humanity."[2] Wars and politics before the Renaissance by and large did not really involve the needs and expectations of ordinary multitudes; they were struggles among the few. Even Machiavelli, the forerunner of modern secular politics and prophet of the politics of change, apparently did not envision the revolution of rising expectations.

The demise of religion and its corollary, the rise of modern science, toward the end of the sixteenth century initially gave rise to the continuing, in fact accelerating, process of overshadowing the traditional meek expectation of a blissful afterlife with the urgent expectation of a better "here and now." Man's journey on earth, which had been considered transitory and insignificant before his final assignment to an ethereal destination, came to assume the magnitude of centrality because he had discovered not only that his universe, which had remained mysterious and unquestionable, was after all intelligible and changeable, but also that he had a native genius to extrapolate secular happiness and comfort from what had previously been a purely spiritual yearning, by manipulating the hitherto uncontrollable. Thus man began to seek on earth what had previously been realizable only in heaven. This new realization of man's own capabilities first generated the modern idea of natural right which was concerned primarily with the purely normative political dimension of man's life, for example, the relationship among citizens, the relationship between government and governed. This was the origin of modern democracy and mass society. It was soon discovered, however, that the mere enunciation of abstract principles of the political relationship between man and society could not produce either comfort or happiness. The political kingdom turned out to be a fragile facade behind which still lurked disease, deprivation, exploitation, and premature death. Humanization of the political relationship of man was not enough. As a result, demands for humanization of social and economic relationships emerged and spread with ever increasing velocity. Today, in a few fortunate nations, mostly in Northwestern Europe and North America and Japan, the basic foundations for such humanization have, it seems, been well established. The main problem in these few nations consists in how to build a more equitable, truly humane existential universe on those foundations. From the viewpoint of the world at large, however, the humanization of man's political, social, and economic relationships is, at best, only beginning. Rising expectations are rising demands for this humanization, and are manifested in the form of numerous ideologies, such as socialism, communism, nationalism, and their combinations and offshoots. This modern development is now at its zenith, with the effect of drastically altering man's outlook on his universe, on his own capacities, and on the role of politics.

Such was the historical origin of the politics of national development and modernization that first appeared in the West. In its intrinsic manifestation, the politics of development and modernization in contemporary developing nations is basically the same. It is, in an important sense, a secular quest for "the good life," to use a classical expression, the quest for an existential universe in which man may at long last live well and die well and which, therefore, is the logical opposite of the Hobbesian state of nature. What makes the secular quest for "the good life" in the latter half of the twentieth century different from its earlier counterpart in the West is the level of its urgency and intensity, both within political leadership and among the masses, which often defies any rational calculus as to the feasibility of progress and development. And it is this dimension of the contemporary politics of national development that creates an enormous range of technical complexities for those three aspects of politics discussed earlier. It is well at this point, therefore, to take a brief but careful glance at the nature and process of national development in today's world.

THE POLITICS OF NATIONAL DEVELOPMENT

Conflict, that perpetual human and social phenomenon, exists in every society. No society, however abundant and peaceful, is free from it. Else politics would wither away, as the Marxian purist would say, and the "administration of things" would come into being. Yet, no society can maintain itself, let alone develop itself further, in the absence of some means for the creation and maintenance of internal order. Conflict and order, therefore, imply each other. Otherwise, politics would be irrelevant.

The kind of conflict that plagues nations in the process of national development, however, is of a special type both in its content and in its magnitude. The major content of conflict in a developing nation today consists in the enormous, often apparently insurmountable disparity between the kind of society it is and the kind of society it struggles to become, between what it has to do to become such a new society and what it in fact is capable of doing in its attempt to achieve the goal. Corollary to this phenomenon of enormous disparity is the fact that political systems of developing nations are in the difficult process of modern institutionalization; hence they are lacking in adequate levels of adaptability to change, of flexibility to cope with volatile circumstances, and of ability to promote development. National development, therefore, is at once the goal and the process of attaining the goal. As goal, national development is the desired future state of affairs—a politically, socially, and economically integrated society with built-in capacities for continuous adaptation and growth, and regularized processes and methods for the resolution of conflict and the generation of change.

National development as goal, however, is not to be regarded as some teleological terminus. It is simply the type and level of material welfare and more or less viable close, mutually beneficial interdependence of all significant segments of society that have emerged in some of the highly industrialized, politically consensual nations. It is this type of society that the developing nations try to become. It is the type of society that, apart from being materially comfortable and dynamic in economic activities and productivity, has established the kinds of general rules and procedures that admit of orderly, continuous, evolutionary changes as well as legitimate claims and demands of various groups in society without compromising their own integrity and utility. It must be pointed out, however, that the level of "built-in-ness" is subject to debate. At least we have as yet no way of determining the extent to which the capacities for continuous and orderly change and growth in a given society may be adjudged "built-in."[3] There is, furthermore, no permanent guarantee that the political system of an advanced nation, such as that of the United States, will continue to be resilient and viable, as witness the current political and social turmoil in this country. It may, indeed, suffer decay rather than further development. But there is little to be gained by quibbling about some empirico-definitional problem that does not lend itself to satisfactory resolution. What is important about national development as goal, however one may choose to describe it, is that it is what those seeking development and modernization want to pursue.

As process, national development is a series of complex and novel changes—economic, social, and political—to be brought about by the application of modern industrial and organizational technologies and, more crucially, by the skills, imagination, and resolve of political leadership. The result, hopefully, is to institutionalize self-generative dynamics for further evolutionary change and self-adaptive capacity of politics and society, to create the desired future state of affairs. This process, in terms of the efforts and sacrifices required, is perhaps the most ambitious in man's whole history. The essential feature of national development as goal, as Huntington cogently argues, is stability. That of national development as process, however, is instability.

The content of conflict that grips the developing society differs from that with which politics in a developed society must deal in that it arises out of efforts to make drastic changes in the basic life style of the individual and of society. Furthermore, politics as the process of conflict resolution becomes disrupted because of the change in the context and nature of conflict. Politics in a traditional society, as Kautsky observes, is largely "a conflict for the spoils of office carried on either by aristocrats themselves or by cliques of men who, in their policies, always represent the aristocracy."[4] This pattern of conflict clearly delimits both the kind of conflict relevant to the political arena as well as the type of participants in conflict. The basic stability of a traditional society is a function of the divorce of the tiny political arena, the small number of political actors, and the parochial nature of conflict from the rest of society, from the great majority of the population. Here, participants in conflict share one view as to the direction and role of politics, namely, the protection and preservation of the existing society with all the elements of the status quo. Political struggle is not about policies concerning society but only about office. In contrast, politics in a transitional, or developing, society is "a contest among conflicting policies in which even the peasantry and old middle class may here and there participate, in which the aristocracy seeks to save what it can of its predominant social, economic, and political position, and in which each of the new classes attempts to fashion a new society and its political institutions in its own image."[5]

Now, conflict as the essence of politics is about divergent, often mutually exclusive political programs and socioeconomic policies to transform the existing society. And the fundamental cause in this change in the nature of politics—the emergence of modern politics—is, as was suggested earlier, the entry of the perennial issue of poverty into the political universe, in short, the politicization of poverty.[6] This contextual change in political conflict, moreover, produces an equivalent change in the nature of the "facts" that are relevant to politics, for the introduction of a new type of issue or conflict in the political arena necessarily entails the accordance of relevance to a varying range of phenomena (and nonphenomena) that have hitherto benumbed themselves in the societal limbo.[7] Power (or office), which is the immediate object of struggle in the political arena, is merely an indispensable means, rather than an end in itself, toward the ultimate end, which is the implementation of certain types of policies and the manipulation of relevant facts. The political arena thus rapidly expands; the complexion of the political universe undergoes an irreversible change; the categories of conflict increase; and new types of actors, more likely than not with rules of their own, or none at all, enter the arena.

This significant shift in the character and content of politics, which inevitably accompanies the process of national development, calls into question all tradition, custom, and the modus operandi according to which society has long existed. The level of governmental ability that has hitherto been adequate for the maintenance of stability and the resolution of conflict is now found to be insufficient for and incongruent with the requirements of change and the types of new conflict that constantly emerge from the now volatile circumstances. The continuity of fundamental human and social relationships is painfully disrupted. All these phenomena combine to create and aggravate acute instability in society. Flux and volatility become the all-pervasive features of individual and group behavior, political relationships, and social organization. The existing political institutions are inadequate, to begin with, and their shortcomings in turn are further compounded by increasing instability. Such circumstances as these are not conducive to the emergence of meaningful direction and coherent mobilization of resources for the task of national development.

The magnitude of conflict in the process of national development lies in the fact that the resolution of conflict and the effective undertaking of development require more or less total and explicit social and political control from above as well as mobilization of all significant segments of society under such control.[8] No longer can the process of development be left to follow its "natural course," as might have been the case with some of the already advanced nations in the nineteenth century. "The era of political spontaneity is behind us," argues Brzezinski. "Today, social engineering as a means of effecting social change characterizes all societies, and especially the emerging nations."[9] This revolutionary dimension of the general context of efforts warranted by the process of national development calls for the kind of relationship between government and governed as well as among various groups in society that, because of its penetration and intensity, inevitably generates a high degree of mutual incongruence and strain, thereby severely aggravating and compounding the conflict already there and rendering the task of politics that much more taxing and perilous. Again, the basic cause of conflict unique to the developing society is the critical imbalance between the goal desired and society's ability to fulfill the conditions for the attainment of that goal.

Despite the profusion of ideologies briefly mentioned above, they are actually less relevant to the problem of goal than to the issue of process. Most students of modernization and development seem to agree that different ideologies have pertinence to the question of choice of methods to achieve the goal, and some of them have developed typologies of political systems on the basis of manifest proclivities toward particular methods of modernization.[10] This general recognition of the relevance of ideologies to the question of methods, rather than to that of goal, seems quite appropriate. For, while ideologies surely affect the arrangement and relationship among various components of the desired future state of affairs (at least in the minds of their proponents), they are more immediately and operationally influential upon what government and society in fact do rather than upon what they desire to achieve. Within the context of the process of national development, an ideology is essentially and functionally an intervening variable rather than an independent variable, although many definitions of ideology may lead us to conclude that it is indeed an independent variable.[11] In fact, all ideologies today aim at the common good and welfare. Their common goal is a materially abundant and politically harmonious society whose benefits are to be shared by all rather than by the few. In this respect, there is little significant difference among the competing, apparently mutually hostile ideologies pursued by many nations. For this reason, the goal commonly sought-after connotes a certain specificity of purpose and concreteness of content, although the logical implications of the content are often neglected or misunderstood by the proponents of certain of these ideologies. In any case, there are two important aspects to this more or less universally shared goal that should be considered at this point. One is the process by which development as goal is projected and pursued, and the other is the general content of the process of development itself which creates difficulties of enormous proportions for society.

THE RESISTANCE TO NATIONAL DEVELOPMENT

It seems still relevant, even after a variety of studies have been made about innovative behavior and achieving society, to ask how national development as goal for society is being projected and promoted. For while the goal of national development is the attainment of a certain desired state of affairs for man and society, national development as process is a hazardous and costly enterprise that calls for painful sacrifices and unaccustomed efforts. In the words of Olson, "Though all of the members of the group therefore have a common interest in obtaining this collective benefit (namely, goal), they have no common interest in paying the cost of providing that collective good."[12] The important consideration, then, is not so much whether or not a given end is desired as whether or not efforts and sacrifices can be engendered, and how.

And the few lead the many. This is an historical fact of interminable durability. Pericles said that democracy is a government of the many and not of the few. However, he was speaking of Athenian democracy where, indeed, there was direct participation in decision making by the many (that is, by citizens). The essence of the democracy he spoke of was not so much the idea that all citizens must directly participate in decision making as it was the commitment that democratic government must rule in the interest of all rather than of the select few and that, for this purpose, every citizen must possess equal right to political participation. The first part of the commitment is shared by all good governments, whether democratic, monarchic, or aristocratic. The second, however, is the operational characteristic of democratic government. In no other form of government is every citizen granted the *equal* right to political participation, except, perhaps, anarchy where, of course, politics is impossible. The principle of equal right to participation that substantively obtains in democracy should not be confused with an idea that all in fact participate. Moreover, for necessary organizational reasons, only the few constitute the elite and political leadership in democracy as in any other form of government. Thus the few, inevitably, lead the many.[13] The only difference between democracy and other political systems consists in the fact that, in the former, the many have the right to compete freely for membership in the few and that the incumbent few have no tenure other than that which the many deign to grant them for varying lengths of time. In this sense as well as others, democracy can be defined as the minority rule and the majority rights.

Political leadership of society, whether democratic, aristocratic, or monarchic, at least initially derives its power and authority from the support or acquiescence of one or more dominant segments of society. Without such support, it would not be in power, at least not for long, even if it were despotic. Whether such support is qualitatively or quantitatively determined is another matter. In a hierarchical society, it is generally enough that the top political elite or the ruling group receive support from its immediately subordinate group or groups. In a pluralistic democratic society, on the other hand, the support its political leadership must enjoy should be wide and extensive, cutting across group lines. In a society where no meaningful political structure exists, the ruling group would need the support of those who possess the means of physical coercion, such as the military and the police. Thus, we can establish a variety of typologies of political systems and political leaderships on the basis of support bases and/or natures of support.

Whatever the kind of support it may have, political leadership exists for the promotion of a certain goal for society.[14] In the briefest manner of speaking, the goal of political leadership is one of the following: the maintenance of the status quo, the restoration of the status quo ante, the pursuit of a status nuovo. Every authoritative political decision is made for the purpose of one of these three goals.[15] That any of these goals, when it becomes the goal of society officially projected and pursued by political leadership, encounters opposition of one kind or another is inevitable, for any decision causes discontent and relative deprivation for some groups in society while it may at the same time benefit some other groups. So political leadership has to protect itself as well as the goal it seeks from the negative impact of its opposition, and this is the most essential task it must perform. Take, for example, Spain since the Civil War. Franco's regime, at least in the early stage of its existence, aimed at restoring the status quo ante. Once it had solidified its position by fulfilling this objective, the regime began to pursue a new goal, namely, the maintenance of the established status quo (the status quo ante restored). In recent years, there were indications that the main goal of Spanish society as pursued by the regime had become some sort of a status nuovo, seeking, albeit rather gingerly, to introduce certain basic reforms through a new constitution to the people, allowing some minimal range of freedom, and undertaking a more vigorous policy of economic modernization. Most recently, however, it seems we are witnessing another attempt to restore the status quo ante, with the regime reverting to the prereform practice of severely restricting freedoms and curtailing or suppressing demands for reform and political improvement. In each of these four (if that many) periods, the goal desired and pursued by the regime was supported by some segments of Spanish society, acquiesced in by some others, and opposed by still others. The regime's survival and the pursuit of its goal depended, therefore, not only upon the support and acquiescence it received but also upon its ability to vitalize such support as it received, to convert acquiescence into support, and to control, neutralize, or even convert opposition as well. The Spanish regime was successful to the extent that it could garner and increase support and neutralize or reduce opposition.

The goal, or societal goal, as a relevant category of analysis in this regard may be defined as one among many projected goals competing for adoption by society that becomes—with or without significant modification, either with public support or by official fiat—the goal of that society within a given temporal and spatial context. It is the goal to be promoted and pursued by political leadership in order to maintain or alter the status quo with regard to the allocation of goods, services, and statuses, and general societal well-being.

The major concern here is with the politics of development, hence the pursuit of a status nuovo as the societal goal. The politics of national development is preeminently the politics of a status nuovo. It is the type of politics that, because of the magnitude and the special content inherent in it, is the most difficult enterprise for political leadership to undertake. Indeed, one is reminded of Machiavelli's paradigmatic observation that "there is nothing more difficult to carry out nor more doubtful of success, nor more dangerous to handle, than to initiate a new order of things."[16] The vicissitudes of many a contemporary developing nation, as of many an unstable state in Renaissance Italy, have vindicated Machiavelli's misgivings. The special qualities of national development as a drastic status nuovo to be pursued, hence also as a process, engender intense opposition to political leadership and promote sociopolitical instability. As mentioned earlier, national development means a certain desired future state of affairs, namely, a politically, socially, and economically integrated society with built-in capabilities for continuous and orderly adaptation and growth. As such, it demands that certain requisite conditions be fulfilled. In other words, national development is also the process of meeting these prerequisites for the realization of the goal as national development. As process, therefore, national development is the transition from society as it is to society as it would like to become. Since the existing capacity of society is largely the residue of past experiences, tradition and customs, it is adequate, if at all, only for the task of coping with the known and customary problems in that society as it has been. National development as process, however, warrants the acquisition of a higher, different level of capacity for society so as to bring about changes of various degrees of intensity and magnitude in fundamental social, interpersonal, economic, and political relationships as well as in the channeling of human and material resources into those activities that have hitherto been altogether outside the functional purview and capacity of society.[17]

Perhaps this problem of the acquisition of a higher and newer level of societal capacity called for by national development as process may be divided into two areas in which opposition and resistance to political leadership and its efforts for development emerge. One is the area of the problem of perception, where certain categories of people in society, especially those who have been the beneficiaries of society, now feel deprived of traditional sources of material and psychic gratification and where even the multitudes feel increasingly severed from the comfortable psychological habitat which surrounded them with the traditional symbols of community and security. In short, national development as process inevitably gives rise to psychological dislocation and a crisis of identity. The other is the area of material allocation. National development as process demands not only the diversion of material resources from the traditional channels of allocation and patterns of consumption to new ones which would generate progress but, for this very reason, cause deprivation, either in an absolute or relatice sense, on the part of significant segments of society.[18]

The imperatives inherent in the process of national development and the policies political leadership formulates for their satisfaction according to its perception of them engender resistance and opposition to national development as the process of achieving national development as the goal. People "may agree in support of political objects in the abstract but differ markedly in what they are willing to give up in the behavioral economy to see their ends achieved."[19] There is, therefore, a critical lack of meaningful and positive support for national development as process and, simultaneously, powerful resistance against it, both deliberate and subconscious. Lack of support and presence of resistance (necessarily of politically significant groups), while conceptually separable, are analytically closely related, for one suggests the other. Resistance, at least the deliberate type, may be identified, for example, as demand or the kind of demand whose satisfaction is detrimental to the intention of political leadership (or the regime broadly) and/or destructive of the goal or policy it pursues. That a group of people opposes or resists a given policy means that it demands its repudiation and/or promotion of an alternative policy. In this sense, lack of support (or withdrawal of support) and demand are functionally interchangeable. In the process of national development, they have the effect of seriously straining the ability of political leadership and circumscribing its area of maneuver and critically burdening the institutional resources of the government. Both demand and support functions in this regard are relevant to the problem of the allocation of values, material and symbolic; and the crucial importance of these categories of consideration in relation to national development as process consists in the fact that the "means for the attainment of the goal always signify sacrifices of resources that could otherwise be consumed for immediate or short-run psychic and appetitive gratifications."[20] For this reason, it is difficult for national development, even under the best possible circumstances, to proceed smoothly. Its pace of progress is more likely than not to fluctuate to varying extents of seriousness. The pace could just as easily be reversed. Progress can never be automatic; nor can it be inherent.

The content of national development as process is vast in scope and far-reaching in its effects. We cannot enumerate here in detail all the components and ingredients of the process, but it is nevertheless necessary and useful, in addition to the discussion above, to take a brief look at a few other general features of the process in order to understand some of the more critical problems involved in it.

Perhaps three of the most important features (or requirements) of national development as process are change, the integration of change, and the ability to control and direct change. National development means change in a variety of dimensions of society: political, social, economic relationships, hence political, social, and economic institutions and activities, and patterns of allocating values. Thus national development also calls for change in the realm of sociocultural values and patterns of human and institutional behavior. Sociocultural values determine ideas about the nature of politics, the nature and capacity of man, the role of the individual, the purpose of society, and the types of relationships that should obtain among men, among groups of men, and among various roles they are to play in society. Modernity as an element of national development requires an idea of politics as vehicle for human and social progress and welfare rather than as an instrument for perpetuating the existing conditions; an idea that man is the creator as well as the actor of his own drama, struggling to maximize his potentialities; an idea that each individual has the right to exert influence upon decisions affecting his condition; an idea that society is a cooperative, rather than fragmented, enterprise serving the welfare of man; and an idea that each social and political role must be filled and performed not for the selfish benefit of its incumbent but primarily for the benefit of those whose interests it is created to serve. Change in these basic ideas or perceptions is brought about in various ways, of which two are exposure to information (such as travel abroad, movies, and other mass communications and information media through which new ideas and visions are transmitted unwittingly or deliberately, and personal contact of one kind or another) and manifest political socialization (through which political leadership can attempt to inculcate those ideas and attitudes in citizenry that help promote national development both as goal and process).

Change in sociocultural values manifests itself in patterns of human and institutional behavior. Most observably, it is expressed in new patterns of recruitment for various jobs and roles in society, social and occupational mobility, and the allocation of values both authoritative and private. For example, ascription gradually gives way to rational and universalistic criteria as the basis for recruitment. Social and occupational mobility increases as talent and achievement become the criteria for measuring the worth and utility of the individual. Rewards are allocated more and more on the basis of secular achievement rather than of hereditary status or religio-moral principles.

Changes in sociocultural values and in patterns of behavior are mutually supportive and generative because, while change in the first generates change in the second, change in the latter reinforces and consolidates the former. The problem, however, is that value change and corresponding behavior change do not occur simultaneously or evenly throughout society. Some segments of society feel critically deprived of material benefits and their accustomed position of influence as a result of a new pattern of allocation of values or recruitment. Thus there is always resistance, overt or covert, against new ways of doing (behavior) and new modes of thinkging (values). If the forces opposed to new ways and new modes are strong, then those changes in value and behavior may eventually be suppressed or eradicated, as in a resurgence and triumph of reactionaries, for example. If change in values and patterns of behavior is to persist, then there must be some means by which it may be effectively integrated and absorbed in society and in the process of national development. This condition means that, on one hand, something must be done to ward off attack and opposition against the emergent change in value and behavior and, on the other, some organizational device must be provided to consolidate and reward the change. Certain existing institutions, political as well as economic, may prove to be detrimental or resistant to these needs, in which case they may have to be reorganized, restructured, or even abolished. Likewise, some new institutions may have to be established for the same reason; two such institutions that readily come up to mind are a modern civil service and a conscript army. But unless proper caution is employed, a presumably modern civil service and an army may easily succumb to pressures of old parochial values and patterns of behavior.

There is another consideration about change which is vital in the process of national development in order to increase the ability of government and the capability of society to absorb and integrate change, hence to promote progress on the path of national development. This element is the need to encourage the continuous generation of appropriate types of change and to direct and control the course, content, and rate of change in the realm of sociocultural values and patterns of human and institutional behavior, and to prevent the kind of change that will undermine the process of national development. All too frequently, change in value and behavior emerges randomly and rampantly, which the process of development at a particular stage can neither tolerate nor absorb. There is the crucial need to control and direct all changes so as to render them positively contributive to national development. In short, the forward movement in the process of national development requires that change be steered and regulated in such a way as to prevent it from undermining the ability of government and society.

An instance of change in sociocultural values and subsequent change in human and/or institutional behavior, for example, may give rise to the kind of demand that the existing level of the ability of government/society is unable to satisfy without jeopardizing its integrity and viability. The so-called revolution of rising expectations is the most critical and pervasive example of such change which has seriously undermined and eroded both the existing ability of government and its potential growth and viability in many a new nation. There are also instances of change which have the effect of either undermining the viability of change that has already occurred or seriously inhibiting the emergence of further needed change. Moreover, since change in value and behavior necessarily leads to change in the kind and volume of demands, it also necessarily signifies change in the extent and content of support for government and political leadership. In more senses than one, demand and support are two sides of one same coin. Certain types of change have the effect of increasing support; others have the opposite effect. It is for these reasons that change should be carefully engineered, steered, and controlled if national development as process is to proceed without serious and destructive obstacles of its own making.

There is one unique and critical danger in the process of contemporary national development as discussed above. Ours is an age in which exposure to knowledge and visions of modernity and its material lure is an extremely rapid and widespread phenomenon in those very nations that are undergoing national development as process. Movies, transistor radios, and other elatively inexpensive methods of mass communication have all conspired to create a highly tense situation in those nations in which the gap between what is desired and what is in fact available is excruciatingly wide and, more often than not, widening. Change in value and subsequently in behavior induced by such exposure to unattainable lure and by awareness of the gap is almost invariably dangerous to the task of national development because it far exceeds in kind and volume the existing capacity of society and ability of government to absorb and integrate it. In the meantime, the rate of increase in the capacity of society and government to absorb and integrate change is far slower than the rate of change taking place.[21] Demand that is the ultimate manifestation of change in values is far beyond the ability of government or society to satisfy.[22] There is, therefore, a critical and fundamental disequilibrium between what is demanded and what can be delivered, between what should be done and what is in fact done. Such disequilibrium seriously hampers, if not completely halts, the process of national development. Moreover, it is frequently the case that the political system itself still lacks sufficient capability to regulate, control, and manage existing as well as growing conflict arising from various groups in society as the result of disruptive clashes between change-inducing forces and change-resisting forces. Thus, not only is there the widening gap between the rising expectations of people and the ability of government to meet them, but there is this second significant, equally explosive, and growing imbalance between the putative ability to control the rate of change and the actual rate of change. It is, therefore, not unreasonable to argue that there is an inverse relationship between the extent of these disequilibria on one hand and the degree of political stability and rate of development on the other.

Added to the problem of these critical disequilibria is the sense of urgency that characterizes the majority of today's developing nations (or, more properly, their political leaderships). They are intent upon accomplishing in a decade or a few decades what it took most of the advanced nations nearly two centuries (strictly speaking, four centuries) to accomplish.[23] This impatience often results in these leaderships actually forcing the kind of change in society which they are really unable to accommodate or absorb and which, in the long run, may well retard development and progress. Either immediately or ultimately, it will further compound the disequilibria that already exist in society.

The basic predicament of politics in the developing areas is thus enormously compounded and complicated. It is only in a few regions of the globe that such conditions as may facilitate the attainment of the goal of national development seem to obtain. Elsewhere, the disparity between the goal sought and the actual conditions obtaining is devastatingly vast. The authoritative allocation of values, as the essential function of the political system, therefore, is extremely difficult to make because of the extraordinary disequilibria that exist in society. Conflict to be resolved, therefore, is proportionately vast and deep. There is another dimension to the basic task of politics in this regard, namely, the need to reduce and bring under control these critical disequilibria and at the same time to promote the smoothest and fastest possible pace of progress toward the goal of national development.

A MEANING OF NATIONAL DEVELOPMENT

So far we have talked about some of the problems and issues that seem more critical in the process of national development and modernization, without really focusing on any single issue that might be regarded as the most crucial or as the controlling factor. In terms of a more familiar and popular approach in comparative analysis, national development or modernization means, after everything else has been said about it, a continuous and sustained increase in the capability of the political system to deal effectively with existing and emergent needs and demands of society, to resolve attendant conflict both horizontal and vertical, and to adapt itself to continuous change both internal and external to itself. In short, a good political system is one that governs well, and a bad political system is one that cannot. A successful political system, whatever its structural form may be, is one that can maintain a reasonable balance between its competence and its environment. As its environment constantly changes, especially in the process of national development, in terms of the volume and kind of inputs, the system must be able to increase the level of its competence accordingly in dealing with them. The failure of many a developing nation to make appreciable rates of progress in national development consists, one may argue from this particular viewpoint, in the failure of its political system to adapt itself to the changing circumstances of its environment by increasing its competence proportionately.

Such, at any rate, seems to be the argument most frequently made and accepted quite widely among students of comparative politics.[24] It is suggested here that the argument is substantively inadequate and quite misleading for two reasons. One reason is that the self-adaptive capacity of the political system or government should be and is predicated upon a certain minimal degree of institutionalization of the political system, for adaptability of any system implies certain continuity and consistence. If the political system of a developing nation is already adaptable, presumably national development will cease to be such a critical and perilous proposition, for it has already become sufficiently institutionalized. Under circumstances that are rapidly changing, the institutionalization of a political system is impossible unless it is adaptable. Adaptability, in short, signifies institutionalization, and vice versa. Political underdevelopment means lack of adaptability (in a stable traditional government) or adaptability *and* institutionalization (in the government of a developing nation). In posttraditional society, adaptability and institutionalization *combined* signify political development. To say that a given political system is self-adaptive or not, therefore, is to say little about the process of development and modernization. The really important concern in the study of developing nations is how a political system (or government) can be institutionalized (that is, how political development may be promoted and achieved), for the idea of institutionalization subsumes the notions of adaptability, flexibility, viability, and increasing competence for governance. And this issue leads to the second reason for questioning the adequacy of the generally accepted argument about the problem of national development.

Since no political system or government in posttraditional society is or can be *ipso facto* institutionalized (hence adaptable), namely, institutionalization is something to be engineered, and not given, its institutionalization (and what is subsumed under it) is to be realized through deliberate and discreet efforts of something other than the political system or government itself. It is political leadership, and nothing else, that can institutionalize the political system or government. The process of national development in a most vital sense is the process of political leadership's attempt to institutionalize the particular political system it chooses for the progress and development of its society. It is the process of political leadership's efforts to render the political system accepted, legitimate, adaptive, flexible, and able to govern, and to adjust these qualities as occasions require. This, indeed, is the crux of the task of national development. And it is primarily this dimension of the process of development and modernization that is the subject of the present inquiry.

The crucial importance of the role of political leadership in the process of national development may be observed in yet another way. A cursory general review of the recent history of modernization and development clearly suggests that there is really much more to the process of national development than economic, geographical, sociological, and psychological considerations. Relative rates of development of any number of nations cannot thoroughly be explained solely in terms of considerations of objectively ascertainable and hopefully quantifiable variables, [25] such as literacy rate, per-capita income, rate of industrialization, pattern of growth in communication and dissemination of information, process of socialization and elite recruitment, and extent of functional specificity. Nor can they be adequately assessed in terms of political culture, value systems, absence or presence of consensus, and an "identitive" relationship between government and governed. It is really not too difficult to see that some nations have achieved remarkably high degrees of development even though objectively ascertainable conditions for such development were often lacking. At the same time, there are nations that have failed to make any appreciable headway in spite of the fact that they are endowed with a variety of resources and conditions that presumably should enable them to develop much more rapidly. This sort of discrepancy in patterns of development and modernization, however, tends to be explained away by more of the same approach, namely, finding presumably more complex and subtle factors which belong to those same categories of consideration that have failed to achieve an adequate level of explication. The approach to the study of modernization and development that relies upon those categories of consideration tends to lead one to conclude that national development is to be expected if what are regarded as necessary, usually objectively ascertainable conditions for development obtain.

The basic untenability of such conclusions consists in the fact that the mere presence of those positive conditions, or preconditions, for development does not obviate the continued and persistent existence of resistance in society; otherwise, development would already have been undertaken. Nor does it mean—and this is important—that these positive conditions automatically and indiscreetly generate and direct national development. If we are to exclude any considerations but those of economic, social, organizational, and other relatively objectively ascertainable factors for national development, there would be only one final explanation for it: those positive factors, representing forces of modernization, naturally and inevitably overcome and eradicate resistance to the extent that resistance ceases to be a functional obstacle for modernity. It is patently doubtful, however, that this sort of presumed historical progression has ever been the case even in those nations of what Horowitz calls "the First World."[26] There is, in the process of national development, the inevitable clash between the forces of modernity and those of tradition, between those factors that promote development and those that resist it. The mere presence of a favorable factor does not necessarily—in fact, seldom does—mean that it is more potent than its functional opposite in society. Under the circumstances, if national development is to take place, the inevitable conflict between the two opposing forces or sets of forces must be either eliminated or reduced to the point where progress may become continuous and sustained. It is not to be expected, however, that any meaningful direction or creative solution will emerge out of the natural and indiscreet interaction between the hostile opposing forces. Some approaches to the study of development and modernization seem to be based on the assumption that successful nations are successful because they have fewer obstacles or, what amounts to the same thing, more favorable conditions for development. Apart from smacking of the tautological, the assumption fails to take into account the crucial fact that national development warrants engineering, direction, and discreet types of resource mobilization. It is indeed necessary for us to remember that "[c]hoice and policy are the stuff of political history and political science."[27] The increasing and, in more ways than one, significant convergence of political science with other social-science disciplines[28] has apparently led us inadvertently to commit the kind of contextual error that Weldon once pointed out: "You cannot discover the rules of whist by citing those of bridge."[29]

POLITICS AS LEADERSHIP CONTROL

From the discussion thus far of the process and problems of development and modernization, we can perhaps draw a view of politics which is not intrinsically different from the view discussed earlier, but which perhaps better elucidates some of those crucial problems unique to the politics of national development. Functionally speaking, politics may be viewed as the process of establishing, exercising, and maintaining control over whatever political leadership wishes to and is able to control. A so-called political system or government, then, is an analytically ascertainable structure of the process through which such control may be exerted by political leadership, one of whose chief characteristics is the possession of the ultimate means of sanction against defiance of such control.[30] What is under the control of political leadership (or government or regime, to use a more common and perhaps more comprehensive term) varies, on the surface and in particulars, from society to society and from time to time. Apart from certain essential aspects of society that are more or less universally regarded as necessary and legitimate objects of control—such as national defense, internal order, the enforcement and modification of existing laws and regulations, and the adjudication of disputes arising out of differing interpretations of those laws and regulations—the extent of control exerted or attempted by political leadership over society differs according to the needs perceived by that leadership and the levels of capacity to control possessed by leadership.[31]

A totalitarian political leadership does not intrinsically differ from a democratic political leadership in this regard. The former perceives the need of pervasive control over society, its economic and private spheres included, and, for this purpose, attempts to acquire the level of control capacity it requires. Whether it in fact succeeds in acquiring and maintaining the necessary level of control capacity is another matter. A democratic, laissez-faire political leadership, on the other hand, generally remains limited in its power and control capacity, and tolerates pluralism in society and dispersal of power, not because it is intrinsically different from its totalitarian counterpart, but because it perceives no overriding need for expanding its control over society except in cases of national emergency, such as war. In both cases, the fundamental nature of control as the central feature of politics is the same. Only application and use are variable. Because the resolution of conflict is never conclusive, but merely a temporary adjustment preparatory to another round of conflict, so is control that political leadership exercises never complete. What is termed the authoritative allocation of values is a continuous process of attempted control, throughout which the extent of control fluctuates and at no point of which control is complete.

The politics of national development, then, is the process of political leadership's attempt to establish, exercise, and maintain its control over those crucial aspects and tasks of society that warrant manipulation, mobilization, and direction. The institutionalization of political institutions and processes is the fruit of successful establishment, exercise, and maintenance of such control. In a sense, the process of national development is the process of political leadership trying to institutionalize the level of control capacity required for the long-run stabilization of society. Whether or not a developing nation can manage to progress, instead of stagnating or regressing, depends upon whether or not its political leadership can manage, first, to acquire sufficient control necessary to impose the minimal level of stability and order without which no coherent, long-range program of socioeconomic development can be implemented and, second, to engineer the type of political institutions and social and economic reorganization that will render stability and order lasting and provide the dynamics for continuous forward growth of society. There is, therefore, a sense in which we may say that political leadership of a developing nation should combine the qualities of what de Jouvenel calls *dux* and *rex*.[32] Fundamental to this view of politics in general and the politics of national development in particular, then, is a notion of the manipulative capability of political leadership, hence, in an important sense, the autonomy of the role of political leadership. What Matossian calls "the manipulation of the disagreeable Present" is the essence of the task of the politics of national development.[33]

THE DIFFICULTY OF INQUIRY

Viewed in this manner, politics as process of control (hence manipulation) contains a number of factors that are highly elusive and do not lend themselves to ready description and analysis. This presents serious conceptual and methodological problems to anyone who tries to study the process of politics, especially the politics of developing nations. And this fact is eloquently corroborated by the singular paucity of studies of the manipulative dimension of political leadership in the now rather large body of literature on political elites.[34]

Since the publication in 1952 of *The Comparative Study of Elites*,[35] a large number of studies have appeared on the elites and political leaderships of a variety of nations.[36] The dominant focus among them, with a few exceptions, however, has been the structure and recruitment of political elites, that is, such aspects of political leadership as socio-economic-cultural backgrounds, patterns of elite recruitment, intraelite relationships, and relationships between elites and masses.[37] These studies are certainly valuable in describing patterns and rates of recruitment and mobility and their relationships to societies and cultures. They are also admirable in their common adherence to the canons of empiricism. They are, however, quite narrow in scope because they operate within a severely circumscribed, analytically "safe" frame of reference. There is evidenced a general reluctance to engage in efforts, however dangerous, to deal explicitly with political and strategic dimensions (that is, the role, as distinct from the structure) of political leadership, though speculative statements and propositions concerning these dimensions are often inconspicuously tagged onto quantitative and empirical findings. This failing may be due to the predominant influence of the current behaviorist orientation in political science. "If you can't count it," as the saying might go, "it doesn't count."[38] Other studies of political leadership are concerned with such aspects of the political elite as decision-making processes and the attitudes and styles of political leadership.[39] Unfortunately, however, they are no more generative of clear understanding of the crucial role of political leadership in politics, and especially in the politics of national development, than the studies of structure and recruitment patterns. While these types of elite studies have been of considerable significance in increasing knowledge about, and often generating interesting insight into, a variety of political elites in different societies, they may already have reached the peak of their utility and value in generating any fundamental kind of knowledge in the field of comparative politics. In other words, we already know (and this, to a large measure, thanks to those studies) who are members of a given political elite, where they come from as well, perhaps, as what they think, how they view their roles and society, and how they interact among themselves and with various groups in society. What we do not know enough about, concerning political leadership as a category of analysis, is what it in fact does as well as what it should do in relation to the vital problems it needs to cope with and the crucial issues it must attempt to resolve. The dominant approaches to the study of elites mentioned above are generally incapable of providing this needed knowledge, for they are underlain with a traditional, largely unsupportable assumption of some kind of positive correlation between elite structure/recruitment and ideology/policy.[40]

What the present volume attempts, then, is a step, albeit hesitant and uncertain, in the direction of inquiry into this political-strategic (that is, manipulative) dimension of political leadership, especially in the politics of national development. There is no attempt to count what we "can't count." However, it is suggested that what we can't count does count and that how it counts can be demonstrated without counting. Furthermore, the basic problem at this point is not yet one of definitive and comprehensive description and analysis (even if such were feasible), but rather of indicating a direction of inquiry, a particular viewpoint which may be useful, a particular way of approach, which may help clarify certain crucial kinds of relationship that are inherent in politics in general and politics in the developing context in particular. The role of political leadership, especially in the dimension of the role that we are concerned about, is complex indeed. It is complex in terms of the number of relevant factors and variables germane to it. It is complex also in the sense that most, if not all, of those relevant factors and variables do not lend themselves to ready quantification or to facile analysis. Yet it may still be possible to extract certain key elements of leadership behavior and role that are most directly and immediately pertinent to its central task and construct them into an intelligible conceptual whole which, while never able nor meant to reproduce or replicate as an intellectual construct the whole of leadership behavior and role, nevertheless is capable of eliciting a useful, though highly heuristic, understanding of certain basic principles underlying the role of political leadership. In other words, such an attempt may produce a certain coherent disciplined point of view through which the object of inquiry becomes intelligible and its pattern clear, instead of remaining amorphous, confusing, and obscure.[41]

THE MEANING OF POLITICAL LEADERSHIP

The broad overview thus far attempted of certain of the problems of national development, albeit based on rather loose generalities and perhaps an oversimplified and more or less impressionistic review, suggests, nevertheless, that the role of political leadership (in its political-strategic, hence manipulative, dimensions) is indeed the most crucial factor to be ascertained in the process of national development. An important, and as far as this effort is concerned, crucial idea emerges from it: that political leadership is the arbiter of, rather than one participant or factor among many in, the process of national development. This notion is in direct contradiction to the view of political leadership held by contemporary students of politics, which is perhaps best exemplified by Simon that political leadership is like "a bus driver whose passengers will leave him unless he takes them in the direction in which they wish to go. They leave him only minor discretion as to the road to be followed."[42] The relationship of political leadership to the process of national development is completely different from that of the bus driver to his passengers. The passengers know not only their destination but also the general route through which the bus may travel (usually the shortest possible route). They also most likely know how the bus should be driven as well as traffic rules and regulations. Masses of people in a developing nation, on the other hand, have only the vaguest idea as to their destination, let alone how and on what kind of road to travel in order to reach that destination. Nor do they know how the vehicle of national development and modernization should be driven. Simon's analogy, therefore, is not only contextually inappropriate but substantively irrelevant. Ours, indeed, is a concept of the autonomy of political leadership, even within the context of the idea of "political system." In the first place, the political system can be institutionalized only by political leadership (conversely, a well-institutionalized political system may be easily undermined and eventually destroyed by political leadership). Even when it is apparently institutionalized and stable, it does not and cannot operate, let alone adapt itself to change, by itself, for it is not a perpetual-motion machine. Whatever its structural complexity and functional sophistication may be, the political system, after all, is an institution, or a set of institutions, manned and operated by human beings, individuals. In short, it is only as good as those who run it. The competence of a political system, in the end, is the competence of its incumbents. Its adaptability is the adaptability of those who manage and direct it. It is thus that the role of political leadership is decisive in the process of national development.

It is always a hazardous business to try to define concepts and terms. There is danger of attack, on whatever is defined, on a variety of grounds such as logical, empirical, and semantic. While foolproof definitions are impossible of attainment, however, it is still necessary that the attempt be made to define what is meant by political leadership at least in such a way as to render it appropriate to the context of the argument that follows in the subsequent chapters of the present volume. Thus, by political leadership, is meant, in each nation, the body of topmost decision-makers whose legal and/or actual responsibility it is to make final authoritative decisions on each of the issues and problems it is concerned about. In this sense, political leadership, as concept and category of analysis, is constant, while its actual membership or personnel composition is variable. The latter varies from society to society, depending upon such factors as historical tradition, past political experience, foreign influence, ideological predilection of society, or simple happenstance. For example, in one nation, political leadership may consist of its actual head of government, for example, the prime minister, and his cabinet (as in Great Britain) while, in another, legal incumbents of the topmost political roles are in fact agents of the real wielders of power who choose to remain behind the scenes (as in the first few years of Meiji Japan). In a Communist nation, political leadership is most likely found in the powerful chairman of the council of ministers and/or the first secretary of the party supported by the presidium (for example, Brezhnev and Kosygin) while, in a multiparty parliamentary system, it can consist of a coalition of leaders of several parties (for example, Italy or Malaysia until recently). In a more traditional society, political leadership may be said to reside in the monarch and his close counselors (for example, Saudi Arabia). In a dictatorship, it rests with the dictator and his cronies (many Latin American examples). Political leadership may be collective, as in the case of a military junta or a revolutionary command (for example, Egypt 1952–1954), though its collective feature may not last very long, in which case political leadership will come to rest elsewhere. In terms of structure and personnel composition, therefore, we can think of many kinds of typologies of political leadership, but specific structure is not very important here. Whatever structural form it may take, political leadership is, in an important sense, comparable to the rational faculty of an organic entity. Political leadership may be viewed as the directing center, so to speak, of all actions and decisions pertaining to the political universe. It is the brain of the political system. It mediates between the organic needs of the system and the forces of its environment; it determines how the functions of the various constituent parts will be coordinated; it arbitrates as to how government itself ought to behave under a variety of circumstances; and it attempts to regulate the relationship between government and governed. It is thus that political leadership orders society, directs individual and group behavior, to determine and control events. Political leadership is part of the so-called political system; at the same time it is independent of it—hence its autonomy in the political universe and in the political process. Herein lies the unique role of political leadership in the process of national development.

Another important aspect of this unique autonomous quality of political leadership may be seen from a certain normative viewpoint. Participants in the political process, such as groups, the bureaucracy, the military, and other politically active and articulate segments of society, however they may be categorized, are, by their very nature, concerned about the protection and promotion of their respective interests as they perceive them. Their activities in the political arena are partial and particular. They are, in fact, the sources of conflict which in turn calls for constant resolution and the authoritative allocation of values. They are, in this sense, also the materials which political leadership attempts to mold into the coherent, albeit imperfect and temporary, whole it desires to generate. In contrast, the interest that political leadership ought to serve and usually does try to serve, even though frequently in a manner that eventually proves self-defeating or unwise, is general. It is general in nature because it is ultimately the interest, not of this group or that, nor of this coalition of interests or that, but of the corporate entity called "the nation." It transcends all particular and partial interests that are intrinsically impermanent. This, indeed, is the most fundamental difference between political leadership and other participants in the political process. This also, is the basis for the distinction between governing and being governed, between authority and obedience. The first and most fundamental requirement of legitimacy, then, is political leadership's commitment to the promotion of this general interest.

The political universe is the context of actions of political leadership; the so-called political system is the major, yet manipulable instrument that broadly structures and defines the behavior of political leadership; and politics is the method by which political leadership performs its role. It is thus that political leadership determines goals, selects methods, and gives direction. Society develops or fails to develop according to the extent to which its political leadership is intelligent, creative, skillful, and committed. Without this requisite function of political leadership, there is no progress, no direction, no development.

NOTES

1. For many conceptually different ways in which politics can be viewed and studied, see, for example, Samuel P. Huntington, "The Change to Change: Modernization, Development, and Politics," *Comparative Politics*, III (April 1971), 306.
2. E. J. Hobsbawm, *Primitive Rebels* (New York: Norton, 1959), p. 1.
3. Samuel P. Huntington, in his *Political Order in Changing Societies* (New Haven: Yale University Press, 1969), presents a tightly reasoned argument concerning the requirements for "built-in-ness" (or "institutionalization," to use his word), but application of his concept to empirical analysis will be altogether different matter. See his Chap. 1.
4. John H. Kautsky (ed.), *Political Change in Underdeveloped Countries* (New York and London: Wiley, 1962), p. 24.
5. *Ibid*.
6. For the predominance of poverty as a distinguishing feature of modern politics, see also Hannah Arendt, *On Revolution* (New York: Viking, 1965), p. 54.
7. For consideration of the nature of facts in the political universe, see, for example, Jacques Ellul, *The Political Illusion* (New York: Knopf, 1967), pp. 97–103.
8. "The reasons for heavy public or governmental involvement in the phenomena of economic, social and political change are as myriad as the kinds of development actually under way. In many places, government is the only significant social sector willing to assume the responsibility for transformation." Joseph LaPalombara, "An Overview," in LaPalombara (ed.), *Bureaucracy and Political Development* (Princeton: Princeton University Press, 1963), p. 5.
9. Zbigniew Brzezinski, "Communism and the Emerging Nations," in J. Roland Pennock (ed.), *Self-Government in the Modernizing Nations* (Englewood Cliffs, N.J.: Prentice-Hall, 1964), p. 81.
10. See, for example, David E. Apter, *The Politics of Modernization* (Chicago: University of Chicago Press, 1965), Chap. 11; C. E. Black, *The Dynamics of Modernization: A Study in Comparative History* (New York: Harper & Row, 1966), Chap. 4; A. F. K. Organski, *The Stages of Political Development* (New York: Knopf, 1965), Chaps. 3, 4, and 5; and W. W. Rostow, *The Stages of Economic Growth: A Non-Communist Manifesto* (London: Cambridge University Press, 1963), Chaps. 8 and 9.
11. For various definitions of the term "ideology," see, for example, Karl Mannheim, *Ideology and Utopia* (New York: Harcourt Brace Jovanovich, 1954), p. 49; Harold Lasswell and Abraham Kaplan, *Power and Society* (New Haven: Yale University Press, 1950), p. 123; Harold Lasswell and Daniel Lerner (eds.), *World Revolutionary Elites: Studies in Coercive Ideological Movements* (Cambridge, Mass.: M.I.T. Press, 1965), p. 17; Sebastian DeGrazia, *The Political Community: A Study in Anomie* (Chicago: University of Chicago Press, 1948), pp. 81–82; Talcott Parsons, *The Social System* (New York: Free Press of Glencoe, 1963), p. 349; and Apter, *The Politics of Modernization*, p. 314.
12. Mancur Olson, Jr., *The Logic of Collective Action: Public Goods and*

the Theory of Groups (Cambridge, Mass.: Harvard University Press, 1965), p. 21.

13. See, for example, Maurice Duverger, *Political Parties* (New York: Wiley, 1963), p. 425; Gaetano Mosca, *The Ruling Class* (New York: McGraw-Hill, 1939), Parts I and II; Carl J. Friedrich, *Man and His Government: An Empirical Theory of Politics* (New York: McGraw-Hill, 1963), pp. 161–162; and Peter Bachrach, *The Theory of Democratic Elitism: A Critique* (Boston and Toronto: Little, Brown, 1967), *passim*.

14. Fred H. Willhoite, Jr., "Political Order and Consensus: A Continuing Problem," *Western Political Quarterly*, XVII (June 1963), 295.

15. A summary form of some of these observations first appeared in Taketsugu Tsurutani, "Stability and Instability: A Note in Comparative Political Analysis," *Journal of Politics*, 30 (November 1968).

16. Niccolò Machiavelli, *The Prince*, in a Modern Library edition of *The Prince and the Discourses* (New York, 1950), Chap. VI, p. 21.

17. Neil J. Smelser, "Mechanisms of Change and Adjustment to Change," in Jason L. Finkle and Richard W. Gable (eds.), *Political Development and Social Change* (New York, London and Sidney: Wiley, 1966), pp. 36–37.

18. "It is thus of the very nature of the modernizing process that at every step of the way the impulses making for modernization are in active contention with powerful forces tending to retard and to frustrate the transformation of the traditional society into full constructive modernity. There is nothing which decrees that the forces of modernization will win eventual or automatic victory." Max F. Millikan and Donald L. M. Blackmer, *The Emerging Nations* (Boston and Toronto: Little, Brown, 1961), p. 19.

19. David Easton, *A Systems Analysis of Political Life* (New York: Wiley, 1965), p. 168.

20. Tsurutani, "Stability and Instability," p. 913.

21. For one of the most cogent discussions of this problem, see Samuel P. Huntington, "Political Development and Political Decay," *World Politics* XVII (April 1965).

22. Easton, *A Systems Analysis of Political Life*, p. 108. See also Claude Ake, *A Theory of Political Integration* (Homewood, Ill.: Dorsey Press, 1967), pp. 96–99; and Smelser, "Mechanisms of Change and Adjustments to Change," in Finkle and Gable (eds.), *Political Development and Social Change*, pp. 38–39.

23. It is probably true that the scientific and organizational technology now available tends to compensate for the time lag for these nations. This, certainly, is one of those dimensions of national development calling for investigation. Nevertheless, the problem of basic sociopolitical change remains intrinsically the same.

24. For a further methodological comment on some of the more familiar approach to the study of development and modernization, see Chapter II.

25. See Stein Rokkan's comments on "the 'whole nation' bias" and "the 'economic growth' bias" in his *Citizens, Elections and Parties* (New York: McKay, 1970), p. 49.

26. Irving Louis Horowitz, *Three Worlds of Development: The Theory and Practice of International Stratification* (New York: Oxford University Press, 1966).

27. Ardath W. Burks, "Politics of Japan's Modernization: The Autonomy of Choice," in Robert E. Ward (ed.), *Political Development in Modern Japan* (Princeton: Princeton University Press, 1968), p. 539.

28. Or, as one critic of functionalist and systems approaches remarked, "the uncritical assimilation of nonindigenous concepts borrowed from related but minimally formalized behavioral sciences." A. James Gregor, "Political Science and the Uses of Functional Analysis," *American Political Science Review*, LXII (June 1968), p. 426.

29. T. D. Weldon, *The Vocabulary of Politics* (Baltimore: Penguin Books, 1960), p. 39.

30. Perhaps a typical structuralist description of the same idea may be: "Government is the regulation of public affairs. This regulation is a set of processes which defines government functionally, and which also identifies its content as the affairs which are regulated, and the resources used to regulate them." M. G. Smith, "A Structural Approach to Comparative Politics," in David Easton (ed.), *Varieties of Political Theory* (Englewood Cliffs, N.J.: Prentice-Hall, 1966), p. 115.

31. For the functional choices of political leadership in this regard, see, for example, Amitai Etzioni's introduction to J. P. Nettl and Roland Robertson, *International Systems and the Modernization of Societies: The Formation of National Goals and Attitudes* (New York: Basic Books, 1968).

32. See Bertrand de Jouvenel, *Sovereignty: An Inquiry into the Political Good* (Chicago: University of Chicago Press, 1957), pp. 21-22, 50-53, 299-300.

33. Mary Matossian, "Ideologies of Delayed Industrialization: Some Tensions and Ambiguities," in Kautsky (ed.), *Political Change in Underdeveloped Countries*, p. 254.

34. Perhaps the best and most concise review of the literature thus far is to be found in "Editor's Introduction" to Lewis J. Edinger (ed.), *Political Leadership in Industrialized Societies* (New York, London, and Sidney: Wiley, 1967).

35. Stanford: Stanford University Press, 1952.

36. See, among others and in addition to the studies contained in Edinger (ed.), *Political Leadership in Industrialized Societies*, Karl W. Deutsch and Lewis Edinger, *Germany Rejoins the Powers* (Stanford: Stanford University Press, 1959); Frederick W. Frey, *The Turkish Political Elite* (Cambridge, Mass.: M.I.T. Press, 1965); W. L. Guttsman, *The British Political Elite* (London: MacGibbon and Kee, 1963); Lasswell and Lerner (eds.), *World Revolutionary Elites*; Robert T. McKenzie, *British Political Parties* (New York: Praeger, 1962); Dwaine Marvick (ed.), *Political Decision-Makers* (Glencoe, Ill: Free Press, 1961); Robert C. North, *Kuomintang and Chinese Communist Elites* (Stanford: Stanford University Press, 1952); Richard L. Park and Irene Tinker, *Leadership and Political Institutions in India* (Princeton: Princeton University Press, 1959); Lucian W. Pye, *Politics, Personality and Nation Building* (New Haven: Yale University Press, 1962); Robert A. Scalapino and Junnosuke Masumi, *Parties and Politics in Contemporary Japan* (Berkeley and Los Angeles: University of California Press, 1962); Lester G. Seligman, *Leadership in a New Nation* (New York: Atherton, 1964); Marshall R. Singer, *The Emerging Elite: A Study of Political Leadership in Ceylon* (Cambridge, Mass.: M.I.T. Press, 1964). For a recent comparative, cross-cultural study of elites in terms of social-background characteristics, see William B. Quandt, *The Comparative*

Study of Political Elites, A Sage Professional Paper, Comparative Politics Series No. 01-004, Vol. I, 1970.

37. Exceptional in this regard are two recent works: W. Howard Wriggins, *The Ruler's Imperative: Strategies for Political Survival in Asia and Africa* (New York: Columbia University Press, 1969); and Warren F. Ilchman and Norman Thomas Uphoff, *The Political Economy of Change* (Berkeley and Los Angeles: University of California Press, 1969). Wriggins' focus is on what he calls "strategies" that a number of contemporary national leaders in Asia and Africa have used to win or stay in power and to impose their wills on their nations. While largely descriptive and oriented toward the treatment of individual leaders rather than political leadership as a category of analysis, his work does highlight the concern with leadership *behavior*. As such, one might say that Wriggins' work, in a historical and methodological sense, belongs to the genre of Machiavelli's *The Prince* and Richard Neustadt's *Presidential Power*. Ilchman and Uphoff, on the other hand, make an extremely fascinating attempt to apply economic concepts to the study of developing nations in general and the problem of political management in particular. They propose what they call "the new political economy," the central concept of which is "the productivity of politics" (that is, policy outputs) that is the function, as in economics, of behavioral interactions among a number of crucial resource, management, and situational variables. Again, the central concern of their book is with techniques of political leadership, although methodologically they are far more rigorous and sophisticated than Wriggins.

38. Peter H. Merkl, *Political Continuity and Change* (New York: Harper & Row, 1967), p. 14.

39. Edinger, in his introduction to *Political Leadership in Industrialized Societies*, identifies two major categories of current approaches to the study of political elites, which roughly correspond, to, but are more detailed than, the two major kinds of elite studies mentioned here. See Edinger, p. 12, Table 1.2.

40. Daniel Lerner, "The Coercive Ideologists in Perspective," in Lasswell and Lerner (eds.), *World Revolutionary Elites*, esp. pp. 463–465. On the absence of such meaningfully positive causal relationships, see also Deutsch and Edinger, *Germany Rejoins the Powers*, and North, *Kuomintang and Chinese Communist Elites*, among others.

41. For justification of this view, see, for example, Abraham Kaplan, *The Conduct of Inquiry* (Scranton, Chandler, 1964), pp. 302–310, and Eugene Meehan, *The Theory and Method of Political Analysis* (Homewood, Ill.: Dorsey Press, 1965), Chap. 5.

42. Herbert Simon, *Administration Behavior* (New York: Macmillan, 1947), p. 134, and quoted in Edinger (ed.), *Political Leadership in Industrialized Societies*, p. 14.

II
National Development and Governmental Capability

Successful undertaking of the task of national development calls for the generation and maintenance of two vital phenomena that are frequently mutually exclusive or at least find coexistence difficult. They are stability and change. On one hand, there ought to be some minimal degree of order and stability in a society if it is to develop and modernize. In the absence of such order and stability, no meaningful long-range programs of reform and change of society can be implemented. Social engineering is impossible in a condition of chaos. On the other hand, however, programs of change and reform that are essential to development and modernization have a natural tendency to disrupt and undermine order and stability. They do so because they often necessitate painful sacrifices and unaccustomed efforts on the part of the population. Traditional society is stable so long as it is free from the need of change. Once change is introduced, its tranquillity begins to disappear. How to promote change, hence development and modernization, while still maintaining (or creating and maintaining) stability, then, is the most crucial problem for any developing nation. It is indeed the central task for political leadership, for it is political leadership alone that can mediate these two necessary but often incongruent requirements for national development by rendering them mutually reenforcing. The capacity for national development of any society consists ultimately in its political leadership's manipulative skill in, creative intelligence for, and unwavering commitment to, generating and maintaining order and stability on the one hand, and, on the other, effectively mobilizing and creatively utilizing the human and material resources that exist in society for the task of national development. Mere existence of those human and material resources in society, however abundant, does not in itself generate progress, let alone guarantee it. Society will stagnate, even regress, if political leadership is lacking in skill, intelligence, commitment, and resolve.

Chapters II and III will examine the relationship between material, human, organizational, and institutional resources of society on the one hand and the role of political leadership to utilize, channel, and direct these resources on the other. In the present chapter we shall comment on the nature of what is called governmental capability and the relationship among its components, as well as suggest some of the methods of measuring those components that may be useful for purposes of comparative analysis. In Chapter III, we shall look into the nature of the impact of political leadership on different levels of governmental capability and its crucial role in enhancing the total societal capacity for national development.

AN APPROACH TO INQUIRY

To state a problem is simple; to examine it is very difficult. Students of comparative politics, especially of the politics of the developing nations, have known the problem of development and modernization; they have also stated it in a variety of ways,[1] and the particular statement of the problem above and in Chapter I will not be the last. While the problem stated is one and the same, however, particular ways in which it is stated, particular manners in which it is described, necessarily require different ways of examining it. If the problem is stated (or described) in terms of tension and struggle among groups, it might then be examined within the framework of, say, a group theory. If it is stated as some sort of organic maladjustment or homeostatic disequilibrium, some students might choose to employ a systems approach. Or, if the problem is viewed from the standpoint of structural imbalance and functional immaturity, then one type of functional approach or another might be considered relevant. Some investigators would use a configurative approach since they tend to view the problem as volatile interactions of a variety of forces that are perforce unique to each particular society. I do not intend here to examine relative conceptual and methodological merits and defects of these methods of examination and analysis of the problem. I simply mention these different methods as arising out of different ways in which the problem of development and modernization can be and has been stated. Since this volume, too, looks at the problem in a particular way and states it in a certain manner, the method of examining it will necessarily be different from others. This, of course, is not to say that the approach is wholly novel. Consciously or unconsciously, explicitly or implicitly, what is attempted here, if it has anything to recommend at all, is at least a by-product, a small part of the cumulative result, of what has been done in the field of comparative politics in general and in the study of development and modernization in particular. It will therefore include old ideas as well as some new ones, some well-known concepts and categories, albeit modified to various degrees for purposes of this inquiry, as well as some that may be considered original. What I attempt, then, is to construct a certain framework of investigation and analysis which employs those ideas and concepts, hoping that they can be meaningfully integrated into the framework. In doing so, I run certain risks of exposure to criticism and attack on conceptual and methodological grounds. While such criticism and attack will, in large measure, be deserved, it is perhaps not inappropriate at this point to state some of the reasons for the particular framework of analysis that will be constructed in this book.

Some of the concepts that will be initially utilized are derived from a very familiar approach in comparative politics—the functionalist developmental approach of Almond and Powell.[2] I intend to utilize this approach because it is useful as a take-off point and also lends itself to the kind of modification that I believe is necessary. The mere fact of borrowing even a few of the conceptual categories from Almond and Powell may invite the same kind of criticism that has been leveled against functionalist approaches and methods in the past decade.[3] By way of clarifying the purpose of the endeavor in the present inquiry, it may not be too digressive to comment on the criticism—though I do not identify myself as an Almondian functionalist.

There are many aspects to the criticism directed to functionalist approaches, but among the critics' main concerns are: (1) functionalism is fraught with conceptual ambiguity and ambivalence; (2) it is empirically untestable; (3) it is based on some teleological assumptions; and (4) it lacks explicatory and, subsequently, predictive capability. These, among others, are formidable methodological attacks, and devotees of functionalist approaches have yet to offer persuasive counterattack and refutation.[4] At the same time, however, it may be suggested that the criticism is a bit more than the criticized deserves, for underlying the criticism is an assumption that students of comparative politics should already be able to construct a theory of political system that is as scientific, that is, methodologically as flawless and logically as coherent and consistent, as a theory of organic chemistry. To meet such an expectation is clearly beyond the level of competence and growth that has been achieved in the discipline of comparative politics. Nevertheless, it is true that conceptual ambiguity or ambivalence accompanies an approach that employs too many major categories of analysis. Lines of conceptual demarcation become difficult to see, and analytical overlapping difficult to avoid. For the sake of clarity as well as economy, perhaps it is desirable first to limit the number of major categories of analysis and, as Holt and Turner suggest, treat others "as empirical correlates" of the limited number of categories or dimensions.[5] And this I shall try to do in this inquiry. Limiting the number of categories has the advantage of avoiding certain analytical redundancy and subsequently achieving a higher degree of precision and clarity. That functionalist propositions and hypotheses are empirically untestable results primarily from the singular dearth of efforts to utilize extant empirical data as well as from the fact that certain definitional criteria are empirically undemonstrable. Untestability is also in part a consequence of the first weakness, conceptual ambiguity. For example, it is impossible, within the functionalist context, to tell when a political system is maintained or not maintained. Clearly, mere existence of a system (in terms of its physical trappings, personnel, possession of means of coercion, and so on) does not indicate whether the system is maintained or not, although that would be a much simpler and more testable criterion, because system maintenance is said to depend upon the proper operation of certain "functions," which, in turn, is difficult empirically to ascertain. One would have to end up saying that a political system is *more or less* maintained so long as it exists. Part of the attempt in this inquiry, however, is to employ categories that are different from the functionalist categories of system maintenance and functions that accompany it and that lend themselves to some meaningful empirical testing. Verification can be done, in part, because the number of relevant major categories of analysis is limited.

Concerning the third criticism, the present framework of analysis is not based on any assumption of teleological terminus or a notion of irreversibility, even of unidirectionality of development and modernization. The observable fact is simply accepted: that new nations in Asia, Africa, and Latin America are struggling to emerge from the condition of deep political instability and economic underdevelopment or poverty, to become materially comfortable, politically stable, and socially harmonious. Within certain types of debate, one can make an argument that any notion of progress necessarily implies a teleological view because no idea of progress is possible without the knowledge of that toward which progress is to be made. Perhaps it is partly for this reason that some students of development and modernization prefer to use the word "change" (as in "social change" instead of "modernization"), but that does not solve the problem, if indeed there is a problem. Change, one could argue, also implies a certain direction, if not a teleological terminus (as change to the better). For the purpose of metaphysical or philosophical disputation, these may be very crucial considerations. But for the present purposes, such considerations only obstruct the attempt to discover many dimensions of the empirical phenomenon of concern and to analyze them. We have not yet reached the stage in our knowledge where those considerations will become indeed relevant. Various ideas (statements) about development and modernization simply suggest the kind of direction which most nations in the second half of the twentieth century seem intent upon pursuing.[6] These nations are pursuing this direction not because they envision some kind of utopian *telos*, but rather because they wish to escape from the unpleasant present conditions. Furthermore, it is the contention here that the progression of these nations is not linear or unidirectional, but rather is pregnant with constant danger of digression and regression.[7] Else, national development would be foreordained. Indeed, the idea of the crucial importance of political leadership (that is, its autonomy in the political process and political arena and society) arises out of the conviction that the process of development and modernization is neither teleological nor irreversible, for any approach that assumes either of these inherent qualities "has an inherent tendency to play down the importance of policies, or rather to organize them into the predetermined sequence of events."[8]

Of the fourth criticism: there is not pretence in this inquiry to being more than simply exploratory. Explicative and predictive capacities call for the level of theoretical growth and sophistication which the relatively young discipline of the study of modernization and development has yet to achieve. Being exploratory in its basic nature and intent, the effort in the present inquiry can hope to generate only heuristic findings. In more senses than one, I propose at this moment still to operate at the level from which more ambitious and experienced scholars are doubtless trying to emerge. And this simply because there are many loose and unexamined ends to be clarified and tied together at this particular level before aspiring to a higher level of analytical precision, methodological rigor, and theoretical abstraction and formalization that many critics of the study of development and modernization demand. Admittedly, the struggle will be at a rather low level of theoretical development, perhaps reflecting the complex and volatile nature of the subject of inquiry, but the hope is that the attempt will be of some importance in increasing our understanding of the nature and process of development and modernization and that it will elicit some meaningful insight as well as testable hypotheses which will in the end contribute to the generation of a higher level of theoretical abstraction and formalization in the field of comparative political analysis.

THE CATEGORIES OF ANALYSIS

For the sake of convenience, let us begin with a brief elaboration of a few categories of analysis initially derived from Almond and Powell. It will be noted that these few categories of analysis are being significantly modified or augmented in their explicit meanings and dimensions for present purposes.

Almond and Powell cite five "capabilities" that they argue the "political system" should possess, and four support functions that society at large should perform. It is proposed, here, however, that only three of these nine major categories of analysis are really useful in talking about the kind of capability every polity should possess. In so doing, I also propose both to narrow and to enlarge the scope of inquiry into the role of polity: narrow in terms of the number of major variables, and enlarge in the sense of positing more empirical correlates to each of the major variables. The three major categories of analysis selected here for governmental capability are: regulative, extractive, and distributive. These three encompass the general range of ability to govern that every government should possess.

The reason for excluding the other categories of analysis proposed by Almond and Powell is relatively simple. What they call "responsive capability" will, in this inquiry, be posited in a distinct notion of political leadership as one of its major attributes. The reason for this consideration is this: In the first place, certain types and levels of "capacity to respond" are inherent in any system, institution, or organization. They are indeed one of the purely systemic or "administrative" aspects of any government, institution, group, or organization. As such, they are also implicit in each of the three aspects of governmental capability, namely, regulative, extractive, and distributive. For example, a graduated income tax (or any tax, for that matter, though each operates differently), as a component of the extractive aspect of governmental capability in many a nation, automatically responds to fluctuation in the national economy, that is, change in its environment. If people's incomes fall, income-tax collection automatically falls by extracting proportionately less from them. If, on the other hand, incomes rise because of economic growth or prosperity, tax collection will rise by its ability automatically to adjust tax rates. A simple sales tax also possesses a mechanical ability to "respond" to change in its environment: if more goods are sold, the tax "extracts" more from its environment; if business declines, it automatically extracts less. In either case, it is "responding" or adapting itself to certain environmental change.[9]

The mechanical ability to respond and to adapt to different conditions inheres also in other aspects of governmental capability. The police department of a town or city, as an agent of the regulative aspect of governmental capability, regardless of who happens to be chief, deploys a concentration of policemen when a serious crime takes place, but otherwise follows peaceful routine. The mechanism of judicial process grinds in a certain way under one set of circumstances, but operates differently in another: for example, a petty crime is punished in one way, and a serious one in another. All these represent different patterns of response to different occurrences, that is, changes in environment. Take the national flag, for example, as another component of the regulative aspect of governmental capability (the "symbolic capability," according to Almond and Powell). It, too, possesses a significant degree of built-in ability to "respond" to fluctuations in its environment, for it automatically elicits a heightened level of patriotic sentiment and identification when it is displayed on special occasions or in times of external crisis (namely, in times of confrontation with another polity which has its own flag).

The distributive aspect of governmental capability, too, possesses considerable degrees of ability to respond automatically and mechanically. Unemployment compensation, for example, will be given to a larger or smaller number of people according to environmental change: if more people are laid off, more money will be spent on compensating their unemployed status; when the number of the unemployed decreases because business picks up (another instance of environmental change), then the outlay for unemployment compensation will accordingly decline. Likewise with social-security payments when they are by law adjusted to changes in the cost-of-living index. There are numerous other examples of the "response" capability that is built into these aspects of governmental capability. In general, one can argue that any administrative agency, whichever aspect of governmental capability it may represent, responds in a predictable and wholly routine fashion to certain types of demands, conditions, or environmental stimuli. In this sense, certain amounts of response capability are inherent in all governmental capability.

In the second place, there is a far more important kind of response capability which resides solely in the category of political leadership, in the sense that responses, or patterns of response, of government to environmental change and fluctuation are the function of a combination of predilection, ideology, perception, manipulative skill, political intelligence, and creative vision (or the absence of any of these qualities) of each particular political leadership in the face of a given problem under a given set of circumstances. This, indeed, is what is meant by the statement that to govern is to choose. This second type of response is really what Almond and Powell are concerned about and, inasmuch as this "capability" is what determines the levels and manners of operation of the three aspects of governmental capability, it should be a category of consideration quite distinct from the general governmental capability. Leadership's response capability (under which such correlates as conversion processes may be subsumed) determines the patterns of generation, maintenance, and exercise of not only the government capability but also the total societal capacity for development. In this respect, it stands above and separate from what Almond and Powell call "system capabilities."

In this analysis I have chosen to eliminate from consideration the four support functions that, according to Almond and Powell, should be performed by society. The main reason for doing so is that they seem to lead to unnecessary conceptual redundancy and analytical overlapping. Capability of a government (or political system) should logically comprehend what may be termed the support functions that Almond and Powell treat as different categories of analysis. A polity, according to both the first and the second view of politics advanced in the preceding chapter, provides the context, the arena, in which resolution of conflict takes place and political leadership attempts to establish, maintain, and exercise control. A polity (or political system—the term is useful because of its wide currency, for which an alternative, equally popular, would be simply government), in this sense may be small in its conceptual size and extent, or it may be extensive, depending upon the variety and volume of conflict that it admits of, upon the size or proportion of the population it accepts or allows as participants, and upon the extent of control its leadership attempts to exercise over society. In this sense, the political system of today's developing nation (or, for that matter, almost any nation today) is conceptually much larger and more extensive than, say, the political system of Victorian England, of the Roman Empire, or of *ante bellum* America. At any rate, society's support functions, which Almond and Powell (attempt to) delineate from their "system capabilities," are part of the components and ingredients of the general governmental capability. That a government has a high level of extractive capability, for example, by definition means that society *supports* government by surrendering to it what it extracts. That law is enforced (the regulative aspect of governmental capability) simply means that, somehow, people by and large obey law. To speak of governmental capability or any of its three major aspects and its corresponding support function of society separately as if they were two empirically distinct phenomena seems unprofitable and serves no useful purpose. Thus, this inquiry subsumes Almond's and Powell's society's support functions under general governmental capability and treats them, when necessary, only as its empirical correlates. Further, Almonds' and Powell's "symbolic capability" is subsumed under the regulative aspect of governmental capability for reasons that are mentioned below.

THE THREE COMPONENTS OF GOVERNMENTAL CAPABILITY

The three necessary aspects of capability that government should require in order to govern, then, are regulative, extractive, and distributive. It may be suggested here that they lend themselves to partial empirical verification.

THE REGULATION OF BEHAVIOR

The regulative aspect of governmental capability refers to an ability to control the behavior of individuals and groups of individuals as well as to regulate their relationships and interactions. This capability is most directly related to government's task of creating and maintaining order and stability in society. Hence, it is the first requirement of any government. It has, as such, two major aspects: (1) an ability to elicit positive affect toward, and voluntary support for, the polity through such feelings as respect, patriotism, deference, awe, or even love and through such methods as education, communication, civic and political participation; and (2) an ability to provide and enforce an effective network of laws and regulations concerning the behavior of individuals and groups. In the recent literature on comparative politics, the first of these aspects of governmental regulative capability has usually been treated as a dimension of political culture. Political culture is the pattern of three essentially psychosymbolic orientations toward political action: cognition, affect, and evaluation.[10] As such it comprehends what Almond and Powell treat as the system's symbolic capability as well as their category of society's symbolic support function. In some nations, these orientations are said to be positive (that is, the political system or existing form of government has a high level of the ability to elicit positive affect and voluntary support from the population at large), where people generally regard their polity, those who run it, and even themselves as participants in the political process or as simply members of the nation state in a very favorable light. They think the polity is proper and productive in terms of the allocation of values, that those who run it, for example, government officials and elected representatives, are by and large doing a reasonably good job, and that they themselves are partaking of the political process in a manner that is tolerably satisfactory to them. In such nations, the ability to elicit positive affect toward the political system is *ipso facto* high. Consequently, people are willing to obey the laws and regulations made and enforced by their government. In contrast, in a nation where the political culture is negative in character (that is, where people feel their government is a fraud, that the government officials and elected representatives are corrupt, indifferent, or wicked, and that they themselves really can do little or nothing about the situation), the ability to elicit favorable feelings and attitudes toward government, its institutions and programs, is very low. The importance of this first aspect of governmental regulative capability consists in the simple fact that the higher this psychosymbolic ability, the more easily can the behavior of individuals and groups be controlled and their relationships regulated, that is to say, the easier it is to maintain order and stability in society. The most intimate microcosmic example in which this psychosymbolic ability is clearly observable is the family in which, at least under ordinary circumstances, love, affection, and respect are the basis of unity, order, growth, and continuity. Thus, other things being equal, a government that in its structure, operation, and conduct is congruent with the expectations, values, preferences, and desires of society has the appropriate and viable type and level of (the psychosymbolic aspect of) the regulative capability.

Unfortunately, however, the kind of political system or government that may be deemed proper in its structure, operation, and conduct for the purpose of carrying out national development is more often than not quite incongruent with the expectations, values, preferences, and desires that exist in a developing nation. This means that the psychosymbolic dimension of the regulative capability is very low. Hence, this first ability of the regulative capability must be created, engineered, and manipulated if the total level of the regulative capability is to increase. Again, the crucial importance of the skill and intelligence of political leadership becomes obvious. The central consideration of political leadership aside for the moment, this psychosymbolic dimension of the regulative capability consists in an ability (1) to maintain whatever congruent and integrative tie may exist between the political system and society, (2) to manipulate symbols—verbal, behavioral, and institutional—so as to render the political system palatable and legitimate (or strengthen its legitimacy), and (3) to create new psychic and symbolic channels through which positive orientations of society may be elicited and maintained toward the polity and those who run it. Through these channels, symbols should be constantly manipulated and manifest political socialization carried out, to generate and strengthen the sense of nationhood and common citizenship and the feeling of identity of interest between government and governed as well as among various groups in society, so as to minimize social conflict and to strengthen the affective, cognitive, and evaluative orientations of people toward the polity, its role incumbents, and its processes. Each of the major symbols upon whose efficacy the political system relies for its legitimacy and stability in this regard should possess more or less constant positive relevance, however illusory, to society at large (for example, the notion of patriotism, deference for the authority of the court, respect for the office of the chief executive, even though the nature and tradition of each of these may differ from society to society). Special occasions such as national emergency or international crisis may call for a heightened mobilization of this dimension of the regulative capability, but a minimum degree of constancy and relevance must be rendered permanent, to the extent that challenge against these fundamental symbols either from within or without would be rendered highly difficult, if not altogether impossible. Many developing nations have dangerously low levels of the psychosymbolic dimension of the regulative capability. The prevalence of personal charisma in these nations as the only psychosymbolic entity capable of eliciting support and deference is the result of the general failure of these nations to develop this vital dimension of the regulative capability. It is unfortunate for these nations that personal charisma is incapable of continuity and permanence.

The other dimension of the regulative capability is the ability to provide and enforce an effective network of laws and regulations concerning the behavior of individuals and groups of individuals as well as relationships among them. Criminal laws, legal norms protecting fundamental human rights, and regulatory provisions concerning political organizations and activities are examples of such laws and regulations. Needless to say, it is not enough that these laws and regulations be promulgated. They must be effectively and impartially enforced. And such effectiveness and impartiality depend upon coherent organization of law-enforcement agencies, recruitment of properly qualified personnel, rules for internal operation, and professional ethics and morale of those agencies and personnel. Effectiveness is also a function of congruence between law and culture and of optimum economy in the use of coercion. It is at this point that the mutual inseparability of those two aspects of the regulative capability becomes clear. Both the psychosymbolic and the legal-coercive aspect of the regulative capability are means of suasion and combat for the proper behavior of the citizen and his obedience to government. Both are functions of control by government. They are mutually complementary, supportive and supplementary. Combined, they constitute governmental capacity for control of individual and group behavior. Effective enforcement of laws and regulations is vitally assisted by the positive quality of the psychosymbolic aspect of the regulative capability; positive affective, cognitive, and evaluative orientations of people are engendered and enhanced by effective, impartial enforcement of laws and regulations. In the absence of the psychosymbolic aspect of the regulative capability, government would have to rely exclusively on its legal-coercive aspect, which, in the end, would lead to bureaucratic tyranny and totalitarianism or to anarchy. In the absence of effective legal-coercive ability, the psychosymbolic ability of the regulative capability would be seriously undermined. People more willingly obey laws when they have positive and favorable feelings toward their government; their feelings toward their government become positive when they know that laws are impartially and effectively enforced for their mutual and common benefit. Conversely, they resist and evade laws and regulations when they know that law enforcement is partial or when they feel hostile toward their government, and, in the end, effectiveness of law enforcement will be reduced or the government will be impelled to resort to what Machiavelli called "extraordinary measures."

Many contemporary developing nations do not possess the level of this regulative capability that is essential for their stability and for the implementation of their development policies. In the first place, they lack an adequate level of the ability to engender and improve psychosymbolic orientation of people toward their governments. Second, the relative qualities of their law enforcement are such that they are all too frequently unable to prevent or punish the deviant behavior of individuals and groups of individuals that clearly undermines governmental authority and viability. Lack of an adequate level of regulative capability produces and, in turn, is aggravated by two phenomena: legal and political. Unlawful activities of all types will increase, for people have respect neither for law nor for government. Serious as well as petty crimes become rampant; violence and other types of open defiance of law spread. Indeed, in the absence of any sense of identity of interest between government and governed, some people and some groups of people may come to feel that it is really a good thing to break laws since the laws, in the eyes of many, are not just. This sort of tendency is likely to be encouraged when what Deutsch and his associates call the "politically relevant strata" of society refuse to accept the legitimacy of government.[11] Criminals are coddled; some of them even become heroes, modern-day Robin Hoods.

The kind of political phenomenon that results from the lack of an adequate level of the regulative capability overlaps with its strictly legal counterpart, but nevertheless manifests a clearly political orientation and is clearly political in its impact on the political process and government. One example of such a political phenomenon is the violation of the manner of political participation that are either prescribed or encouraged by government. Society at large, but especially its core areas or "politically relevant strata" should participate in the political process in such ways as would increase and maintain the authority, legitimacy, and capacity of the political system and should at the same time refrain from the kind of political activities that would undermine or destroy those psychosymbolic, legal, and political abilities of government. If participants in the political process, actors in the political arena, behave in certain ways and according to certain rules, written or unwritten, political participation would have the effect of constantly energizing and improving the political system, strengthening those two dimensions of the regulative capability of government, and, within the context of new nations, promoting the process of national development. At least, such was the hope of practically all newly independent nations that entered the community of nations after World War II. Political participation has, however, been found to be a two-edged sword. In the absence of meaningful congruence between the underlying traditional culture of society and the kind of modern form of government imposed upon it, expansion of political participation allows or encourages the types of political activities that seriously undermine the need to generate the regulative capability and to establish order and stability in society. Sudden emancipation of the masses in developing nations after independence has unleashed into the political arena all sorts of groups that have neither the knowledge of how to cope and associate civilly with one another nor the understanding of the difficult task of nation-building.[12] They are politically not only untutored but often also irrational. Their behavior, therefore, is likely to disrupt political order, critically aggravate the existing cleavages among their respective groups, and seriously compound the already strenuous psychosymbolic relationship between government and governed, thereby further encouraging deviant behavior in society and in the political arena.

One aspect of the importance of this type of politically, if not legally, deviant behavior of participants in the political arena consists in its impact on the issue of support and demand. While political participation properly channeled and conducted would have a positive supportive value to the political system and its leadership, and hence be contributive to the process of national development, deviant, disruptive patterns of political participation are undesirable precisely because of their "demand" effect on the political system. The latter type of political participation engenders the kind of demand on government which the latter is unable to satisfy without undermining its capabilities, the regulative among them, and hence ultimately reducing its regulative capability. In other words it generates the type of change in value and behavior that the system cannot admit of or absorb. For example, labor agitation for higher wages and shorter working hours constitutes more than mere participation in the political arena and the political decision-making process. It means a demand on the political system which the system can ill afford to satisfy in view of the existing levels of its various capabilities and resources. Even if the government were able to meet such demands it could do so only at the expense of further progress in national development and of its own growth and viability. "Someone who joins a mob screaming for the head of the prime minister engages in a political act no less than one who dutifully salutes as he marches past the minister's grandstand in the independence day parade."[13] Similar kinds of deviant and undesirable behavior of groups in the political arena may be seen in activities and demands of regional groups, ethnic or communal groups, and certain economic groups, as well as in the kind of modus operandi (or, perhaps more properly, the absence thereof) among them in many a developing nation. In any event, within the context of the contemporary developing areas, there is a tragic irony to this phenomenon. The phenomenon has often been caused by the very effort to modernize society, to develop and increase governmental regulative capability, for example, by introducing a representative form of government and/or mass political participation and vastly expanded political communication which, unfortunately but inevitably, has produced not a sense of mutual interest among participants in the political arena but rather an intensification and exacerbation of traditional cleavages within society.

There is a glaring absence of any meaningful sense of identity and common interest between government and governed as well as among various groups in society. Whatever little sense of national pride and common purpose may have existed during and shortly after the struggle for independence has quickly disintegrated. The "bright and shining sword" of self-determination and independence[14] has produced not the political kingdom but something of a political hell for many new nations.

Measuring the regulative *capability* of a given government or political system is a difficult proposition. The two aspects of the capability, namely, the psychosymbolic and the legal-coercive abilities, call for different kinds of measurement. For example, the psychosymbolic ability cannot be ascertained or measured from available statistical data on a cross-national level. First, public-opinion polls are available in only a few nations, being either unknown or virtually prohibited in other nations. Second, even where they are available, their reliability and ability to elicit meaningful and usable data on the psychosymbolic aspect of the regulative capability of a government or political system are highly questionable, because of the kinds of questions asked and techniques used in such surveys. All this means that students of comparative politics have to devise their own methods, formulate their own questions, and select their own respondents in a number of countries in order to generate meaningful data and findings. So far, there are at least three outstanding (and apparently very expensive) examples of attempts to measure and compare relative qualities of this particular aspect of the regulative capability on an extensive cross-national basis. The first, in order of publication, is a study of political cultures of five "democratic" nations, made by Almond and Verba; the second is an inquiry into the process and effectiveness of preadult political socialization in four Western countries, by Dennis and associates; and the third is Inkeles' investigation of political orientations of "common man" strata in six developing nations.[15] One distinguished "within nation" study of the similar problem is McClosky's work on psychological and political attitudes of American voters and politically more relevant strata.[16] All four studies are highly suggestive of the kinds of questions that should be asked in order to elicit meaningful data and other information. Unfortunately, however, there are two main drawbacks with any meaningful effort to study the psychosymbolic aspect of the regulative capabilities of a number of nations. One is cost, in terms of funds, manpower, and time. This, indeed, is the main reason for the paucity of cross-national empirical studies of political culture and the psychosymbolic aspect of governmental regulative capability. The second drawback is the high probability that, with the possible exception of few nations, the psychosymbolic aspect of governmental regulative capability fluctuates significantly and frequently (see Chapter III). Thus, by the time an extensive empirical investigation is completed by somehow overcoming the first handicap, the second drawback leads to a situation where what has been learned is no longer pertinent. The prospects for many students of comparative politics being able not only to engage in cross-national comparative studies of this dimension of the regulative capability, but also to generate comparable data are, therefore, not very bright.

Ways of measuring and comparing various degrees of the legal-coercive aspect of the regulative capability are more readily available. To be sure, they are not very satisfactory, especially since accurate data are generally difficult to obtain and, in some cases, virtually impossible to obtain. More difficult still to come by are up-to-date data. Nevertheless, proximate indices, while they should always be viewed with caution, are obtainable and they often *suggest* at least broad comparative contours of a number of nations in terms of their relative extents of the legal-coercive aspect of the regulative capability.[17] On the basis of some of those indices, therefore, it is possible to ascertain levels of stability and order (the major function of the regulative capability) of a number of nations.

Table 1 is a tentative and, unfortunately quite outdated, index of regulative capability (albeit in large measure confined to the legal-coercive aspect of it). Group violence signifies the absence or decline of the ability to control the behavior of groups of individuals and to regulate their relationships and interactions. Groups in society, then, act deviantly, that is, try to resolve conflict among them, not through the mediative procedures that exist in the formal political and legal channels, but instead among themselves by use of brute private physical force in direct action. In the first place, laws and regulations are defied by these groups, and in the second, high frequencies of group violence suggest that the government has little ability to punish such defiance. In this sense the type of index used in Table 1 is significant in the attempt to examine relative levels of the regulative capability in many nations. Another interesting aspect of the table is that there is a close association between group violence and political instability, hence between regulative capability and political stability. Banks and Textor delineate three categories of nations in terms of governmental stability: stable, unstable, and unassertainable (due to insufficiency of data and information).[18] Twenty-six of the twenty-seven nations in the fourth column of Table 1 happen to be classified in Banks and Textor as stable. (The only

48 *National Development and Governmental Capability*

Table 1. **An Aspect of the Regulative Capability: Deaths from Domestic Group Violence per 1,000,000 Population, 1950–1962.** (In rank order for each column.) (*N* = 74)

Over 101 (*n* = 11)	11–100 (*n* = 18)	1–10 (*n* = 18)	Below 1 (*n* = 27)
Cuba	Paraguay	Ethiopia	Turkey
Hungary	Guatemala	Pakistan	Czechoslovakia
Indonesia	South Korea	Yemen	Russia
Bolivia	Syria	Jordan	France
Iraq	Ceylon	Nepal	Uruguay
Colombia	Iran	Poland	Italy
Philippines	South Africa	Mexico	Saudi Arabia
Argentina	Dominican Republic	Bulgaria	Spain
Burma	Peru	East Germany	Japan
Honduras	Panama	Israel	West Germany
Venezuela	Costa Rica	Thailand	United States
	Afghanistan	Chile	Australia
	China	El Salvador	Austria
	Ecuador	Greece	Canada
	Haiti	Egypt	Denmark
	Lebanon	Brazil	Finland
	Nicaragua	Portugal	Ireland
	India	Belgium	Liberia
			Netherlands
			New Zealand
			Norway
			Romania
			Sweden
			Switzerland
			Taiwan
			United Kingdom
			Yugoslavia

Source: Adapted from Bruce Russett *et al.*, *World Handbook of Political and Social Indicators* (New Haven, Conn.: Yale University Press, 1964), Table 29, pp. 99–100. Copyright 1964 by Yale University Press. Reprinted by permission.

exception is Turkey which, to Banks and Textor, was unstable apparently because of the coup of 1960.) At least thirteen of the eighteen nations in the third column (say "at least" because Yemen is classified by Banks and Textor as unassertainable; unstable ones are Pakistan, Jordan, Nepal, El Salvador, and Brazil) were adjudged as governmentally stable. On the other half of the spectrum of group violence in Table 1, we find, again comparing the table with the Banks-Textor measurement, that only five of the eleven nations in the first column (nations with more than 101 deaths per 1 million people) were classified in the stable category (Cuba, for some reason, is unassertainable) while only seven of the eighteen in the second column were regarded as governmentally stable (Paraguay, South Africa, Costa Rica, Afghanistan, Haiti, Nicaragua, and India).

It should also be noted that most nations in the fourth column are either highly industrialized, modern political systems which have had continuous political stability and order as the result of having a homogeneous political culture or being governed by regimes whose explicit characteristic is an extremely high degree of authoritarian coercion (Communist nations plus Taiwan and Spain). In one sense, this fact suggests the important impact of high levels of extractive and distributive capabilities (to be discussed below) on the regulative capability. In another, perhaps equally important sense, it suggests the vital importance of organizational and manipulative abilities of political leadership. At any rate, this observation leaves three nations in the fourth column that belong neither to the group of highly industrialized, more or less consensual, open societies nor to that of totalitarian nations. They are Turkey, Saudi Arabia, and Liberia. These could be simply dismissed as exceptions to the rule, but a brief comment on them may be more appropriate. One can argue that Saudi Arabia and Liberia, despite their superficial difference in terms of formal political structure and process, are equally underdeveloped and unmodern, one ruled by a *de facto* absolute monarchy and the other governed by a parochial, paternalistic autocrat who masquerades as the popularly elected president of a republic. The populations in both nations are politically indifferent, apathetic, hence politically quiescent. Both nations are in actuality traditional societies, where political change and socioeconomic development have yet to commence, rather than transitional or modern societies. These are some of the reasons for the apparent governmental stability and general order in Saudi Arabia and Liberia. Turkey is more difficult to explain. She is perhaps the most advanced of the nations in the Islamic world, but is by no means a fully "modernized" or "developed" nation in the sense that most of the nations in the fourth column are. At the same time, the Turks, since the days of Kemal Ataturk, have become gradually but steadily politicized and mobilized into the political arena, and, in this regard, one may argue that they are relatively sophisticated and mature politically. This characterization, however, seems to apply only to the process of voting. The manner in which Turkish governments governed, at least before 1962, seemed to be more authoritarian than democratic, and, paradoxically, that may well have been the main reason for the general stability that obtained in Turkey before 1960 when the regime of Premier Adnan Menderes was overthrown by a bloodless, swift military coup (apparently this is the reason for the Banks-Textor classification of Turkey as governmentally unstable). Even then, however, the transition, albeit extraconstitutional, was largely nonviolent, though Menderes, President Bayar, Foreign Minister Zolulu, and other close associates of the deposed prime minister were tried, convicted, and either executed (Menderes and Zolulu) or incarcerated (for example, Bayar).

At the other extreme of the scale of group violence are eleven nations of which all but one are generally regarded as "developing," hence presumably lacking in adequate levels of extractive and distributive capabilities, that is, in terms of the possible inference that can be derived from the cases of the column four, namely, the relationship between the regulative and other capabilities. They were, at least during the period covered by the table, with the exception of Hungary, either unstable autocracies/dictatorships or unstable, often tottering "democracies" or nations in which these two unstable types of regime followed each other. The only nation among them in which orderly constitutional succession of regimes was consistently witnessed was the Philippines, but that was perhaps the only thing that was orderly about Philippine politics. There was the serious internal war in the form of frequently open clashes between the Hukbalahap, seeking economic and social reform, and the inefficient, highly corrupt (except perhaps during the short incumbency of Ramon Magsaysay), unstable "democratic" political system. Hungary was, and still is, one of the East European Communist political systems and, as such, it had a high level of regulative capability, as is characteristic of any Communist nation. The main reason for the high rate of death from group violence was the revolt of 1956, after the sudden demise of Matias Rakosi, which spread rapidly from Budapest to other parts of the country and which was subsequently crushed by the armed might of the Soviet Union. Elsewhere, among the nations of the first column of Table 1, the overthrow of legally constituted regimes, coups, or countercoups were the major political feature during the period under review, all clearly indicating a serious lack of regulative capability on the part of government.

The nations of the remaining two columns of the table may be viewed in similar fashions. By and large, those belonging to the third column are either more developed or governed by well-organized, cohesive authoritarian regimes or monarchies, while those in the second column are, again speaking generally, economically less developed or less well-off or ravaged by critical internal social or economic or ethnic fragmentation/polarization or governed by ineffective authoritarian regimes. In short, those in the second column resemble those in the first column, while those in the third column are closer to their counterparts in the fourth column in terms of the general level of development, internal political organization, and socioeconomic composition.

Table 2 attempts to state more explicitly that the level of group violence has a definite and measurable relationship to governmental instability as manifested in extralegal changes of regime, attempted coups and countercoups and widespread political violence. It should be borne in mind that the orderly succession of government does not necessarily signify either a high level of regulative capability or a high degree of

Table 2. Group Violence and Governmental Stability, 1950–1962.
(Percentages in parentheses.)

Deaths from Domestic Group Violence per 1,000,000 Population	Number of Nations	I Nations with Extralegal Change of Government	II Nations with Attempted Coups or Countercoups	III Nations with Widespread Political Violence	Nations with I, II, and/or III
Over 101	11	9[a] (82)	3[b] (27)	6[c] (55)	11 (100)
11–100	18	7[d] (38)	2[e] (11)	8[f] (44)	11 (61)
1–10	18	3[g] (17)	1[h] (6)	2[i] (12)	6 (33)
Below 1	27	1[j] (3.6)	0	1[k] (3.6)	2 (7.1)
Total	74	20 (27)	6 (8)	17 (23)	30 (40)

[a] Cuba, Bolivia, Iraq, Hungary, Colombia, Argentina, Burma, Honduras, Venezuela.
[b] Indonesia, Colombia, Honduras.
[c] Cuba, Hungary, Indonesia, Philippines, Honduras, Venezuela.
[d] Guatemala, South Korea, Syria, Iran, Peru, Ecuador, Haiti.
[e] Syria, Panama.
[f] Guatemala, South Korea, Ceylon, South Africa, China, Haiti, Iran, Lebanon.
[g] Pakistan, Thailand, Egypt.
[h] Ethiopia.
[i] Poland, East Germany.
[j] Turkey.
[k] France.

political stability. Conversely, the mere fact of a coup in a nation does not necessarily mean that the nation is more unstable and less able to regulate than another nation that is free from such an event. Statistics suggest, however that there is a significant association (which suggests a certain general tendency) between a high rate of violence and a high frequency of symptoms of political instability (lambda = .50 in Table 2). This correlation means that both are manifestations of serious insufficiency of regulative capability, for another correlate of the regulative capability is an ability to maintain certain norms in the political arena, for example, ability to maintain constitutional and other norms of orderly political processes. Thus, nations that maintain high levels of operative stability of constitutional procedural norms for succession and tenure security of government also more effectively regulate relationships and interactions among divergent groups in society.

Another dimension of the regulative capability is the ability to control and regulate the behavior of individuals. In this sense, comparative crime statistics ought to tell much about relative levels of regulative capabilities of various nations.

THE EXTRACTION OF RESOURCES

The regulative aspect of governmental capability most directly and immediately relates to order and stability in society and in the political arena, which is the first prerequisite for any polity. Long-run stability, viability, and development of society, however, requires generation, mobilization, manipulation, and utilization of human and material resources for the strengthening of stability, the introduction of needed change, and the promotion of continuous economic, social, political, and human development. The extractive aspect of governmental capability, then, refers to an ability of government to make available to its direct and indirect disposal the kinds and quantities of resources it needs and intends to manipulate and utilize for the development and stability of society. One example of the expression of such ability may be taxation or any other form of exaction for purposes of generating governmental revenue. Government should have a system of taxation to insure a fairly constant and predictable level of revenue, to allow for a rational budgetary policy, and to finance its administration of laws and regulations, pay salaries and wages to its officials and workers, and pay the cost of acquiring, exercising, and maintaining its control over whatever aspects or activities of society it wishes to control. Government should also have some methods or means to recruit and train the best available talents in society for expanding government services and for those posts and roles it institutes and maintains at different levels. It should also have the means to draft people into the military service to provide for national defense and internal security. These, among many other, dimensions of the extractive capability should be fairly constant and permanent if the polity is to attain stability or remain stable and be able to promote progress and development. None of them should be haphazardly organized and subjected to shifting whims of either society or factions within government, for the stability of society and government requires a high degree of predictability of governmental process and behavior.

Extraction in the process of national development is different from that in established societies. It means patterns and sources of extraction quite different from those of the past. It calls for different patterns of institutional behavior on the part of government. National development and modernization requires large amounts of investment capital as well as large and different types of human resources.[19] Certain sectors of society will therefore inevitably suffer greater exaction and deprivation than others. For example, since the agrarian sector is generally the only area of a traditional society from which initial development capital must be generated (that is, barring massive foreign aid and investment), peasants and landowners may well feel greater relative and absolute deprivation than other sectors. There will, therefore, emerge resistance—overt, as in the flat refusal to pay taxes or in physical attacks on tax collectors, or covert, as in concealing portions of agricultural produce. Where a democratic or representative form of government exists, the same resistance will manifest itself in the form of legislative opposition. Apart from the agrarian sector itself, the traditional upper class (which is largely tied to land) possesses much of the national wealth that should be mobilized or taxed for investment in development and modernization, but members of that class are not accustomed to such practice or sacrifice. Collection of taxes from the emergent urban sector will be no easier task, especially when many of the taxes are new. Even when there is no deliberate effort on the part of many groups in society to resist or subvert the government, the amount of material and monetary resources that can be exacted may not be adequate for carrying out certain policies and programs for development. Society may be too poor to support any ambitious enterprise in the direction of rapid national development.

Extractive ability is also manifested in many indirect ways. Even in a nation where much of the economic activity is legally in private hands, government, through the laws and regulations it establishes, plays a crucial role in determining the direction of business and economic activities and the manner in which they operate. In this sense, capital formation and investment in modernization and development, whether by private concerns or by government, properly pertain to the extractive aspect of governmental capability. Therefore, much could be learned about levels of the extractive capability of many governments by examining the proportions of the gross national product that are plowed back into investment.

Then there is the problem of extracting nonmaterial resources and utilizing them for development and modernization. This activity calls for patterns of recruitment and role assignment as well as of behavior that are drastically different from those in the past. In many societies, formal education traditionally meant training for governmental bureaucracy or the military. These were prestigious occupations that were generally the monopoly of the upper class of society. Development and modernization, however, require many different types of occupations and professions, hence different kinds of education; recruitment from all strata of society into these occupations and professions is required, and role assignments and scales of rewards within them not on the basis of ascriptive criteria but on the basis of ability and achievement. All this calls for significant, even radical value change among the people concerned, but such change, if left to take its own natural course, is an exasperatingly slow process. In the meantime, the necessity of new patterns of mobilization and utilization of human resources for the purpose of national development is likely to encounter varying degrees of overt and covert resistance. The traditional warrior class that monopolized the officer corps will resent the recruitment and promotion of able and aggressive men from lower classes. Aristocrats who were accustomed to an automatic recruitment into and promotion within the high civil service by virtue of their birth and social position would naturally oppose the idea that it is talent and achievement and not birth that counts as the criterion for recruitment and reward. Moreover, many qualified people resist recruitment into many types of work that are necessary for society's development but are undesirable to them. Those who are equipped, through education, ability, or experience, with such modern skills as managerial, technical, and professional should be willing to work for the implementation of many programs and policies. In reality, this is not the case. Many educated people abhor the prospect of working in rural areas or in provinces away from the capital city where modern conveniences and amenities are available. Even if they are willing to work in rural areas, moreover, they are willing to perform only certain roles —such as officials, clerks, accountants—not as public-health workers, community development leaders, agronomists, organizers of peasant cooperatives. University students still seek training for these few traditionally lucrative or prestigious occupations, instead of for critically needed skills in the fields of engineering, agronomy, medicine, teaching, and rural development. Educated and trained people are concentrated in the capital where they covet only a few types of work such as the civil service, law, and journalism, which they feel confer upon them maximum social prestige and opportunities for large, often illicit, incomes. As a result, those coveted professions and occupations in urban areas are overloaded with redundant personnel, while many other categories of critically needed jobs which are far more essential to the task of national development suffer from serious shortages of qualified manpower.

Few explicit attempts have thus far been made by political scientists to measure and compare extractive capabilities of governments,[20] but it is still possible to suggest a number of statistical indices which could be manipulated to generate some general understanding of the extent of extractive capability of many a polity. One simple example of such statistical indices may be the total governmental revenue as a percentage of the GNP. For the year 1967, as an instance, Table 3 provides figures for national-government revenues of thirty-two randomly selected (16 developed, 16 developing) nations. While our common-sense knowledge of these nations would tell us that most of the nations in the two columns at the left are well developed (hence with high extractive capabilities)

Table 3. Government Revenue as a Percentage of National Income, 1967. ($N = 32$)

Over 40.1 ($n = 8$)	30.1–40.0 ($n = 8$)	20.1–30.0 ($n = 8$)	10.1–20.0 ($n = 8$)
Austria	Australia	Taiwan	Colombia
Canada	Belgium	Spain	Costa Rica
Chile	Italy	Japan	Greece
Denmark	Malaysia[a]	South Korea	Guatemala
Finland	Switzerland	New Zealand	Honduras
France	Britain	Panama	Paraguay
West Germany	United States	Portugal[b]	Philippines
Sweden	Uruguay	Venezuela	Thailand

[a] 1966.
[b] as % of GNP.

Source: *Yearbook of National Accounts Statistics 1968*, Vol. 1 (New York: United Nations, 1969).

and that the great majority of those in the other two columns are either developing or underdeveloped (hence with lower levels of extractive capabilities), the table in itself can give only partial knowledge of the real relative extents of respective extractive capabilities. Inasmuch as direct taxation, especially of personal and corporate income and property, is more difficult to institute and enforce than indirect taxation, a better knowledge of the relative extractive capabilities of various nations may be elicited from data on what proportion of each nation's government revenue is derived from such direct taxes. Table 4 indicates that there is even greater disparity of extractive capability among those nations than is apparent in Table 3. By and large, those nations ranking high in Table 3 also rank high in Table 4. For example, of the sixteen nations in the two columns at the left in Table 3, thirteen are also in the first two columns of Table 4. On the other hand, seven of the eight nations in the column at the extreme right in Table 3 (lowest proportions of national incomes as government revenues) are also located in the "below 40%" categories in Table 4. It does not seem unreasonable, therefore, to say that there is a direct correlation between development and extractive capability. It is important, however, to note that the difference in extractive capability between modern countries and transitional nations is not only in the *level* of revenue relative to national income but also in the *pattern* of generating much of the revenue; consequently, the difference between the two types of nations in this regard is not only quantitative but also qualitative. Since the ultimate test of

Table 4. Direct Taxes as a Percentage of Government Revenue, 1967. ($N = 32$)

Over 60.1 ($n = 5$)	50.1–60.0 ($n = 11$)	40.1–50.0 ($n = 6$)	30.1–40.0 ($n = 2$)	20.1–30.0 ($n = 4$)	10.1–20.0 ($n = 3$)	Below 10.0 ($n = 1$)
Belgium	Australia	Canada	Costa Rica	Guatemala	Greece	Taiwan
New Zealand	Austria	Colombia	Paraguay	Honduras	Philippines	
Sweden	Chile	Denmark		South Korea	Thailand	
Switzerland	Finland	Panama		Malaysia[a]		
United States	France	Portugal				
	West Germany	Venezuela				
	Spain					
	Italy					
	Japan					
	Britain					
	Uruguay					

[a] 1966.

extractive capability consists in whether or not government can extract from where the wealth is (but where it is politically most difficult to extract), it may be argued that the difference between the two types of nations in Table 3 proves much greater in Table 4. The nations in the "40.1–50.0" column are a mixed bag. Canada and Denmark are, by most standards, developed nations and they do show larger proportions of revenues coming from direct taxes (48.2% and 49.6% respectively) than do the other four nations (Colombia 41.2%, Panama 41.0%, Portugal 48.0%, and Venezuela 45.0%), but the difference between the two types of nations in the column is not great.

In order to establish an empirically more persuasive relationship between development and extractive capability, therefore, it would be necessary more closely to examine contents and sources of revenues as well as the rates at which various taxes, particularly of the direct kind, are levied. Indirect or hidden taxes are generally less offensive to economically and politically influential strata than are direct taxes, especially of the progressive kind. And this consideration should have direct bearing on the task of evaluating and measuring relative extractive capabilities of various polities. It is nevertheless significant that, taken as groups, there is a clear gap of extractive capability between sixteen "developed" nations and sixteen "developing" countries. The group of developed nations derive close to three-fifths of governmental revenues from direct taxes (56.9%) in comparison to less than one-third (31.3%) for developing nations. An equally significant gap between these two groups of nations may be observed in another index that is suggestive of extractive capability: gross domestic capital formation as a percentage of national income. This variable suggests developmental investment, though an accurate assessment of it could be made only by careful examination and evaluation of the content and purposes of such capital formation. At any rate, the developed nations show an average of 29.4% of national income as gross domestic capital formation for 1967, while the other sixteen nations indicate an average of only 23.4%. Numerically, the difference between the two is only 6, but the cumulative effect of this difference over time would prove to be enormous. This finding is salient especially in view of the fact that developing nations need to devote a proportionately much larger portion of national income to investment than do modern, developed countries.[21]

The ability of government to extract nonmaterial resources is even more difficult to ascertain, let alone measure. Table 5 is presented merely as suggestive of the kinds of variables that may elicit some meaningful understanding of the level of governmental ability to extract non-

Table 5. A Dimension of Extractive Capability: Primary-Secondary School Teacher-Population Ratios, 1965. ($N = 46$)

Below 150 ($n = 17$)		151–200 ($n = 9$)		201–300 ($n = 12$)		Over 301 ($n = 8$)	
United States	100	Bolivia	158	Congo (Braz.)	213	Burma[a]	428
Albania	128	Taiwan	158	Cyprus	201	Ethiopia	2,091
Argentina	86	Colombia	188	El Salvador	203	Haiti	561
Austria	130	Ecuador	178	Guatemala	254	Indonesia[a]	302
Canada	92	Ghana	166	India[b]	289	Nigeria	580
Czechoslovakia	116	Iraq	164	South Korea	262	Sudan	871
Finland	103	Philippines[a]	168	Libya[a]	210	South Vietnam	424
France	109	Syria[a]	193	Nicaragua	214	Zambia	431
Ireland[a]	103	Venezuela	154	Portugal[a]	212		
Israel	80			Thailand	213		
Italy	116			Turkey[a]	298		
Japan	120			United Arab Republic	222		
Lebanon	123						
New Zealand[a]	122						
Panama[a]	143						
Costa Rica	124						
Cuba	140						

[a] 1964.
[b] 1962.

Source: *Statistical Abstract of the United States 1968* (Washington: Bureau of the Census, U.S. Department of Commerce, 1968).

material resources in society for its welfare and progress. Even then, much caution is needed in examining the table. For example, the table does not take into account the relative qualities of education and teachers in the nations concerned; nor does it reflect the extent to which education is valued in each nation. In some nations, the relative proportion of school-age children in the population is much greater than in others. And, then, the proportion of school-age population that in fact attends school differs from one nation to another—a situation which, incidentally, may reflect different levels of regulative and distributive capabilities among the nations concerned. Also, education may be urban-centered. On the plane of broad generalizations, however, it can well be argued that those nations that enjoy a favorable teacher–population ratio (hence teacher–pupil ratio, shown in Table 6) have the kind of government that manages to create or maintain conditions which induce large numbers of people to be recruited into the teaching profession, thus suggesting relatively high levels of ability to extract either directly or indirectly.

Table 6. Primary-Secondary School Teacher-Pupil Ratios, 1965. ($N = 75$)

Below 20 ($n = 9$)		21–30 ($n = 31$)		31–40 ($n = 23$)		Over 41 ($n = 12$)	
United Kingdom*	12.1	Sweden*	21.2	El Salvador	30.2	Morocco*	40.1
Norway	15.3	Czecho-slovakia	21.6	Venezuela	30.2	Burma	40.5
Italy	16.8	Poland	22.0	Ecuador	30.6	Turkey	40.7
Israel	17.0	Lebanon	22.0	Thailand	30.6	Algeria*	43.8
Ceylon*	18.7	Bulgaria	22.0	Ghana	31.1	Senegal*	43.8
France	19.3	Hungary	22.3	Nigeria	31.3	Mexico*	46.7
Austria	19.4	Canada	23.2	Syria	31.4	Zambia	47.9
Finland	19.8	Ireland	23.3	United Arab Republic	32.7	Afghanistan*	49.6
Iceland	20.0	Argentina	23.8	Philippines	33.2	Congo (Braz.)	50.8
		Iraq	23.9	West Germany*	33.3	South Vietnam	52.4
		Bolivia	24.8	India	33.3	Chile	52.6
		United States	25.0	Greece*	35.8	South Korea	54.4
		Belgium*	25.4	Taiwan	36.1		
		Japan	25.4	Peru*	36.1		
		Russia	25.5	South Africa*	36.4		
		Libya	25.5	Indonesia	36.6		
		Guatemala	26.1	Liberia*	36.7		
		Australia*	27.3	Jordan*	36.9		
		Portugal	27.4	Sudan	37.0		
		Panama	27.4	Uruguay*	37.2		
		Cuba	27.5	Pakistan*	38.0		
		Albania	27.7	Haiti	38.6		
		Costa Rica	27.8	Ethiopia	39.5		
		Yugoslavia	27.8				
		New Zealand	28.0				
		Brazil*	28.3				
		Colombia	28.1				
		Honduras	28.4				
		Nicaragua	29.1				
		Spain*	29.5				
		Paraguay*	29.8				

*Primary schools only.

Source: *Statistical Abstract of the United States 1968* (Washington: Bureau of the Census, U.S. Department of Commerce, 1969).

Another potentially meaningful index of the ability to extract nonmaterial resources for purposes of national development is the distribution of the student population in higher education by discipline. Developing nations are handicapped by numerous obstacles; one of them is the fact that university students tend to seek those professions and occupations that are traditionally prestigious and lucrative, for example, the civil service and the law, or pursue the kind of education that has traditionally been regarded as cultivating sophisticated gentlemen and ladies. As a result, there is a dire shortage of qualified personnel in those areas of activities that are vitally necessary for the development and modernization of a nation—rural development, agronomy, engineering, public health, and so on. Table 7 is designed to indicate this handicap that plagues many a developing nation. The data suggest another dimension of the fact that developing polities lack adequate levels of ability to extract needed human resources for those activities that are vitally necessary if these nations are to develop.

The tables concerning extractive capability present only a few of the variables suggestive of the extractive aspect of governmental capability. As such, they are meant only to indicate a possible direction in

Table 7. University Students in Humanities, Fine Arts, Law, and Social Science, in Selected Asian Nations.

Nation and Year	Male and Female	Proportion of Students
Pakistan, 1962–1963	M	approx. 2/3
	F	approx. 2/3
India, 1949–1950	M	over 93% (virtually none in education)
	F	over 90%
1961–1962	M	over 55%
	F	over 2/3
Indonesia, 1956–1957	M	approx. 6/10
	F	approx. 1/2 (remainder mostly in medicine)
Burma, 1963–1964	M	approx. 1/2
	F	approx. 3/4
Philippines, 1960–1961	M	nearly 2/3
	F	nearly 1/2 (remainder mostly in education)
Thailand, 1963–1964	M	over 4/5
	F	over 3/5
Ceylon, 1961–1962	M	over 2/3
	F	nearly 2/3
Malaya, 1961–1962	M	approx. 1/5
	F	approx. 1/4

Source: Adapted from Gunnar Myrdal, *Asian Drama: An Inquiry into the Poverty of Nations* (New York: Pantheon, 1968), Vol. III, p. 1778. © 1968 by The Twentieth Century Fund, New York. Reprinted by permission.

which efforts might be made to ascertain, examine, and eventually measure the relative levels of extractive capabilities of polities. Among other indices, apart from economic, to be investigated would be:

1. The distribution, and its changing pattern, of students in institutions of higher learning by field of study.
2. The relative growth of public higher institutions of learning and the placement patterns of their graduates.
3. The relative increases in the rate of enrollment of members of middle and lower classes in institutions of higher learning.
4. The changing patterns of recruitment for the civil service and for military service.
5. The geographical as well as occupational distribution of trained and educated personnel both in terms of social origin and assignment.

THE DISTRIBUTION OF RESOURCES

"Society is a distributive system for the allocation of scarce resources."[22] Good governance then, warrants that wealth, both material and nonmaterial, be shared within society in such a manner as to promote and maintain harmony, stability, and general contentment. The distributive aspect of governmental capability refers to an ability to provide goods and services and other values such as status—directly as in a welfare state or indirectly as in a laissez-faire society—and to allocate rewards and punishments in a manner that society at large can accept. There are two major ways in which this aspect of governmental capability may be manifested. One is direct distribution by government. Government allocates its revenue, through budgetary processes, to a variety of public programs and activities, such as public health, sanitation, educucation, agricultural subsidies and experimental stations, highway construction, irrigation, conservation, postal services, the court system, and social security. It also distributes nonmaterial resources and values, such as personnel (for implementating the various programs), ranks, prestige, authority, and rights as well as promotion, salary increases, and honors. It may also distribute opportunities for higher education through direct scholarship and other financial-aid programs. The second way in which government distributes goods, services, and statuses is indirect. Government induces society at large or its various segments (for example, business, labor) to distribute goods and other values in certain ways or according to certain standards. Laws and regulations concerning the relationship between labor and management are one such example. Laws concerning wages and working conditions are another. Regulations against racial or other discrimination in education, employment, work assignment, and promotion, even in intergroup relations outside economic spheres, are yet another example of government's indirect distribution of values.

In the use or exercise of this capability, government (or its political leadership) ought to consider both how it desires to distribute and how various groups in society want it to distribute. Goods and services, as well as other values desired by men and groups of men, are always in a relatively shorter supply than is adequate to satisfy all the demands and needs of all the groups in society. Distribution, direct or indirect, therefore, calls for discrimination as to which demand is to be satisfied to what extent relative to which other demands. This determination, in turn, requires calculations not only about the existing state of affairs, including the distributive capability itself, but also about the long-run effects. It is in this discretionary area of calculation that political leadership plays a crucial and decisive role. Government must retain flexibility as well as forcefulness in its manner of distributing goods, services, and other values. In order to remain able to govern, it must be able to meet a certain minimal level of material and psychic demands so that society will not withdraw its support. The political system must be, to a significant extent, responsive and accommodative to society's needs and demands in order to remain stable and able to govern. At the same time, it must be able to withstand pressure from powerful vested interests in society. Obviously, some systems today are not capable in this regard. Hence the recurrent revolutions, revolts, civil strifes, coups d'état, and violent demonstrations.

The distributive capability is as difficult to ascertain and measure as the extractive capability. If other things were equal, one could perhaps argue that the higher the level of the extractive capability (for example, as might be indicated by the amount of revenue as a percentage of the GNP), the higher the level of the distributive capability. Likewise, one could then perhaps argue also that the higher the per-capita GNP of a nation, the higher the distributive capability of its government. Such patterns of equation, incidentally, have often been implicit in many published works on the study of developing nations in particular and comparative politics in general. Lipset and others have used such variables as per-capita income, number of persons per motor vehicle, number of doctors per certain size of population, number of telephones, radios, and newspaper copies per so much population as important indices of development and stability.[23] These variables certainly reveal the patterns of distribution of goods, services, and other resources that obtain in certain nations. They tell very little about the level of distributive capability a given government or political system possesses, however. In the first place, some of these variables inform us on the capability of nations that have achieved a high level of development and modernization, such as many Western nations and Japan. They may, however, be less relevant when applied to other nations. Second, the distributive capability and, hence, the actual manner of distribution, of a government should be evaluated in terms of what is needed in its country, within the context of the developmental needs and wants of the nation.[24] For example, in a typical developing (or underdeveloped) nation, automobiles, television sets, hospital beds, and doctors are concentrated primarily in one or a few urban areas. Since the great majority of the people live in rural areas, this concentration suggests an enormous inequality of distribution of goods, services, and other values in the nation. It may well be that such data suggest neither a high level of development and modernization nor a high level of distributive capability, but rather the opposite, namely, underdevelopment and low distributive capability. What the nation needs is not more automobiles, hospital beds, expensively trained and high-salaried doctors, nor more television sets in urban areas, but rather trucks, bicycles, minibuses, inexpensively trained health workers and sanitation experts, small but versatile health clinics, nurses and elementary medical treatment in rural areas. Ten health workers could be trained for the cost of training one son of a well-to-do family to become a physician. For the price of one American-made passenger car, which is useful only to several people in a single wealthy family, a bus (or two minibuses) can be bought, which will benefit a large number of poor rural families or a whole village. Or, for the same price, a large truck can be purchased which can be used for the quick and inexpensive transportation to market of the agricultural produce of an entire village.[25] Likewise, the nation needs not more lawyers and specialized doctors who are useful only to the rich few in the urban milieu, but rather community-development workers, agronomists, and what the Chinese today call "barefoot doctors" who can benefit the many rural poor.[26]

The distributive capability of government or polity, in this sense, then, is adequate to the extent that it is able to redirect resources in society, both material and human, to the more critical needs of society at large. The ultimate example of such governmental capability is an ability to divert wealth from the affluent to the poor and disadvantaged, from the superfluous to the needy. This is also a politically most difficult task to undertake. In this respect, it would be necessary, in any meaningful

Table 8. Income Distribution as a Percentage of Total National Income, in Selected Nations, ca. 1960–1964. (Most figures are approximations.)

Population	United Kingdom	United States	Mexico	Argentina	Brazil	Colombia	El Salvador	Panama	Costa Rica
Top 5%	16.0	20.0	29.5	31.3	31.0	30.5	33.0	34.5	35.0
Top 10%	25.0	30.0	41.4	41.0	41.4	42.8	45.8	44.0	46.0
Next 30% (61st–90th percentile)	34.8	31.2	26.1	25.4	23.9	23.2	22.6	22.6	22.0
Next 30% (31st–60th percentile)	19.7	18.7	11.8	15.3	13.8	14.3	10.5	16.0	12.5
Bottom 5)%	25.5	23.3	15.4	20.5	19.7	20.2	16.0	20.5	18.0
Bottom 20%			3.6	7.0					

Source: Adapted from United Nations Economic Commission for Latin America, "Income Distribution in Latin America," *Economic Bulletin for Latin America,* XII (1967), 41.

attempt to measure relative levels of distributive capability of various polities, to examine patterns of income distribution in each nation (for example, by dividing the population into five 20% groups).[27] Such inquiry would require complex measurements and indices, for which there is a serious paucity of organized data. Tables 8 and 9 present rather sketchy information on nine nations as suggestive of the type of data that would have to be collected in much greater detail in order more accurately to reveal the distributive capabilities of various polities.[28]

Table 10 suggests two other variables which seem to be closely related to the relative levels of distributive capability of a variety of nations: total governmental expenditures on public health and education as precentages of GNP.[29] Why these variables may be relevant to the problem of ascertaining and measuring relative levels of distributive capability may be noted from the fact that in most developing nations, not only are the institution of universal public education and the implemention of public-health programs—to name only two welfare matters—vitally important, but also their adequate funding encounters serious institutional, economic, and political resistance, especially from those institutions within the polity that tend to equate more appropria-

Table 9. Per-Capita Income Ratio, in Selected Nations, ca. 1960–1964.

Top 5% vs. Bottom 50% (approx.)		Top 10% vs. Bottom 50%	
United Kingdom	6:1	United Kingdom	5:1
United States	9:1	United States	7:1
Argentina	15:1	Argentina	10:1
Brazil	15:1	Brazil	10:1
Colombia	15:1	Colombia	11:1
Panama	16:1	Panama	11:1
Mexico	20:1	Costa Rica	13:1
Costa Rica	20:1	Mexico	14:1
El Salvador	21:1	El Salvador	14:1

Note: Equally significant, though much less precise, indicators of distributive capability are compensations for employees as proportions of national incomes. Here, too, the difference between the group of developed nations and that of developing nations is striking. Among the sixteen developed nations sampled in Tables 3 and 4, the range is 55% (Japan) to 75% (United Kingdom) with thirteen nations in the above-61% category, and the remainder in the high-50's. In addition to the United Kingdom, Canada, Sweden, and the United States are in the 71%-and-up category. In contrast, of twelve of the sixteen developing nations for which relevant data are available in the same United Nations source, only three are in the 50% category, while two are below 40%, with the remainder in the 40% (the range for this group is from 25% for Thailand to 58% for Venezuela). In terms of the averages, modern nations devote 65.2% of national income to compensation for employees, while developing countries allocate only 44.1% for their workers. Admittedly, less-developed nations need to invest more and subsequently the gap, for example, 5% versus 50%, is likely to be larger.

Table 10. Expenditures on Public Health and Education Per Capita, 1966. (US $)

Nation	I GNP	II Health	III Education	IV II + III	V IV as % of GNP
United States	3,696	61.9	174.2	236.1	6.4
Canada	2,658	77.2	151.6	228.8	8.6
Belgium	1,903	3.9	91.1	95.0	5.0
Denmark	2,322	78.4	121.7	200.1	8.6
France	2,052	7.1	69.6	76.7	3.7
West Germany	1,990	25.8	63.8	89.6	4.5
Greece	764	5.6	11.6	17.2	2.3
Iceland	2,837	35.7	76.5	102.2	3.6
Italy	1,182	7.4	59.9	67.3	5.7
Luxembourg	2,018	29.9	86.6	116.5	5.8
Netherlands	1,666	17.7	83.9	101.6	6.1
Norway	2,022	33.8	99.4	133.2	6.1
Portugal	436	4.0	5.2	9.2	2.1
Turkey	295	3.4	6.9	10.3	3.5
United Kingdom	1,924	51.5	93.1	144.6	7.5
Warsaw Pact Nations	1,434	76.4	108.8	185.2	12.9
Albania	366	6.3	45.5	51.8	14.2
Austria	1,374	38.7	46.4	85.1	6.2
Finland	1,858	61.2	103.7	164.9	8.9
Ireland	1,020	11.4	31.9	43.3	4.2
Spain	771	8.7	7.7	16.4	2.1
Sweden	2,733	76.4	163.7	240.1	8.8
Switzerland	2,499	44.2	82.3	126.5	5.1
Yugoslavia	457	10.3	21.0	31.3	6.8
Latin America:	415	6.5	10.2	16.7	4.0
Argentina	716	1.4	26.0	27.4	3.8
Bolivia	156	5.9	5.4	11.3	7.2
Brazil	310	5.9	4.6	10.5	3.4
Chile	556	11.8	14.9	26.7	4.8
Colombia	293	2.0	6.4	8.4	2.9
Costa Rica	405	36.5	13.5	50.0	12.3
Cuba	638	19.1	28.9	48.0	7.5
Dominican Republic	266	6.1	5.9	12.0	4.5
Ecuador	237	2.4	6.5	8.9	3.8
El Salvador	284	3.6	6.7	10.3	3.6
Guatemala	292	2.3	4.4	6.7	2.3
Guyana	328	8.9	11.9	20.8	6.3
Haiti	74	.6	.9	1.5	2.0

Table 10 *(continued)*

Nation	I GNP	II Health	III Education	IV II + III	V IV as % of GNP
Honduras	227	2.5	4.7	7.2	3.2
Jamaica	516	8.1	11.5	19.6	3.8
Mexico	493	5.4	8.3	13.7	2.8
Nicaragua	350	9.3	5.2	14.5	4.1
Panama	542	9.3	17.9	27.2	5.0
Paraguay	221	.9	3.3	4.2	1.9
Peru	295	5.0	8.3	13.3	4.5
Trinidad-Tobago	669	14.9	15.9	30.8	4.6
Uruguay	569	5.8	6.5	12.3	2.2
Venezuela	890	29.8	38.1	67.9	7.6
Asia:	149	.9	5.1	6.0	4.0
Burma	67	.7	1.5	2.2	3.3
Cambodia	139	1.3	4.9	6.2	4.5
China	104	1.4	3.6	5.0	4.8
Taiwan	235	.6	5.9	6.5	2.8
Indonesia	100	.2	.9	1.1	1.1
Japan	986	1.4	41.6	43.0	4.4
North Korea	234	1.4	7.3	8.7	3.7
South Korea	131	.8	3.1	3.9	3.0
Laos	70	6.7	1.9	8.6	12.3
Malaysia	311	5.8	12.1	17.9	5.8
Mongolia	439	.9	NA	NA	NA
Philippines	171	.9	8.4	9.3	5.4
Thailand	141	.8	2.6	3.4	2.4
North Vietnam	77	1.4	6.6	8.0	10.4
South Vietnam	126	.7	4.8	5.5	4.4
Afghanistan	88	.1	.8	.9	1.0
Ceylon	147	3.2	5.9	9.1	6.2
India	74	.3	2.0	2.3	3.1
Nepal	75	.9	.2	1.1	1.5
Pakistan	115	.2	1.4	1.6	1.4
Near East:	284	7.0	11.2	18.2	6.4
Cyprus	440	6.6	16.6	23.2	5.3
Iran	252	3.8	6.7	10.5	4.2
Iraq	268	2.6	13.3	15.9	5.9
Israel	1,454	13.7	64.3	78.0	5.4
Jordan	266	2.0	6.7	8.7	3.3
Kuwait	3.462	65.2	95.7	160.9	4.6
Lebanon	476	4.2	13.7	17.9	3.8
Saudi Arabia	380	8.6	20.2	28.8	7.6

Table 10 *(continued)*

Nation	I GNP	II Health	III Education	IV II + III	V IV as % of GNP
Syria	201	11.7	13.1	24.8	12.3
Yemen	103	8.8	.2	9.0	8.7
United Arab Republic	168	8.7	8.4	17.1	10.2
Africa:	171	1.8	5.0	6.8	4.0
Algeria	219	.9	9.7	10.6	4.8
Cameroon	135	1.7	3.2	4.9	3.6
Central African Republic	127	2.0	3.5	5.5	4.3
Chad	75	.9	1.5	2.4	3.2
Congo (Braz.)	145	2.4	3.5	5.9	4.1
Congo (Kins.)	111	2.0	8.7	10.7	9.6
Dahomey	71	2.0	1.7	3.7	5.2
Ethiopia	65	2.0	.4	2.4	3.7
Gabon	372	12.8	15.0	27.8	7.5
Ghana	219	11.7	.4	12.1	5.5
Guinea	80	1.9	3.9	5.8	7.3
Ivory Coast	260	2.0	8.9	10.9	4.2
Kenya	116	2.0	3.6	5.6	4.8
Liberia	207	2.8	4.6	7.4	3.6
Libya	812	1.8	13.1	14.9	1.8
Malagasy Republic	110	1.8	6.8	8.6	7.8
Mali	70	1.9	3.0	4.9	7.0
Mauritania	138	1.8	4.7	6.5	4.7
Morocco	182	1.9	7.2	9.1	5.0
Niger	75	2.0	1.2	3.2	4.3
Nigeria	125	2.0	1.9	3.9	3.1
South Rhodesia	227	3.0	3.9	6.9	3.0
Senegal	200	2.0	6.1	8.1	4.1
South Africa	654	2.0	14.1	16.1	2.5
Sierra Leone	157	2.1	3.3	5.4	3.4
Somali Republic	60	1.2	.8	2.0	3.3
Sudan	105	2.0	3.4	5.4	5.1
Tanzania	75	.7	2.4	3.1	4.1
Togo	113	1.2	1.8	3.0	2.7
Tunisia	209	4.5	8.7	13.2	6.3
Uganda	92	1.9	3.7	5.6	6.1
Upper Volta	55	.8	1.0	1.8	3.3
Zambia	267	2.9	3.9	6.8	2.5
Oceana	2,153	34.3	67.9	102.2	4.7

Source: World Military Expenditures 1966-67, Research Report 68-52, United States Arms Control and Disarmament Agency, Economic Bureau (December 1968), pp. 9-13.

Table 11. Expenditures on Public Health and Education as a Percentage of Per-Capita GNP, 1966.

Over $800		$400–$800		$200–$400		$100–$200		Below $100	
Warsaw Pact Nations	12.9	Costa Rica	12.4	Syria	12.3	United Arab Republic	10.2	Laos	12.3
Canada	8.6	Cuba	7.5	Saudi Arabia	7.6	Congo (Kins.)	9.6	North Vietnam	10.4
Venezuela	7.7	Cyprus	5.2	Gabon	7.5	Yemen	8.7	Guinea	7.3
United States	6.6	Panama	5.0	Guyana	6.3	Malagasy Republic	7.8	Mali	7.0
Israel	5.4	Chile	4.8	Tunisia	6.3	Bolivia	7.2	Uganda	6.1
Western Europe	5.0	Argentina	3.8	Iraq	5.9	Ceylon	6.2	Dahomey	5.2
Kuwait	4.7	Jamaica	3.8	Malaysia	5.8	Philippines	5.4	Niger	4.2
Oceana	4.7	Lebanon	3.8	Ghana	5.6	Sudan	5.1	Tanzania	4.1
Japan	4.4	Mexico	2.8	Algeria	4.8	Morocco	5.0	Ethiopia	3.7
		South Africa	2.4	Dominica	4.5	China	4.8	Burma	3.3
		Uruguay	2.2	Peru	4.5	Kenya	4.7	Somalia	3.3
		Libya	1.8	Nicaragua	4.2	Mauritania	4.7	Upper Volta	3.3
				Iran	4.2	Colombia	4.5	Chad	3.2
				Ivory Coast	4.2	Central African Rep.	4.4	India	3.1
				Ecuador	3.7	South Vietnam	4.3	Haiti	2.0
				North Korea	3.7	Congo (Braz.)	4.1	Nepal	1.4
				El Salvador	3.6	Senegal	4.1	Indonesia	1.1
				Liberia	3.5	Cameroon	3.6	Afghanistan	1.0
				Brazil	3.3	Sierra Leone	3.5		
				Jordan	3.3	Nigeria	3.2		
				Honduras	3.1	South Korea	2.9		
				Rhodesia	3.0	Togo	2.6		
				Colombia	2.8	Thailand	2.4		
				Taiwan	2.7	Pakistan	1.4		
				Zambia	2.6				
				Guatemala	2.3				
				Paraguay	1.9				

Source: World Military Expenditures 1966–67, Research Report 68-52, United States Arms Control and Disarmament Agency, Economic Bureau (December 1968), pp. 9–13.

tion for such programs with less appropriation for them and from those sectors and groups that have to foot the bill. It is partly in these senses that a relatively high level of governmental expenditure on health and education may be viewed as a sign of a relatively high level of distributive capability. Therefore, what was presented in Table 5 can also be viewed as one of those indices that pertain to the distributive capability.

Table 11 shows no clear correlation between the level of per-capita GNP and that of expenditure on public health and education. Among those five groups of nations divided according to level of per-capita GNP, there is little significant variation in the proportion of the GNP expended on public health and education. On the average, figures for respective groups of nations are: 5.9% for the richest group, 4.6% for the second-richest, 4.6% for the third, 5.0% for the next, and 4.6% for the poorest group of nations. What is interesting and significant is the variation that obtains in each group of nations, suggesting that the level of expenditure on public health and education is essentially the function of political leadership in each nation. In the group of richest nations, the range of variation is from a low of 4.4 to a high of 8.6 (or 12.9); in the second group, it is from 1.8 to 12.4; in the third, 1.9 to 12.3; in the fourth, 1.4 to 9.6; and among the poorest nations, the expenditure ranges from 1.0 to 12.3. Clearly, a high per-capita GNP does not automatically nor necessarily generate a high level of expenditure on public health and education. The same may well be true of other items of expenditure relevant to distributive aspect of governmental capability. In short, there is no correlation between wealth and public policy. The distributive capability, like the other two capabilities, is ultimately a function of political leadership.

THE RELATIONSHIP AMONG THE THREE COMPONENTS

At a casual glance, it often appears that these three aspects of governmental capability are mutually not only convergent but also complementary. Their mutual covergence—the fact that they are in reality operationally not neatly separable is obvious. For example, the extraction of resources is necessarily predicated upon the ability to regulate and control individual and group behavior. In order for a tax to be collected (extractive), government must induce people to obey relevant tax laws (regulative) first, or create the kind of sociopolitical climate in which people become accustomed to obeying the tax law and paying taxes as a matter of course. Likewise with the distributive aspect of governmental capability. As observed earlier, the distribution of material and nonmaterial wealth and values is a function of interaction between the way government (or, more properly, its leadership) is predisposed to distribute them and the pattern of demands of various groups in society. If, therefore, government wants to distribute in a way that will promote national development, it must have the ability to enforce its will (namely, to regulate and control the behavior of individuals and groups). The regulative aspect of governmental capability is clearly influenced by the way in which the other two aspects of governmental capability are maintained, exercised, and augmented. (For example, political stability is unlikely unless a certain tolerable degree of societal welfare is maintained.) To that extent, then, there is a mutually complementary relationship among those three aspects of governmental capability.

Thus, other things being equal, the distributive capability will be enhanced in proportion to the degree of increase in the extractive capability. The regulative capability will likewise be positively increased when there is a significant rise in the distributive capability, and so on. Certain data support this kind of equation. For example, radical and persistent inequality of land distribution in transitional society (which may be viewed as a significant symptom of a low level of distributive capability) seems seriously to inhibit the growth of order and stability, namely, the regulative capability of a polity, as can be seen in Table 12. Another set of data indicates, as in Table 13, a discernible general tendency that seems to obtain in the relationship between the distributive and regulative aspects of governmental capability. Table 13 examines nations that spend more than 5.1% of GNP on public health and education (see Table 10) and those that spend less than 2.5%, in terms of extraconstitutional change of regime or the existence of observable

Table 12. Inequality and Instability, ca. 1948–1958.

Gini Index of Inequality in Distribution of Agricultural Land	I Number of Nations ($N = 50$)	II Unstable Nations	III II as % of I
.801+	16	10	63
.601–.800	21	5	23
.400–.600	13	0	00

Source: Gini indices and Column I adapted from Bruce Russett et al., *World Handbook of Political and Social Indicators* (New Haven, Conn.: Yale University Press, 1964), Table 69, pp. 239–240. Copyright 1964 by Yale University Press. Reprinted by permission.

Table 13. Welfare and Stability, 1966.

Expenditure on Public Health and Education as % of GNP	I Number of Nations (N = 49)	II Unstable Nations	III II as % of I
Below 2.5	12	8	66.7
Over 5.1	37	6	16.2

political instability during the immediate years around 1966 (the year of data). Excluded are those nations whose regimes had extremely high levels of legal-coercive ability (Communist nations, Spain, Portugal, Cuba, and Paraguay). Nations that fall between these two groups in terms of the level of expenditure on public health and education are difficult to examine at this point and, for present purposes, they need not be examined in detail. The suggestion here is merely that levels of distributive capability, under certain circumstances, seem to have some ascertainable relationship with levels of regulative capability. Provisionally, a certain positive general tendency can also be seen in the relationship between the extractive and distributive aspects of governmental capability as well. For example, fifteen of the seventeen nations in the column at the extreme left in Table 5 are also among those nations which demonstrate very high levels of distributive capability in terms of Table 10 (more than 5% of GNP for public health and education), while six of the eight nations in the column at the extreme right in Table 5 are among those nations with lowest levels of the distributive capability (less than 3% of GNP for public health and education). The remaining two columns of nations in Table 5 follow the general tendency of relationship between the extractive and distributive capabilities: eight of the nine in the "151-200" column in Table 5 have relatively high distributive capabilities, (between 3 and 5% of GNP for public health and education), while seven of the twelve nations in the "201-300" category in Table 5 show markedly low (but, by and large, not as low as those in the column at the extreme right) levels of distributive capability in terms of Table 10.

These observations, however, are only partial; they are, in an important sense, even misleading. What may, within the context of these tables, be regarded as exceptions are perhaps even more important than the general tendencies that appear consistent. General tendencies are pertinent only when nations are treated as groups. There is a wide range of variation among individual nations in each group in terms of relationships among the three aspects of governmental capability. The crucial question is: What accounts for such wide variations? It is easy to accept that nations with similar conditions and circumstances (in terms of per-capita wealth, for example) would, other things being equal, manifest similar tendencies. A rich nation, for example, would (be able to) spend much more on health and education than would a poor nation. It would also (be able to) recruit more and better-trained personnel to the teaching profession, than would its less affluent counterpart. And, for these reasons, it should enjoy a higher level of political stability as well. These considerations, however, do not take into account factors that make for variation among individual nations, for other things are seldom equal. We must, in this sense, examine at least two phenomena in order to gain a better understanding of the problem of national development in general and of those significant variations among nations in each grouping in particular. One is the question of why some rich nations spend less—for example, on public health and education—than other less-well-off nations? That is, why do some nations that should perhaps demonstrate higher levels of distributive capability in actuality demonstrate *lower* levels of distributive capability than nations that are worse off? The other question is: Why do nations that demonstrate higher levels of distributive and extractive capability also manifest *lower* levels of regulative capability? The first of these questions, namely, the frequently incongruous relationship between the material wealth of society and the distributive aspect of governmental capability, will be fully explored in Chapter III. Suffice it at this point to state that the relationship is the result of low levels of commitment, intelligence, and skill on the part of political leadership. The remainder of the present chapter considers the second of these two important questions, namely, the inverse relationship between distributive capability and regulative capability (or between rising well-being of society and declining political stability).

The question at issue here has been examined by a number of students of the politics of national development. Duff and McCamant, for example, argue that "the most important reason why economic development sometimes fails to produce political stability is that while the economy is making it possible for the political and economic systems to satisfy the demands of the population, it is also raising the level of expectations."[30] As discussed in Chapter I, the rate of rise in expectations is often faster than the rate of increase in the ability to satisfy expectations and demands. In short, as the governmental ability to satisfy demands and needs increases, the gap between expectation and actuality also widens. Thus, even if the level of regulative capability were raised by the skillful manipulation by political leadership, "the new political order could only persist if it were underpinned by the higher level of economic well-being that would be demanded by the newly participant groups, who would be likely otherwise to reject the established system and turn to anti-constitutional alternatives."[31] Here, clearly, the rate of increase in political participation exceeds the rate of increase in general welfare. Moreover, certain patterns of increase in the ability to meet needs and demands produce negative impact which can undo whatever positive increases may have been experienced by the distributive, regulative, or extractive capabilities. This is the kind of situation reflected in Perlmutter's observation: "Modernizing groups have invested greater intellectual efforts, administrative craftmanship, and wealth into the center. In the end, the neglected periphery retaliates."[32] Thus, consideration of how these capabilities are to be increased and in what manner relative to one another and to environmental needs becomes vital to the calculus of political leadership. Rates of increase in these capabilities as well as ways in which they are increased and exercised must be closely coordinated with the changes in perception, values, and individual and institutional behavior that are taking place in society. An ability to achieve a greater equalization of income, for example, suggests a high level of distributive capability of government, but if it is exercised without due regard for the perceptions and values that persist in society, or without skillful manipulation of them, the result may be a decline in stability, hence in the regulative capability, by generating discontent among certain groups in society that are rendered politically relevant. The Aristotelian dictum about rebellion being caused either by inequality among equals or by equality among unequals is not irrelevant to contemporary society. It is not to be supposed that, once a certain level of regulative, extractive, or distributive capability is reached, government (or more specifically its leadership) will retain it. In the first place, such achievement is neither inherent nor automatic: it is a result of political leadership's efforts and manipulative skill. In the second place, once a level of any of the capabilities is reached, whether or not it is maintained, let alone increased, depends upon the conduct of political leadership, as will become clear in Chapter III.

One additional, though perhaps minor, consideration about these three aspects of governmental capability is what may be called supplementarity or substitutability in their mutual relationship in some instances. For example, a relative lack of regulative capability (always to be judged in relation to environmental needs) may be compensated for or substituted by a relatively higher degree of distributive capability. Compensation may be achieved, as will be discussed in Chapter IV, by what may be called selective bribery, utilized to induce compliance with the law. The United States government, in recent years, has provided a largess, all of a sudden, one may say, to the urban ghetto in order to counteract its relative inability to enforce law and order, namely, in order to compensate for the relative inability to regulate and control the behavior of those ghetto dwellers who have decided to defy law and order. Conversely, a relatively low level of distributive capability (a result of the low extractive capability), which would generate discontent and resistance, could be compensated for by a high level of regulative capability, as witnessed in certain authoritarian nations. These, even if they work, are of temporary value, however. As discussed earlier in this chapter, the governmental ability to distribute goods and services consists ultimately in an ability to distribute as government deems necessary and desirable, and not to distribute under duress or pressure for compromise. The level of superficial ability to regulate and control that is achieved by bribery, however selective or discriminating it may be, cannot last. It is bound to dissipate as the benefit of the bribery dissipates in the eyes of those who have been bribed. Likewise with repression as a method of achieving a certain level of regulative capability in the absence of an adequate ability to satisfy material and other needs and expectations of society (for example, Haiti, Portugal, Spain, Paraguay, Ethiopia). The kind of stability thus established, while it may last for some time, however, is obviously not related to the task of development and modernization, for it is incapable of meaningfully expanding the extractive capability and increasing the distributive capability.

THE ROUTINIZATION OF GOVERNMENTAL CAPABILITY

One important consideration concerning the three aspects of governmental capability is the idea of routinization or institutionalization. The political stability and developmental viability, that is, meaningful change, of a nation require the continuity of a certain basic set of rules of behavior and the predictability of behavior both individual and institutional. A powerful and charismatic political leader may be able to bring about and even maintain certain levels of stability in society during his incumbency. But that is not enough. Machiavelli, the forerunner of the students of national development, clearly recognized this problem when he wrote that "the welfare, then, of a republic or a kingdom does not consist in having a prince who governs it wisely during his lifetime, but in having one who will give it such laws that it will maintain itself even after his death."[33] Orderly society, especially orderly and changing society, calls for its citizenry to behave civilly and to participate in its political processes constructively. In order for people to behave civilly and constructively in the political arena, however, it is necessary that they have some reasonably accurate notion as to what the government can and cannot do, as well as what the government will or will not do. That is to say, people should know at least approximately the level of each of the aspects of governmental capability. And this means that the governmental capability, in all its three dimensions, must be routinized and institutionalized, not in a rigid and static sense but in a dynamic way so as to enable the government flexibly to adapt itself to changing environmental needs. If the three dimensions of governmental capability are inconstant, inconsistent, and unpredictable, not only will they adversely affect the pace and pattern of national development but also they will produce the effect of eliciting and encouraging deviant behavior on the part of participants in the political arena. Individuals and groups would begin to act deviantly because they would not know whether the government was capable of acting either to punish or to accommodate them.[34]

One of the most essential ingredients of good government is efficiency, but efficiency of governance is predicated upon predictability of behavior. The predictability of governmental performance establishes and stabilizes governmental legitimacy in the eyes of people. In this sense, government requires the trust of people, but "trust involves predictability; and predictability requires regularized and institutionalized patterns of behavior."[35] If governmental behavior (in all its three dimensions) is predictable and consistent, then people not only will know how to go about registering their needs and demands by behaving in a nondetrimental fashion, but "the existence of such structures increases men's value opportunities, i.e., their repertory of alternative ways to attain value satisfaction"[36] without resorting to deviant behavior. The actions of participants in the political arena, then, become predictable and consistent as well, thus generating stability. It is in this sense that the process of national development may be interpreted as the process of routinizing and institutionalizing the ways in which the government acts and the viable growth patterns of the three dimensions of governmental capability. One of the major sources of political instability and subsequent digressive tendencies in the pattern and rate of national development is the fluctuation in the level of governmental performance (in its three aspects of capability), both in the absolute sense and in the sense relative to change in the environment. Fluctuation in the level of performance engenders a serious disequilibrium between the expectations of people and the competence of government. Or the kind of expectation for value allocation that the government is unable to make will emerge. In either case, the relationship between government and governed becomes strained, thereby creating or aggravating instability.

Another dimension of political stability is the regularization of behavior of individuals and groups of individuals in the political arena. Patterns of behavior of people must be largely routinized and habituated. Government, by exercising the three aspects of its capability, should induce people, for example, to become accustomed to the idea that taxes levied must honestly be paid as well as to actually paying them. Government must help people internalize the sense of civic duty involved in taking time from what they are doing in order to go to the voting booth on election day, accept as a matter of course that they should customarily read and listen to political and other public news, and believe that obeying laws and regulations is for their own personal benefit as well as for the benefit of society at large. Individuals and groups alike must learn that they benefit from certain patterns and ways of interacting with one another in the political arena. These politically relevant habits and routines are indispensable if the polity is to attain and maintain stability. The polity must be assured of a certain definite level and pattern of predictable behavior in society, much in the same sense that society must be assured of a certain minimal level and pattern of predictable governmental performance. "A stable functioning polity," observes Needler, "is one in which there is a limited set of patterns of normal behavior, which recur predictably in given sets of circumstances."[37] Thus, the mutual predictability of behavior, or, in the words of Talcott Parsons, "the complementarity of expectations,"[38] among social groups as well as between government and governed is indeed a vital and indispensable factor for political stability. It is also indispensable for orderly national development. Stability, in an important sense, then, is synonymous with habit formation and the routinization of certain patterns of interactions. Mere stability can be had without meaningful change; mere change is possible without meaningful stability. Change that promotes genuine national development, however, is unlikely without genuine stability, and genuine stability is impossible unless it is accompanied by meaningful and orderly change.

NOTES

1. For a variety of definitions of the issue of political development and modernization, see Lucian W. Pye, *Aspects of Political Development* (Boston and Toronto: Little, Brown, 1966), Chap. 2.
2. Gabriel Almond and G. Bingham Powell, Jr., *Comparative Politics: A Developmental Approach* (Boston and Toronto: Little, Brown, 1966).
3. For some cogent examples of the criticism, see A. James Gregor, "Political Science and the Uses of Functional Analysis" *American Political Science Review,* LXII (June 1968); William Flanigan and Edwin Fogelman, "Functional Analysis," in James C. Charlesworth (ed.), *Contemporary Political Analysis* (New York: Free Press, 1967); Carl G. Hempel, "The Logic of Functional Analysis," in Llewellyn Gross (ed.), *Symposium on Sociological Theory* (Evanston: Northwestern University Press, 1959); Robert E. Dowse, "A Functionalist's Logic," *World Politics,* XVIII (July 1966); and Richard Rudner, *Philosophy of Social Science* (Englewood Cliffs, N.J.: Prentice-Hall, 1966).
4. One recent attempt at defense against the criticism is presented in Gabriel Almond, "Political Development: Analytical and Normative Perspectives" *Comparative Political Studies,* I (January 1969).
5. Robert T. Holt and John E. Turner, *The Political Basis of Economic Development: An Exploration in Comparative Political Analysis* (Princeton: Van Nostrand, 1966), p. 17. See also Samuel P. Huntington, "The Change to Change: Modernization, Development, and Politics," *Comparative Politics,* III (April 1971), p. 303.
6. For ideas of progress and change, see, for example, Robin G. Collingwood, *The Idea of History* (New York: Oxford University Press, 1967), esp. pp. 144–146, 321–334.
7. See also Fred Riggs, "The Dialectics of Developmental Conflict," *Comparative Political Studies,* I (July 1968), pp. 197–199.
8. Gunnar Myrdal, *Asian Drama: An Inquiry into the Poverty of Nations* (New York: Pantheon, 1968), Vol. III, p. 1852.
9. Almond obviously recognized this later when he wrote about the response capability that "it" is not the same kind of category . . . as are the first three [that is, regulative, extractive, and distributive]." Almond, "Political Development," p. 463.
10. Gabriel A. Almond, "Comparative Political Systems," *Journal of Politics,* XVII (August 1956), 391–409.
11. Karl W. Deutsch *et al., Political Community and the North and the North Atlantic Area* (Princeton: Princeton University Press, 1957), p. 48.
12. This kind of phenomenon is not the monopoly of developing or underdeveloped nations. It is also recognized in advanced societies, and the recent political events in America have suggested serious implications of such participation. See, for example, Robert Lane, *Political Life* (Glencoe, Ill.: Free Press, 1959), pp. 341–343.
13. Alex Inkeles, "Participant Citizenship in Six Developing Countries," *American Political Science Review,* LXIII (December 1969), 1123.
14. Rupert Emerson, "The Problem of Identity, Selfhood, and Image in the New Nations," *Comparative Politics,* I (April 1969), 293.
15. Gabriel Almond and Sydney Verba, *The Civic Culture: Political At-*

titudes and Democracy in Five Nations (Princeton: Princeton University Press, 1963); Jack Dennis *et al.*, "Political Socialization to Democratic Orientations in Four Western Systems," *Comparative Political Studies,* I (April 1968); and Inkeles, "Participant Citizenship in Six Developing Countries."

16. Herbert A. McClosky, "Consensus and Ideology in American Politics," *American Political Science Review*, LVIII (September 1964), 361-382; reprinted in Robert A. Dahl and Deane Neubauer (eds.), *Readings in Modern Political Analysis* (Englewood Cliffs, N.J.: Prentice-Hall, 1968).

17. In recent years, there have been a number of attempts made both to discover meaningful measurements and to compare cross-nationally in this regard: Ivo K. Feierabend *et al.*, "Correlates of Political Stability," a paper presented at the annual meeting of the American Political Science Association, September 3-7, 1963; Ivo K. Feierabend *et al.*, "Dimensions of Political Unrest," a paper presented at the twentieth annual meeting of the Western Political Science Association, March 25, 1966; Ivo K. Feierabend and Rosalind L. Feierabend, "Aggressive Behaviors within Polities 1948-1962: A Cross-National Study," *Journal of Conflict Resolution*, X (September 1966); Ted Gurr and Charles Ruttenberg, *The Conditions of Civil Violence: First Tests of a Causal Model* (Research Monograph No. 28, Princeton University Center for International Studies, April 1967); Betty A. Nesvold, "Scalogram Analysis of Political Violence," *Comparative Political Studies*, II (July 1969); and Ted Gurr, "A Causal Model of Civil Strife: A Comparative Analysis Using New Indices," *American Political Science Review*, LXII (December 1968).

18. Arthur S. Banks and Robert B. Textor, *A Cross-Polity Survey* (Cambridge, Mass.: M.I.T. Press, 1963), Computer Printouts 99 and 100.

19. For limitations and obstacles to extraction (and distribution) of material resources, see, for example, Charles W. Anderson, *Politics and Economic Change in Latin America* (Princeton: Van Nostrand, 1967), Chap. 3.

20. One recent such attempt is Ernest A. Duff and John F. McCamant, "Measuring Social and Political Requirements for System Stability in Latin America," *American Political Science Review*, LXII (December 1968), 1125-1143.

21. For this particular as well as other economic and investment needs of modernizing societies, see W. W. Rostow, *The Stages of Economic Growth: A Non-Communist Manifesto* (London: Cambridge University Press, 1963).

22. Reo M. Christenson *et al.*, *Ideologies and Modern Politics* (New York: Dodd, Mead, 1971), p. 2.

23. See, for example, Seymour Martin Lipset, *Political Man: The Social Bases of Politics* (Garden City, N.Y.: Doubleday, 1963) Chap. 2.

24. "If the family is taking adequate care of its own needy members, the state may well abstain from action in this field. But when economic security or other human needs—education, for example—are not being taken care of to the extent that the resources of society would justify, then whether and how effectively the political organization steps in is a measure of the society's political development." J. Roland Pennock, "Political Development, Political Systems, and Political Goods," *World Politics*, XVIII (April 1966), 423.

25. One recent and cogent discussion of this problem is Ivan Illich, "Outwitting the Developed Countries," *New York Review of Books*, LV (November 6, 1969). Concerning the similar issue within the United States, see the

superb argument in Nick Kotz, "Hunger and the Market Place," *Harper's Magazine*, CCXL (January 1970).

26. For an interesting account of highly effective Chinese rural medicine, see Edgar Snow, "Report from China—III. Population Care and Control," *New Republic*, CLXIV (May 1, 1971).

27. In this sense, the distributive capability of the American polity has increased significantly since the 1930's. According to Heilbroner, the per cent share of total national income by the top 1% of the population declined from nearly 19% in 1929 to 7.7% in 1945 and that of the top 5% of the population from 30% in 1929 to 20% in 1957. During the same period, all but the top 20% of the population enjoyed more than 78% increase in average income (highest increases were for the lowest three-fifths of the population: 101%, 116%, and 107% respectively). See Robert L. Heilbroner, *The Making of Economic Society* (Englewood Cliffs, N.J.: Prentice-Hall, 1962), p. 172. For changes in patterns of income distribution in twelve Western nations including the United States, see Karl W Deutsch, *Politics and Government* (Boston: Houghton Mifflin, 1970), pp. 92–93.

28. See, among other studies, P. D. Ojha and V. V. Bhatt, "Pattern of Income Distribution in an Underdeveloped Economy: A Case Study of India," *American Economic Review*, LIV (September 1964); Simon Kuznets, "Quantitative Aspects of the Economic Growth of Nations: Distribution of Income by Size," *Economic Development and Cultural Change*, XI (January 1963); Harry T. Oshima, "The International Comparison of Size Distribution of Family Incomes with Special Reference to Asia," *Review of Economics and Statistics*, XLIV (November 1962).

29. Expenditure on education as a variable for distributive capability is used also by Duff and McCamant, "Measuring Social and Political Requirements."

30. Duff and McCamant, "Measuring Social and Political Requirements," p. 1127.

31. Martin Needler, "Political Development and Socioeconomic Development: The Case of Latin America," *American Political Science Review*, LXII (September 1968), 896.

32. Amos Perlmutter, "The Praetorian State and the Praetorian Army," *Comparative Politics*, I (April 1969), 388. In Chapter V, this and other similar phenomena are discussed in detail under the heading "The Differential Impact of Developmental Policies."

33. Niccolò Machiavelli, *The Discourses*, in a Modern Library edition of *The Prince and the Discourses* (New York, 1950), Bk. I, Chap. XI, p. 148.

34. For a concise discussion of the relationship between group behavior and government response, see Andrea L. Weber, *Factors Influencing Political Violence in "Third World" Nations* (unpublished M.A. thesis, Washington State University, 1971), pp. 41–45.

35. Samuel P. Huntington, *Political Order in Changing Societies* (New Haven: Yale University Press, 1969), p. 24.

36. Gurr, "A Causal Model of Civil Strife," p. 1105.

37. Martin Needler, *Political Development in Latin America: Instability, Violence, and Evolutionary Change* (New York: Random House, 1968), p. 12.

38. See Talcott Parsons, *The Social System* (New York: Free Press of Glencoe, 1963), p. 249; Lucian W. Pye, *Politics, Personality, and Nation Building* (New Haven: Yale University Press, 1962), p. 293; Reinhard Bendix, *Nation-Building and Citizenship: Studies in Our Changing Social Order* (New York: Wiley, 1964), pp. 19-21; and David Easton, *A Systems Analysis of Political Life* (New York: Wiley, 1965), p. 276 and Chap. 18.

III

Political Leadership and Governmental Capability

The preceding chapter discussed the three basic dimensions of governmental capability—the capacity to govern—and tried to suggest a direction in which a search for the meaningful measurement of such capability may be made. It is necessary to note at this point, however, that the discussion dealt only with the level of governmental capability that is demonstrated at a given point in time. One of the significant phenomena in developing nations is that the demonstrated level of governmental capability fluctuates more frequently and radically than in modern states. This fact is reflected in such remarks as "What will happen when Mao (Tito, Castro, etc.) goes?" and "So long as so-and-so is in power, such-and-such a country will remain stable." What this attitude suggests is that the level of capability to govern which is demonstrated and ascertained at a point in time (as when an empirical research is conducted by a political scientist) is not necessarily nor usually the same as what may be regarded as the institutionalized, routinized level of governmental capability. In other words, in many a developing nation, the institutionalized, routinized level of governmental capability is usually much lower than the level of capability that is demonstrated. Insitutionalization or routinization, like habit, signifies imperviousness to minor changes and fluctuations of environment or to all but serious kinds of disturbances. And this is the major dimension of national development that is most slow to take place. It is precisely for this reason that a change in political leadership, constitutional or otherwise, for example, often produces a serious national crisis in a developing nation. This phenomenon is frequently observed when a popular, charismatic leader disappears for one reason or another. While he is in power, the government may display a relatively high level of capability to govern and a steady rate of development. General domestic order and stability prevail, violence is not rampant, taxes are paid, the currency reasonably stable, foreign investors invest and foreign aid comes in, developmental policies are made and implemented with reasonable degrees of success and continuity, government officials perform their functions with tolerable competence, and so on. But once such a leader or leadership disappears or loses its grasp of the nation, crises emerge. Laws are defied more and more often, deviant political behavior abounds, administrative fissures and incompetence and corruption suddenly become visible, the economy goes into an inflationary spiral, and modernization loses its momentum. This sort of phenomenon clearly indicates that a large portion of whatever level of governmental capability was demonstrated before was actually uninstitutionalized, unroutinized, hence precarious and temporary, and that there was a wide gap between the level of capability demonstrated and the level of capability actually institutionalized and routinized. The difference between the two, then, was what may be called the "leadership increment."

THE LEADERSHIP INCREMENT AND INSTABILITY

The leadership increment to governmental capability often declines or disappears when there is change in political leadership or policy. This is the major reason that degrees of fluctuation in stability and in rates of growth are generally far greater in developing nations than in more developed societies. The difference in fluctuation will be discussed in statistical terms later in the chapter.

As society develops, then, that portion of governmental capability that has become routinized expands in relation to the level of governmental capability that is demonstrated; conversely, the amount of leadership increment declines in proportion to the level of capability demonstrated. The leadership increment to the governmental capability is that portion of such capability that accrues solely by virtue of intelligent and skillful policy making by political leadership. Therefore, the major cause of actual and immanent instability that characterizes transitional societies consists in the fact that the level of leadership increment to the governmental capability, which is often greater than the level of routinized, institutionalized capability, widely fluctuates with changes in leadership or policy. In a well-developed society, the preponderant portion of the governmental capability that is demonstrated at any point in time is in fact routinized and only the marginal portion of it is incremental as a result of an exceptionally able political leadership. Schematically, such a transition in the relationship between polit-

Figure 1. Relationship between political leadership and governmental capability.

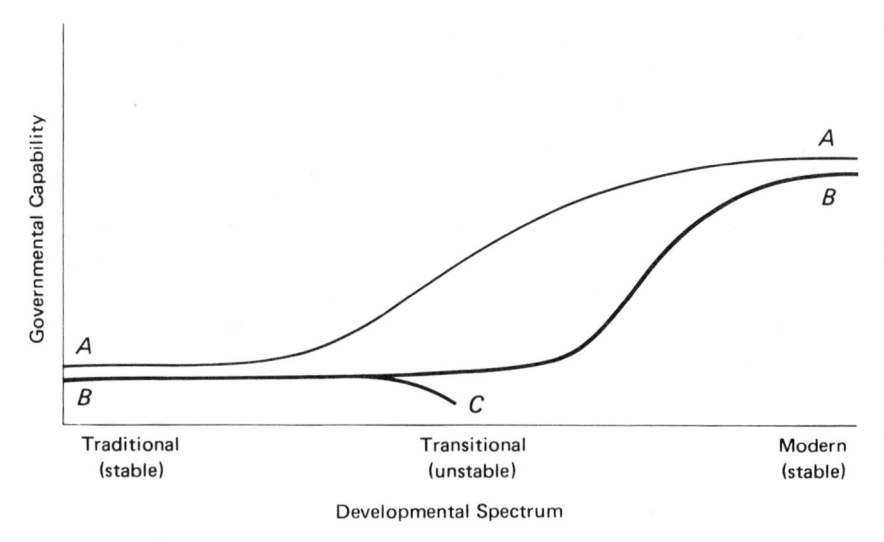

[Graph with axes: Governmental Capability (y-axis) vs Developmental Spectrum (x-axis), spanning Traditional (stable), Transitional (unstable), Modern (stable).]

A = governmental capability demonstrated
B = routinized, institutionalized level of governmental capability
C = declining level of routinized capability as a result of prolonged improper political leadership
A-B = area of leadership increment to governmental capability
A-B > B = basic instability
A-B < B = toward stability

ical leadership and the governmental capability is shown in Figure 1. It is in this sense that we can say that, while in a highly developed society as well as in a stable traditional polity, the basic functional role of political leadership is one of a manager (behaving, in large measure, in an accepted, hence predictable manner), its counterpart in a developing nation is that of an initiator or creator. During the process of modernization, society, in the absence of at least minimally qualified leadership, may in fact decline in terms of its basic, routinized governmental capability, as C in Figure 1. Such a decline and a sharp drop in A (leadership increment to the governmental capability) may translate themselves into such indices as a fall in the annual growth rate of GNP, a drastic rise in the inflation rate and unemployment, widespread lawlessness, and resurgence of class and group hostility. An unintelligent and clumsy political leadership can undo what has been accomplished in terms of a rise in the routinized level of governmental capability. In such cases, the process of modernization may well regress.

The difference in the degree and frequency of fluctuation of the demonstrated level of governmental capability between modernizing nations and modern countries may be noted in Table 14, even though the criteria used here are categorically one-sided (economic) and therefore render any conclusion highly tentative. In a rigorous empirical investigation, a wide spectrum of relevant indices should be examined. The table looks at six modern nations and twelve randomly selected developing nations in terms of their general patterns of fluctuation in annual per-capita GNP growth and inflation rate during the period 1958–1967.

Table 14. Patterns of Fluctuation of Demonstrated Level of Governmental Capability in Modern and Developing Nations, 1958–1967.

Nation	Annual Growth Rate in Per-Capita GNP, %				Annual Rate of Inflation, %			
	I High	II Low	III Range (1–2)	IV Average	I High	II Low	III Range (1–2)	IV Average
Modern:								
Belgium	6	2	4	3.5	5	1	4	2.4
France	5	1	4	3.6	5	0	5	3.1
West Germany	6	0	6	3.4	4	1	3	2.4
Italy	5	2	3	4.0	7	−1	8	3.4
Netherlands	7	1	6	3.6	6	0	6	3.8
United States	6	0	6	3.0	3	1	2	1.6
Developing:								
Argentina	8	−8	16	.6	61	8	53	27.5
Brazil	4	−1	5	1.7	141	5	136	62.3
Burma	9	−6	15	1.7	11	−11	22	.1
India	5	−7	12	.7	19	2	17	7.6
Iran	10	.2	8	4.7	8	0	8	2.8
Malaysia	6	2	4	2.6	4	−6	10	1.0
Morocco	7	−6	13	−.2	5	−1	6	2.5
Nicaragua	10	−1	11	3.1	5	−3	8	1.0
Nigeria	9	−1	10	3.0	9	−5	14	2.3
Thailand	8	1	7	4.4	4	−5	9	.5
Venezuela	5	−2	7	1.1	4	−2	6	.7
Zambia	15	−6	21	3.7	11	0	11	3.6

Source: *United Nations Statistical Yearbook 1968* (New York, 1969).

The third column of each of the two dimensions pertains to the question of stability and governmental capability. In the group of six modern nations, the figures in column III are all low and largely similar among the nations in both per-capita GNP growth rates and inflation rates. As for per-capita GNP, the ratio between column III and column IV is below 2:1 (and in three cases, it is almost 1:1). For inflation rates, the ratio between column III and column IV is again below 2:1 in all but one case (Italy, which, in more senses than one, was the least stable of the six nations during the period under review). These observations, combined with another that each of the six nations at least experienced one change of leadership (the average was 2.6 changes), suggest that these nations are generally stable and enjoy high and consistent levels of routinized governmental capability and largely consistent modernization indices.

The twelve developing nations present a radically different picture in this regard. As a group, these nations show a range of fluctuation (column III) that is more than twice that of the developed nations in annual growth rate of per-capita GNP, and a range that is 5.6 times greater than that for the developed nations in annual rate of inflation. In annual growth of per-capita GNP, only five of the twelve nations come close to the pattern demonstrated by the developed nations, namely, Brazil, Iran, Malaysia, Thailand, and Venezuela. As for annual rates of inflation, again only five of the twelve manifest a pattern that comes anywhere near resembling that of the developed nations: Iran, Morocco, Nicaragua, Thailand, and Venezuela.[1] (In these nations, there were no substantive changes in leadership during the period under review, suggesting, therefore, a more or less constant level of leadership increment.) Apart from this minority of nations, however, the basic and drastic difference between developing countries and modern nations is both clear and significant. It should also be noted that, among the developing nations, the gap between columns III and IV in both items of consideration is far wider than that for the developed countries. In terms of changes in political leadership or regime, the average number of changes for the developing nations is exactly the same as that for the modern nations, that is, 2.6 during the period under review. A provisional conclusion is that these facts concerning the developing nations confirm the earlier proposition (as shown in Figure 1) that, while the routinized level of governmental capability closely approximates the demonstrated level of such capability in a modern nation, the difference between the two levels of governmental capability in a developing country is usually highly fluctuating and that such fluctuation is caused primarily by change in political leadership or its policy and behavior.

One important question at this point which cannot be avoided is: How does one measure B in Figure 1, that is, the routinized level of governmental capability. Routinization (or institutionalization) means that certain patterns of behavior or levels of performance have been consistently repeated over time. How long a period of time it takes is problematical and can be only arbitrarily determined at this point. It can be provisionally suggested that the mean of the demonstrated capability during each five-year period be taken as that level of governmental capability that becomes routinized upon completion of that period. This method, as may be obvious, can be applied to cases in which the routinized level in fact falls as a result of prolonged improper political leadership behavior or policy. Such measurement of the routinized level of governmental capability would then make it possible to generate an accurate measurement of the leadership increment (positive or negative) to the total level of governmental capability during each year of the period concerned, as well as the subsequent five-year period, and to measure the rate of increase in the routinized level of capability from one period to another.

The fact that the wide fluctuations in the two arbitrary indices of annual change among developing nations are not mere economic happenstance unrelated to the behavior and policy of political leadership becomes clear when one examines significant political events prior to and during each major instance of major fluctuation. The case of Argentina may be briefly commented on as such an example.

THE CASE OF ARGENTINA

During the ten-year period 1958–1967, Argentina experienced three separate years of negative growth in per-capita GNP and simultaneously significant increases in inflation: 1959 (per-capita GNP, −8%; inflation 24%), 1962 (per-capita GNP, −4%; inflation, 18%), and 1963 (per-capita GNP, −5%; inflation, 19%). It is interesting to note that these three separate years of drastic decline in economic conditions (which are directly or indirectly relevant to levels of governmental capability in all its three dimensions) were not only all respectively preceded by, but also witness to, serious political-leadership crises. That such leadership crises must have had direct impact upon the nation's economic conditions may be surmised from the fact that other

South American countries, such as Brazil, Bolivia, Colombia, Chile, and Ecuador, during the same period, especially in those three years under review, showed generally stable and even consistent growth rates in per-capita GNP and relatively small fluctuations in annual rate of inflation of their respective currencies.

Perón was ousted in September 1955 by the military, and Argentina entered a period of "the Liberating Revolution" and "de-Perónization" under a military regime headed briefly by the ailing General Eduardo Lonardi and then by the more energetic and forceful General Pedro Aramburu.[2] The Aramburu administration quickly established its political and administrative dominance by proscribing the Peronista party and organizations, vigorously purging Peronistas from the military, industry, labor, and government, barring them from running for public office, smashing widespread labor strikes instigated by Peronistas and Communists, and crushing the few revolts by segments of the military opposed to Aramburu's policies. In the meantime, the provisional government engineered a relatively quick recovery of the national economy, which had suffered from increasingly irrational policies during the last years of Peronism, by implementing some of the recommendations of the prominent economist Raúl Prebisch and by adroit economic diplomacy with Western nations for more trade.

Committed unequivocally to the restoration of constitutional civilian government, General Aramburu and his military government relinquished their power in May 1958 with the inauguration of Arturo Frondizi as duly elected president of a constitutional government. This transition of power, however, was underlain with widespread misgivings, hostility, and suspicion. Frondizi had been elected three months earlier in a general election in a manner that was seriously to undermine the stability established by the provisonal government and to cause him to undertake measures that were politically disruptive and economically disastrous. First, in seeking the presidency, Frondizi, one of the leaders of the Union Civica Radical (UCR), had split it into two hostile groups as a result of his rivalry with Ricardo Bilban, another leader and presidential aspirant, thus weakening his potential base of power. Second, in his desperate search for votes, Frondizi entered into a not-so-well-kept secret agreement with Peronistas in which they offered him their votes in exchange for the lenient treatment of Peronistas and a large wage increase for labor (wages had been virtually frozen by the provisional government). Third, Frondizi was elected with only 45% of the popular vote, though his own party (now UCRI, as opposed to Bilban's UCIP) won two-thirds of the chamber seats and all senatorial and gubernatorial posts. Frondizi's position as president, therefore, was far less stable than might appear on the surface: he had alienated many non-Peronist political forces, antagonized many of his former associates, become at least partly beholden to Peronists, and therefore was suspect in the eyes of the powerful military. Thanks to General Aramburu's refusal to succumb to pressure from within his own military to annul the election, Frondizi became president, but only at the sufferance of the military.

Politically beholden to Peronistas, President Frondizi immediately softened government attitude and policies toward them and decreed a 60% wage raise. The lenient treatment of Peronistas infuriated the military and anti-Peronist forces and the sharp wage hike soon contributed critically to a rise in inflation, which became most pronounced in 1959. In the meantime, three of the major policies Frondizi tried to implement resulted not only in further alienating his initial supporters, including Peronistas and nationalists, but also in seriously undermining and aggravating public welfare and national economy. First, despite his nationalistic and anti-foreign-business campaign platform, President Frondizi negotiated with foreign oil firms for their drilling and refining Argentinian petroleum. From the strictly economic or financial viewpoint, this action may have been justified in view of the fact that Argentina's own public oil corporation established under Perón had been featherbedded and inefficient and had failed to make the nation self-sufficient in petroleum supply. Politically, however, the decision was not only unwise but also disruptive. Suspicion toward and fear of foreign economic influence had been deeply ingrained in the Argentine mind, and Frondizi's election had in significant part been the result of his capitalizing upon this aspect of Argentine politics. Second, in September 1958, Frondizi put through a new educational law which gave degrees granted by Catholic and other private schools the same value as those granted by public institutions. This was regarded as a slap at the long-established tradition of secular education and the separation of church and state, and subsequently, there was widespread protest against the law. Third, Frondizi's "Stabilization Agreement" of December 1958 with the International Monetary Fund generated a long series of events that were soon critically to affect the already worsening economic condition of the country. For the purpose of stabilizing the precarious national economy, the agreement called for a commitment to such unpopular measures as further resuscitation of free enterprise, foreign-capital investment, and austerity. All were in violation of his nationalist, pro-welfare campaign slogans, and the implementation of these measures caused a worsening of workers' conditions, a rise in inflation, an increase in unemployment, and subsequently a decline in GNP. The result was an outbreak of riots, strikes, sabotage, bombing incidents, and other forms of violence and terror throughout the next two years.

In order to counter political opposition and widespread public discontent, Frondizi resorted to increasingly authoritarian means, especially after an alleged attempted coup by his own vice president in November 1958, and ruled the nation under the declaration of the state of siege during much of his incumbency. His resort to such a method of governance was at least partly justified by the fact that there were numerous attempts to overthrow him by violence throughout his residence in the presidential palace.

During 1960 and 1961, the nation enjoyed at least a relative surface calm, as a result of Frondizi's repression, with the military's help, of the terrorist groups, labor strikes, and the Peronistas, who have since organized themselves into a Social Justice Party. In the meantime infusion of foreign capital and loans from the IMF and foreign nations together with domestic austerity were beginning to bear some fruit in the form of a positive growth of GNP and a decline in the rate of inflation. The accumulation of foreign debts, continuous austerity, and the consequent low levels of revenue, however, were to conspire to produce a crisis of drastic proportions in 1962 which spelled the end of Frondizi's reign. By the end of 1962, the government had accumulated a total public foreign debt of $2.7 billion plus a private foreign debt of $800 million, necessitating an annual debt service of $300–$500 million. Meanwhile, the implementation of the stabilization agreement had by then resulted in a record high unemployment of 12% and a continuous wave of bankruptcies, while the government had to bear increasing and excessive deficit spending to the extent that it was frequently unable to pay many salaries and pensions. The desperate condition thus induced even came to cause, for the first time, a net outflow of private capital from the country. One clearly observable result of all this was again a negative growth of both total and per-capita GNP and a rapid increase in the rate of inflation in 1962 and 1963.

By March 1962, the military, which had watched the performance of the Frondizi administration with growing apprehension and distaste, had had enough. Frondizi was unceremoniously deposed, arrested, and imprisoned, and José María Guido, president of the senate, in the absence of the vice president (Gomez who had been accused by Frondizi three years before of an attempted coup and subsequently dismissed), became constitutional successor to the ousted president. General elections were then held in July, and Arturo Illía was elected president, but with only 26% of the popular vote. As a result, his government became a coalition of many small parties, his governance was far from vigorous, and the patterns of deficit spending and inflation inherited from Frondizi by and large continued. One drastic policy change that Illía instituted, however, was to aggravate further the financial condition of the nation, and that was his revocation of Frondizi's foreign petroleum contracts. Illía's act was politically popular, but the inefficiency of the nation's own oil enterprise was quickly to result in the need for huge oil imports, draining its scarce foreign exchange and contributing further to inflation and decline in economic growth.

THE THREE REQUIREMENTS OF POLITICAL LEADERSHIP

The phenomenon of radical fluctuations in the level of governmental capability elicits a question that seems crucial to the understanding of the process of national development: Is there any specific type of political leadership that can be regarded as capable of promoting and accelerating national development? To put the same question a bit differently, what kind of political leadership can most effectively generate and utilize material and human resources for national development, to regulate and direct the pace and pattern of such development? This type of leadership cannot be defined in terms of sociological variables, nor in terms of personnel composition or structure. There is little or no meaningful correlation between the social background of a given elite and its behavior or policy. For example, both Chinese and Russian Communist revolutionaries largely came from the same social strata as did their non-Communist archrivals (the Mensheviks and the KMT): upper-middle or middle class, the intelligentsia.[3] Likewise, there is little significant distinction in terms of social origin between the Nazi elite and the *Bundesrepublik* leadership.[4] The leaders of Meiji Japan (whom one American historian calls "ministers of modernization"[5]) were of the traditional ruling class, yet they were the very ones who most vigorously overrode class interests and promoted modernization of an unprecedented magnitude. In the meantime, specific personnel compositions do not seem to have any identifiable relationship with leadership behavior and policy. Monarchy, oligarchy, democracy, dictatorship, totalitarianism may or may not promote modernization. The typology of political leadership suggested below is therefore based on a consideration, not of social origin or differences in personnel composition, but of certain basic political requirements.

Three basic conditions seem indispensable for successful modernizing political leadership. They are: (1) commitment to what Myrdal calls the "modernization ideals,"[6] (2) political intelligence and skill, and (3) substantive dominance over subnational political elites.

COMMITMENT

No political leadership, however powerful and skillful, can promote national development unless it wishes seriously to do so. Conversely, an initially weak and precarious leadership (because it is threatened by powerful subnational political elites) may, as in the case of the political leadership of Meiji Japan, be able to promote modernization if it is committed to do so and is intelligent and skillful in its effort to overcome initial handicaps and obstacles. Commitment, then, is the first requirement of political leadership of any developing nation. It involves an overriding desire to promote "rationality," "rise of productivity," "rise of levels of living," "social and economic equalization," "improved institutions and attitudes," and "national consolidation"—to borrow some of the ideals specified by Myrdal. All these aspects of national development combined will hopefully produce a politically, socially, and economically integrated society with built-in capacities for continuous growth and adaptation and with regularized processes and methods for conflict management and for generating further change. The promotion of these ideals that point toward modernization, however, is directly opposed to the desire for the maintenance of the status quo and is also in conflict with the general disposition of the populace against efforts and sacrifices for the attainment of the rising levels of gratification they expect. Commitment to modernization, therefore, signifies also independence or dissociation from attitudes, and interests of the multitudes, which are largely parochial, particularistic, and unenlightened concerning the necessity of unprecedented efforts and painful sacrifices for modernization, as well as from the narrow, sectarian interests and values of the particular social classes from which political leadership comes. Not only should political leadership be committed to those modernization ideals but it should also be resolute enough to take many unpleasant and unpopular measures vis-à-vis forces and interests that resist modernization, for purposes of reorienting patterns of extraction and distribution of tangible and intangible resouces in order to promote enterprises and corporate actions that will produce necessary change and progress. To the extent that political leadership is valuationally and attitudinally bound to the class of its origin or to prevailing traditional attitudes and predilections of society, it is uncommitted to the task of modernization.

INTELLIGENCE AND SKILL

Political intelligence and skill, as a category of analysis, is most difficult to define. It is at once elusive as a concept and relative to circumstances as an operative instrument. It constitutes the quality of Machiavelli's fox. It involves creativity, foresight, and the manipulative capability of political leadership. Intelligence has to do with the knowledge and understanding of human nature in general and the characteristics and peculiarities unique to a given society and its inventory of cumulative societal knowledge and experience. Intelligence also includes a critical assessment of actual and potential obstacles, of society's material and human resources, of the various ways in which the resources can be manipulated and utilized, and of the capabilities of existing sociopolitical values and institutions. In short, it is the knowledge and appreciation of situational assets and avenues toward goal attainment. Skill is what translates this understanding and commitment into concrete programs of action by maximizing support and minimizing resistance. As an operative instrument, political intelligence and skill is relative to circumstances because the level of its quality and the extent of its application are determined by the particular needs of a given environment as well as by different levels and qualities of situational assets. In short, the less advanced or more unstable a nation or the faster the pace of modernization desired, the greater the quality and magnitude of intelligence and skill needed.

In the case of a developing nation, any significant decision making is a very difficult and dangerous business because the process of decision making has yet to be institutionalized (that is, accepted and adhered to by most if not all of the political participants) and the political relationships between government and governed as well as among various politically relevant strata of society have yet to be regularized (that is, taken for granted by most of those concerned out of habit or conviction). In the developing nation, the level of predictability of behavior of political participants is still very low. The process of modernization is also the process of political leadership's trying to institutionalize the political process and to regularize the political relationships so as to render the polity at once continually stable and dynamic. The political leadership of a developing nation, then, is the initiator of a new order. As such, it must be creative, skillful, resolute, and farsighted. It must manipulate forces and resources in society so as to mobilize and utilize them for modernization. It must mediate between impulses toward modernity and persistent tendencies toward tradition. It must render conflicting forces and values in society symbiotic, instead of leaving them mutually antagonistic. Political leadership must, in short, possess an "ability to turn situational incompatibilities into assets."[7] In an essential sense, its role is catalytic. Certainly, a function as complex, dangerous, and salient as this calls for a much higher level as well as a more varied kind (relative to circumstances) of intelligence and skill than is perhaps required of the political leadership in a well-developed, stable society, where its role is more that of a manager than that of an initiator.

In a well-developed society, the political process is more or less securely institutionalized, at least to the extent that it is resilient to all but the most serious kinds of disturbances, and political relationships are highly regularized, so that the behavior of political participants is largely predictable. A capacity for orderly change, growth, and adaptation is more or less built-in. The role of political leadership in such a society is that of *rex*, while that in a developing nation is that of *dux*.[8] In the developed nation, political leadership usually does well to follow the accepted, hence predictable, pattern of behavior and policy; in the modernizing state, it cannot afford to, since the accepted, hence predictable pattern of elite behavior and policy in such a society is precisely what should be abandoned. One is the task of careful maintenance and continuous refinement, the other is that of creative imagination coupled with extraordinary skill and resolve, or, in the words of Hannah Arendt, "the act of foundation."[9] Yet, this very fact suggests that political leadership in a developing nation must rely largely upon its own perception, intelligence, vision, untried skill, and uncertain paths. Hence the relevance of Machiavelli's paradigmatic observation that "there is nothing more difficult to carry out nor more doubtful of success, nor more dangerous to handle, than to initiate a new order of things."[10] Thus, how political leadership responds to the requirements of the task of modernization and to the contingencies of volatile circumstances is the function of the interaction between commitment to modernization on the one hand and political intelligence and skill on the other.

DOMINANCE

Much in the same sense that political leadership of a modernizing nation should be independent in its behavior and policy from those attitudes and interests of society and especially of the social class of its origin that impede modernization, it must also be independent of influence of subnational and other political elites. The former is valuational-attitudinal independence; the latter constitutes political-administrative supremacy. In terms of strategic priorities, the latter should be the first concern of a committed and intelligent modernizing political leadership. In view of the fact that, at least in most cases, modernizing political leadership does not initially enjoy such supremacy over subnational political elites, this variable cannot really be separated from that of political intelligence and skill. Indeed, it is political intelligence and skill that alone can bring about the necessary degree of dominance over subnational political elites. In this sense, this third major variable constitutes part of what will be discussed below as situational assets. The very magnitude of this crucial political environmental factor, however, seems to justify its treatment as a major category of concern. The relationship between political leadership and subnational elites, unlike that in a more developed nation, is not a matter of structural-constitutional determination. Rather, it is a clash of historical forces. Provincial warlords, landed aristocracy, the church, potentially or actually separatist forces, and the military frequently constitute forces of overwhelming resistance against modernization in new nations. The initial pattern of such a relationship (namely, the extent to which subnational political elites possess power vis-à-vis political leadership) determines the context within which political leadership can begin to exercise its intelligence and skill. Like Machiavelli's fortune, it provides a starting point for political leadership's behavior and policy. To that extent, the existence of subnational elites inhibits political leadership, at least in the beginning, but, in spite of this and because of this, political leadership can conquer it if it is intelligent and skillful.

Dominance over subnational political elites may be achieved (1) if there happens to be unity between national leadership and other political elites (for example, if both are equally committed to modernization); (2) when the legal or political tradition permits national leadership's direct and substantive control of and dominance over local political and administrative elites; (3) in the presence of a highly charismatic personality within national leadership; (4) by selective bribery; and (5) through the skillful manipulation and integration of originally antagonistic or independent subnational elites into the total process of modernization. Once dominance is achieved, or, for that matter, where dominance already exists, it is up to political leadership's intelligence and skill to maintain it. For political leadership can and often does lose such dominion by carelessness or stupidity. Dominance over subnational elites need not be absolute, however, as in a genuinely totalitarian polity.

It should nevertheless obtain at least to the extent that, for all practical purposes, allows political leadership adequate leeway for the formulation and implementation of developmental programs and policies without running the serious risk of organized opposition or subversion by one or more subnational elites.

A TYPOLOGY OF POLITICAL LEADERSHIP

The three basic leadership requirements discussed above suggest a general typology of political leadership for the developing nations:

Leadership Type	Commitment	Intelligence and Skill	Dominance
A. Effective modernizing	+	+	+
B. Attenuated modernizing	+	+	−
C. Crude modernizing	+	−	+
D. Visionary modernizing	+	−	−
E. Stable conservative	−	+	+
F. Stagnating	−	+	−
G. Extortionist	−	−	+
H. Revolving-door	−	−	−

A. Effective Modernizing Leadership. A country led by this type of leadership is both stable and changing. Political leadership successfully mediates between the need for stability and the need for change. It possesses high levels (relative to its situation) of regulative, extractive, and distributive abilities and mobilizes them well for the promotion of modernization. It is making progress in its task of institutionalizing political processes and procedures and of regularizing political life and relationships. It keeps governmental capability explicit, energetic, and expanding and regulates and directs the process of modernization with a high degree of continuity, consistency, and efficiency. On an impressionistic basis, the following nations, among others, enjoy this type of political leadership: Meiji Japan after 1877, the U.S.S.R. after 1945, China in the first dozen years after 1949, Cuba since 1959, Mexico since the mid-1930's, and Iran since 1958. It may be noted here that one can think of subtypologies of leadership under this category in terms of methods of governance, ideological orientations, and so on.

B. Attenuated Modernizing Leadership. Political leadership of this type is in constant danger of being threatened by powerful opposition either in the open or behind the scenes, and frequently suffers from the subversion or watering-down of its developmental programs and policies by subnational political elites. Sometimes, such opposition or subversion comes from those members of subnational elites who are within the party organization headed by the national leadership. Resistance may be administrative. In other cases, subnational elites or oppositionists align themselves with foreign powers in an attempt to overthrow the national leadership. In countries governed by this type of political leadership, the level of stability often shifts and sometimes even sinks below the safe minimum. Progress in the direction of modernization takes place, but usually at slow, uneven, diluted paces. Where such leadership manages to last over time (without achieving dominance over subnational elites), society is likely to become or remain what Myrdal calls a "soft state." Among nations governed by such leadership may be: Lumumba's Congo (threatened and soon ousted by forces of secessionism); Arbenz's Guatemala (threatened and overthrown by reactionary forces aided by the United States); Mossadeq's Iran (overpowered by royalists, landlords, foreign oil companies, and the American CIA); Nehru's India (constantly subverted and watered down by provincial political leaders and the Syndicate within); and Magsaysay's Philippines (subverted by landed oligarchs and their cohorts in congress).

C. Crude Modernizing Leadership. This leadership is likely sooner or later to commit some serious blunder which could have been avoided and which may therefore doom it or at least distort its future direction. One recent example of this type of leadership is Ayub Khan's regime in Pakistan. Ayub's regime was apparently committed to modernization and had an impressive degree of dominance over subnational elites during much of its incumbency. The mistake, that ultimately was its undoing, was neither the Basic Democracy nor Ayub's slowly declining paternalistic charisma, but rather its failure to heed one of the cardinal principles of the politics of modernization, namely, that there ought to be some tolerable and increasingly favorable balance between the rise in allocation of values, especially material values, and the growth in education, articulateness, and expectations of social classes, especially those strata that are becoming increasingly relevant politically, under circumstances of noticeable material improvement for society at large. In Pakistan, subnational political elites had generally been quiescent, owing, no doubt, to the regime's dominance over the provinces and their political elites, as long as there was no significantly widespread and organizable movement arising out of a feeling of intense material deprivation and discrimination. They surfaced, coalesced, and thus threatened the incumbent leadership only after the regime's continued neglect of the political necessity for proportionate material improvement of the middle class (which had been slowly but steadily increasing in size and in potential political relevance because of industrialization and the expansion of higher education) and, perhaps to a somewhat lesser extent, of the working class had generated a rapidly mounting discontent beyond the point of minimal safety for the stability of political leadership. This was a case of blatant lack or decline of political intelligence and skill. This type of leadership, when its intelligence and skill declines, typically tends to rely increasingly upon coercion in order to maintain itself in power. Among other recent examples of this type of leadership may be found Adnan Menderes, Kwame Nkrumah, and Syngman Rhee. The Stalinist leadership during the 1930's may belong to this category. In many a case, the opposition movement against the incumbent leadership was eventually superseded by a military coup. A society governed by a crude modernizing leadership is capable of maintaining stability and generating change for a considerable length of time, but it is likely to regress at least temporarily once a serious blunder is committed by leadership.

D. *Visionary Modernizing Leadership.* Here, political leadership is definitely reformist, even revolutionary, but lacks the necessary control capability, intelligence, and skill to carry out any sustained efforts for progress. It is the kind of leadership that would become type *C* if it had sufficient dominance over subnational elites. At any rate, it is constantly challenged not only by subnational elites in general but also by powerful reactionary forces in particular which it does not possess adequate ability to counter, let alone neutralize or eliminate. Leadership is likely to be politically naive, ideologically both idealistic and doctrinaire, whose passion outruns its ability and inclination for rational calculus. In an important sense, it is its own mortal enemy. Society governed by such leadership is neither stable nor, for that reason, changing meaningfully. Resources are not mobilized rationally, and though developmental programs may be issued one after another, they are formulated haphazardly and erratically. Political leadership of this type is eventually replaced by another type that has a higher degree of intelligence, skill, and dominance. Whether or not this other leadership meets the first condition of successful modernizing leadership is another matter, however. Sun Yat-sen's republican leadership may be regarded as one such example. Joao Goulart's in Brazil perhaps is another.

E. *Stable Conservative leadership.* Society under this type of leadership is usually well governed and enjoys general peace and order. In the absence of a serious commitment to genuine modernization and development, however, the pace of progress, if any, would be very slow, even though the economy may be very prosperous and national income rising. Increases in national wealth are not likely to be distributed much outside the normal channels and patterns of allocation, thus continually favoring the politically powerful and the socially entrenched. Stable traditional monarchies and their nonroyal contemporary variants usually fall into this category of political leadership. Among current examples are Thailand, Saudi Arabia, Afganistan, Ethiopia, Paraguay, Liberia, Libya before the recent military coup, and the Philippines after Magsaysay.

F. Stagnating Leadership. Feudal kings and their modern equivalents would be in this category. It exists in a precarious, though often durable, balance between its own savvy and skill and, in feudal societies, a certain tradition on the one hand and the ever-present, potentially dangerous power of subnational or regional elites on the other. For its continued existence, leadership must adhere to the kind of modus operandi and modus vivendi that is acceptable primarily to those subnational or regional elites. Drastic change in significant policies is at best extremely difficult to initiate, let alone implement, without the advice and consent of those other elites. Society governed by this type of leadership may or may not be stable, depending upon the substantive patterns of relationship obtaining between the center and the other areas, but there is likely to be little significant modernizing change taking place. Japan during the last generations of the Tokugawa shogunate is one such example. Nigeria before the coup of 1966 is another.

G. Extortionist Leadership. Most likely, this is a dictatorship or autocracy of a very blatant kind which manages to exist mainly by its ruthlessness in the use of coercion and repression. White-supremacist leaderships of South Africa and Rhodesia, reactionary rule of Imam of Yemen before the revolution, Saudi Arabia under Ibn Saud, Egypt under Farouk, Batista's Cuba, Trujillo's Dominican Republic, and Haiti under Duvalier all seem to fall into the category of countries ruled by such leadership. It is extortionist in that its overriding concern is to stay in power and to enrich and otherwise benefit its own members and supporters at the expense of progress and welfare of society at large. It extorts much, materially and symbolically, with coercion or threat of coercion, and distributes little to society. The subtlety and manipulative political skill essential to political leadership are not heeded carefully, and political leadership relies almost solely on the use of brute force to impose its will. Perhaps it is typical of this type of leadership that, while it may last for some time, it is likely to be turned out of office by violence in the form of a coup or revolution. While it lasts, the country may, from outside, appear peaceful and stable, but beneath the surface lurks the imminent danger of violent upheaval. Also, there is little significant positive change taking place in society in the direction of modernization.

H. Revolving-Door Leadership. Society governed by this type of political leadership is usually characterized by civil disorder, deviant individual and group behavior, and a lack of uniformity and consistency in the enforcement of law and policy—in short, nearly a total loss of effective power to govern on the part of political leadership. Personnel change within leadership increases, so that there is little continuity either in the personnel composition of leadership or in public policy and its enforcement. France during the worst periods of the Third and Fourth Republics, the Dominican Republic in 1964-1966, South Vietnam between the demise of Diem and the rise of Ky, the Congo (Kinshasa) after the fall of Lumumba and before the coup of General Mobutu, Thailand before 1958, and Syria in the 1950's before the abortive *mariage de convenance* with Nasser's Egypt all seem to belong to this category of political leadership. Perhaps to be included is Italy since the death of de Gasperi.

The eight types of political leadership as described above are ideal types. In reality, few leaderships (regimes) are exclusively one type. A great majority of regimes at any point in time are likely to be mixtures of two or more types. The typology, nevertheless, seems useful in providing a broad, albeit far from precise, means for assessing what a given political leadership may be capable of in terms of the manner and pace of national development. With the use of the typology, it also becomes easier to understand why certain developmental phenomena occur in transitional societies. In the brief discussion about the phenomenon of radical fluctuation in levels of governmental capability, we noted that, among the twelve randomly selected developing nations, a certain minority of nations (Iran, Morocco, Thailand, Nicaragua, and Venezuela) showed a pattern of relatively limited fluctuation in, for example, annual rates of inflation, which resembled more that of the six modern nations examined than the majority of transitional societies. Now that we have established a typology of political leadership in terms of certain political requirements, it may be possible to see that those relatively stable transitional societies were, during the period considered, ruled by the types of leadership that, in terms of the typology, seem capable of maintaining relatively consistent levels of demonstrated governmental capability. They were ruled by either leadership type *E* (Morocco, Thailand, Nicaragua) or type *A* (Iran) or a mixture of types *A* and *E* (Venezuela). In short, there seems to exist a significant, though by no means perfect, correlation between levels of governmental capability and levels of fluctuation in such capability on the one hand and types of political leadership on the other.

THE PROBLEMS OF MEASUREMENT

The typology may tell whether or not a given society is developing. The next question is: Can the relative paces of development of different nations be ascertained? Inasmuch as the eight types of political leadership are pure types, ascertainment of relative paces of national development and modernization becomes necessary not only in itself but also for the clear identification of types of political leadership actually governing the nations concerned.

Any discussion of conditions and requirements, however, immediately encounters the problem of how to ascertain and measure them. For example, how could we ascertain and measure "commitment"? It is like trying to quantify "moral fortitude" or "love." Likewise with intelligence, skill, and dominance. Since these are the key variables used in establishing the typology of political leadership and since the pace of modernization is essentially the function of these leadership variables, measurement of the pace of modernization is predicated upon measurement of these leadership requirements. Therefore, such dangerous, methodologically vulnerable attempts will be made below. For control of levels or magnitudes of these leadership variables under different circumstances, we will use what will emerge as the situational score or composite index of situational assets.

Measuring levels of commitment to modernization is most difficult. There are several partial ways that randomly suggest themselves, though none would be satisfactory and each quite prohibitive in cost. There are such methods as questionnaire surveys, depth interviews, actual sustained on-the-spot observations of daily conduct of decision makers, and their various combinations. Examinations of speeches and public pronouncements of any political leadership would most likely be unprofitable since every political leadership is rhetorically committed to modernization—as it is to "democracy"—from Haile Selassie to Suharto, from Duvalier to Mao. Also, there is usually a wide gap between the public and the private language of such leadership. Only indirect approaches, then, would be feasible. One such method would be an examination of leadership willingness to deprive or antagonize powerful antimodernization forces and interests in society, as expressed in the frequency and magnitude of policy-making that adversely affects them. Briefly, this equation could be stated as:

$$\text{commitment to modernization (C)} = \frac{\text{number of major decisions adversely affecting antidevelopment forces and interests}}{\text{total number of major decisions made}}$$

This measure would remain too simplistic, for there are many methodological problems that should be resolved if it is to become useful. And resolution of those problems would have to await rigorous empirical investigations of a number of developing nations and their political leaderships. In the first place, there is the problem of the magnitude of each major decision made. In terms of impact on society, especially on those segments or interests that hamper development, each major decision produces different results.

Adverse impacts on antimodernization forces and interests could technically be computed in monetary terms in some cases (for example, taxation, land reform and redistribution, nationalization of certain sectors of economy). In other cases, they would have to be measured in terms of certain human costs (for example, the introduction of an impartial civil-service examination resulting in the failure of a large proportion of candidates from the traditional governing class to be recruited into government services; the emergence of similar phenomena in the military profession as a result of the organization of a conscript army; and a new phenomenon of downward social and occupational mobility for members of the traditional upper classes as a result of replacing the traditional ascriptive criteria by rational universalistic ones). Adverse impacts would be extremely difficult, if not impossible, to measure in still other cases (for example, the deprivation of honor and prestige, which is essentially a matter of subjective perception on the part of those who are affected as well as of those who affect), such as the introduction of free public-school education and universal suffrage. In still other cases, all these three types of costs would be involved. The composite computation of these various types of cost would not be an easy task. To complicate the problem further, certain issues call for policies that, in their negative impact, cut across traditional-modern cleavages, while some others would warrant policies that are explicitly deprivatory of traditional forces and interests. Moreover, in certain instances, a high degree of political intelligence and skill may in fact recommend the kind of decision-making that is deliberately placatory toward some types of traditional forces and interests. Nevertheless, it would be possible for students of the politics of the developing nations to identify those major areas of developmental decision-making that pertain to the breaking up of such traditional, antimodern forces—interests and attitudes which would, if left untouched, seriously impede the process of modernization —and to the promotion of higher societal productivity and the emergence of those forces, interests, and attitudes that positively aid and hasten modernization. Once these relevant categories of policy-making are identified and contextualized, it becomes feasible to apply the suggested method of measuring levels of leadership commitment to modernization. The following might be the kinds of policy areas that would have to be considered for this purpose:

Major areas of *general* developmental decision-making:
1. The rural sector (for example, land distribution, rationalization of agriculture, rural development).
2. The urban sector (for example, industrial development, labor unions, social services, integration of rural immigrants).
3. The cross-sector (for example, public health, education, welfare, recruitment criteria, mobility).

Major areas of *specific* developmental decision-making:
1. Taxation (especially income and property taxes).
2. Budgetary allocation patterns.
3. Nonmonetary policies directly affecting statuses of social classes and interclass and interpersonal relationships.

In any case, the range of commitment score (C) would be from 1 to 10 (for simplicty's sake, decimal points are eliminated).

Similar difficulties attend the second condition for successful modernizing political leadership, namely, political intelligence and skill. As with the first, this quality could initially be assessed indirectly and with much less than a minimal degree of rigor and precision. Nevertheless, it might be possible at least to achieve a partial measurement of the condition by examining the level of efficiency and dispatch with which leadership developmental policies are implemented (or not implemented). It would be possible to ascertain both explicit and implicit intents of such decisions as well as the intended ways and time projections in which they are deisgned to be implemented, and then compare these with the actual processes of execution and implementation. This approach might reveal at least two issues of importance: (1) the technical and situational appropriateness of decisions made (that is, whether or not decisions are so designed or formulated that they can be implemented with dispatch and administrative and political economy), and (2) whether or not there was an accurate perception and evaluation of environmental contingencies as well as situational assets on the part of political leadership. This approach may be stated as:

$$\text{political intelligence and skill (I)} = \frac{\text{actual speed and effect of policy implementation}}{\text{intended speed and effect of major policies made}}$$

Combined with the index of commitment to modernization ideals, this measure might yield a great deal or at least much more than is now known, about the pace at which political leadership is promoting and directing the process of modernization.

Another possible way of at least partly measuring this second leadership condition is to examine the frequency of sustained periods of extralegal or extraconstitutional methods of repression. This measurement might elicit some insight into whether or not political leadership is performing the function of mediating the need for stability and the need for change intelligently and economically, maximizing support and minimizing resistance. The higher the frequency, the lower, one might argue, leadership's intelligence and skill. Likewise with the frequency of violence, riots, and other forms of overt popular defiance and resistance. This suggestion, especially concerning the matter of repression, may well be countered by the argument that an authoritarian or totalitarian leadership can generate change and development while carrying out an extensive policy of repression as in Stalinist Russia, for example. It is apparent that, by ruthlessly repressing all actual and potential opposition and terrorizing the populace into submission, a given regime or leadership can in fact still promote modernization, or at least some aspects of it. An interesting question to ask, however, is whether such repression is actually speeding up the process of modernization or slowing it down. As argued earlier, political intelligence and skill has in part to do with formulating and implementing developmental policies and programs by maximizing support and minimizing resistance. Repression, as that in the second half of the 1930's in Russia, one may argue, is ultimately counterproductive, or at least highly uneconomical and wasteful. In the first place, it necessitates the diversion of much organizational, material, and monetary resources from productive activities and enterprises into an expanding task of coercion. We have no knowledge of the proportion of the Soviet Union's annual budget that was allocated to the running of an extensive network of prisons, labor camps, the secret police, and other instruments and personnel necessitated by what one recent observer calls "the great terror."[11] It is nevertheless reasonable to assume that the cost of repression, even in this restricted budgetary sense, must have been enormous. After all, it could not have been a minor excursion to imprison 5–5½% of a population of between 147 and 170 million in a four-year period.[12] Repression, indeed, cannot but be an exceedingly costly affair. Moreover, the waste or diseconomy that is inherent in repression is also represented by the potential amount of incremental growth and development that society is now increasingly deprived of. Repressed resistance against political leadership often leads to its obtuse manifestation in the form of passive sabotage, decline of energy and incentive, suppression of resourcefulness and initiative, and fear of responsibility and innovation. Not only, therefore, can political leadership not elicit a maximum effort and support from citizens but it thus actually encounters a phenomenon of a diminishing marginal return for repression in terms of progress on the path of development and modernization. The combined cost of diversion of much existing resources into instruments of repression and the decline in the energy and morale of citizens for modernization is likely to be considerable. One student of Soviet economy estimates, for example, that, while labor productivity and investment had increased sharply and the economic situation vastly improved during the few years after the end of repression of the Kulaks and before the Great Purge, the purge years produced a drastic fall in investment, a serious decimation of qualified personnel in many sectors and fields, a rapid rise in free-market prices, a sharp decline in the supply of consumer and other goods, a significant increase in resentment and bitterness, a corresponding decline in morale (not only among common citizens but also among party members), and a paralysis of thought and action among persons in positions of responsibility in all fields.[13] Even Soviet commentators agree that the damage inflicted upon the process of modernization by Stalinist repression was "serious."[14] An obvious implication is that repression, at least of the type that terrorizes an entire society, brings about, not an acceleration of progress, but rather a slowdown. One could argue, then, that the resort to violence is an admission of the insufficiency of intelligence and skill on the part of political leadership.

The range of intelligence-skill score (I) will be from 1 to 10 (decimal points eliminated).

For the ascertainment and measurement of the third condition for successful modernizing political leadership, namely, dominance over subnational political elites, the following criteria may be suggested: (1)

whether the system is unitary or federal; (2) if political parties are significant, whether national leadership in fact possesses control over the selection of candidates for public office and over the choice of party officials in the center as well as in the periphery; (3) whether national-leadership directives, orders, and policies are obeyed and implemented by local political or party elites; (4) whether there are incidences of attempted coups and other forms of subnational oppositionist elite defiance; (5) the frequency of personnel change in national political leadership (for example, the resignation, defection, or dismissal of top members of political leadership such as influential cabinet members, justices, advisers, military commanders); and (6) the frequency with which political leadership makes a significant concession to subnational political elites. Some combination of these criteria would have to be used in order to generate a meaningful measurement and understanding of this third condition for political leadership. If political power and influence at a point in time could be quantified, measurement of dominance would be:

$$\text{dominance (D)} = \frac{\text{power and influence of national leadership}}{\text{total power and influence in polity}}$$

Provisionally we suggest the range of dominance score from 1 to 10, as in the previous two conditions.

Situational assets refer, in brief, to the quality or level of the environment for political action to promote national development. Every nation is "differentially endowed with a supply of resources."[15] It would be possible to say, for example, that nation X has twice the situational assets of nation Y, and so forth. The greater the situational assets, the easier, relatively speaking, the formulation and implementation of developmental policies, hence the faster the pace of modernization that could be expected. It is for this reason that the three measures (C, I, and D) should be adjusted to different levels of circumstances if meaningful measurement of modernization paces is to be generated. Hence the consideration of situational assets. There are broadly three general types of ingredients of situational assets: economic, political, and sociocultural. The economic dimension of situational assets consists of such indices as annual per-capita GNP, annual growth rate of GNP, annual DCF (domestic capital formation), economic infrastructure, number of appropriately trained people as a percentage of the population, and amount of reliable available foreign investment and assistance. The political dimension of situational assets may be evaluated in terms of the existing routinized level of governmental capability. The sociocultural dimension of situational assets can be evaluated in terms of literacy rate, level of communication and mobility, and degree of social fragmentation especially among politically relevant strata. These indices for the three major dimensions of situational assets are merely examples of those that should be carefully examined in actual empirical studies. At any rate, various levels of "development" are various levels of situational assets.

It is possible to measure those variables as well as many other relevant indices and to compute composite scores for a variety of developing nations as well as more advanced nations. Table 15 is a crude and oversimplified example of a computation of situational assets. The range of situational score (S) is from 10 to 40.

On the basis of the four indices namely, commitment score (C), intelligence and skill score (I), dominance score (D), and situational score (S), there evolves the following scheme for measuring a periodic index of modernization (M):

$$M = \frac{\frac{(C \times 2I \times D)}{S}}{2}$$

More weight is given the intelligence and skill score because of its special relationship with other variables in the scheme. The way in which each of the other variables is to contribute to modernization depends solely upon how it is utilized and manipulated by leadership intelligence and skill. In other words, salience of I is incalculably greater than that of C or D or S in producing M. C, I, and D are multiplied in the scheme because their mutual interaction produces the result that is greater than, and intrinsically different in nature from, the sum total of its components. The interaction is both magnificatory and transformative. S (situational score), as mentioned earlier, is used for control of the outcome of the interaction among C, I, and D in order to account for differences in circumstances. The level of leadership performance in promoting modernization should be adjusted to the level of situational assets which largely circumscribes the extent of leadership behavior and policy. In short, an index of, say, 14 for leadership performance under unfavorable circumstances may be in fact equal or superior to another index of, say, 23 under more favorable circumstances. Rates of modernization should be judged against the background of the circumstances under which modernization is being undertaken. M, therefore, is also an index of leadership quality. $\frac{C \times 2I \times D}{S}$ is divided by 2 simply to limit the theoretical maximum index to 100.

Table 15. Example of Computation of Situational Assets, in Selected Nations, ca. 1960–1965.

Nation	I Annual Per-Capita GNP	II Deaths from Domestic Group Violence	III Governmental Stability	IV National Budget as % of GNP	V Teacher-Population Ratio	VI Expenditure on Public Health and Education	VII Internal Cleavage, Hostility	VIII Literacy Rate	IX Communication	X Effective Political Dominance	Situational Score (I–X) (10–40)
United States	5	4	5	2	3	3	5	3	5	3	38
Japan	5	4	5	2	3	2	5	3	5	4	38
Austria	5	4	5	2	3	3	5	3	4	4	37
Ireland	5	4	5	2	3	2	5	3	4	4	37
Canada	5	4	5	2	3	3	3	3	5	3	36
Israel	5	3	5	1	3	2	3	3	4	4	33
France	5	4	3	2	3	1	3	3	4	4	32
Italy	5	4	3	2	3	2	3	3	4	3	32
Portugal	4	3	5	2	2	1	3	2	3	5	30
Argentina	4	1	3	1	3	1	3	3	3	2	24
Thailand	2	3	3	2	2	1	3	2	1	4	22
Venezuela	5	1	1	1	2	3	1	2	2	3	21
Iraq	3	1	1	2	2	2	3	1	3	2	20
Bolivia	2	1	3	1	2	3	3	1	1	2	19
Philippines	2	1	3	2	2	2	1	2	2	2	19
Burma	1	1	3	2	1	1	1	2	1	3	16
India	1	2	5	1	1	1	1	1	1	1	15

Note: Figures in this table are by no means accurate, since they are arrived at arbitrarily. In this book, they remain hypothetical, though in most cases they reflect levels of various items in the nations concerned. In view of the fact that some variables are more important than others, they are given different weights. Moreover, it should be stressed that the variables used as well as the weights attributed to them are at best suggestive.

I: 5 for nations with more than $800, 1 for those with less than $100, other figures for the three different levels of income in between.
II: 4 low, 3 medium low, 2 medium high, 1 high.
III: in terms of extralegal change of regime, attempted coup, political violence. 5 stable, 1 unstable, 3 in between.
IV: 2 high (for example, over 20%), 1 low.
V: 3 low, 2 medium, 1 high.
VI: 3 high, 2 medium, 1 low.
VII: 1 wide, 3 medium, 5 stable.
VIII: 3 high, 2 medium, 1 low.
IX: 5 extensive to 1 very limited.
X: on the basis of constitutional structure, secessionist tendency, powerful sociopolitical groups. 5 very effective to 1 very ineffective.

Below are a few hypothetical examples of the use of the scheme:

Nation X	Nation Y	Nation Z
$S = 27$	$S = 20$	$S = 31$
$C = 6$	$C = 8$	$C = 7$
$I = 7$	$I = 8$	$I = 8$
$D = 7$	$D = 6$	$D = 7$

$$M = \frac{\frac{(6 \times 2(7) \times 7)}{27}}{2}$$

$$M = \frac{\frac{(8 \times 2(8) \times 6)}{20}}{2}$$

$$M = \frac{\frac{(7 \times 2(8) \times 7)}{31}}{2}$$

$$M = 10.9 \qquad M = 19.2 \qquad M = 12.7$$

(The theoretical range of M is from .025 to 100.00.)

ANTICIPATION AND MANIPULATION OF CHANGE

The typology of political leadership and the consideration of relative paces of modernization and development as well as the discussion of two different levels of governmental capability call for a brief comment on patterns of political-leadership response to environmental change and fluctuation. Environmental change and fluctuation enter the political arena in the form of demands and claims from various groups in society. The process of national development involves change in values and behavior which, in turn, translates itself into the emergence of new patterns of expectation on the part of various groups in society toward the kind and level of governmental performance. The emergent urban proletariat, for example, would demand a wage scale that was not known previously; landowners resent taxation on their land, and poor peasants and tenant farmers demand redistribution of agricultural land; previously apolitical strata of society become politically conscious and begin to claim the right to political participation; society at large expresses growing impatience for social welfare and a higher standard of living. What was once unquestioningly accepted becomes intolerable, and what was unthinkable becomes necessary. All these constitute pressure on—inputs into—government and polity, to which political leadership must somehow respond. These are the pressures which, unless properly dealt with, would undermine the governmental capability and reduce the independence and maneuverability of political leadership. These are instances of environmental change which would have to be carefully controlled, regulated, and directed if they are to be rendered constructive to the process of national development. Such control, regulation, and direction are the function of political leadership. They are the function, more specifically, of the ways in which political leadership reacts and responds to those instances of change and fluctuation. In short, they are the function of political leadership's commitment and its intelligence and skill. This particularly manipulative dimension of political-leadership behavior will be discussed in detail in Chapter IV, but at this point, we shall comment on the general problem involved in it, which is succinctly expressed by Almond and Powell: "the responsive capability is a relationship between inputs and outputs."[16]

Ways in which political leadership reacts and responds to environmental change and fluctuation affect both the pace and pattern of development and modernization. This is so precisely because leadership behavior and policy determine whether the process of such development is discreetly engineered, regulated, and directed. While change is essential to national development, it should not be rampant but instead should be carefully designed and regulated so as to lend itself to meaningful and viable integration into the process of development.

Almond and Powell (who consider "responsive capability" as one of their five "system capabilities") discuss four general forms of response to be employed by political leadership. In the present conceptual framework, those forms of response are of leadership behavior and policy and not part of the "system capabilities." The four general forms of response are, according to Almond and Powell, repression, indifference, substitution, and accommodation.[17] These are pure types; in actuality, most instances of leadership response are likely to be a mixture of these pure types. Under each particular set of circumstances, therefore, political leadership must carefully calculate relative immediate and long-range costs and relative benefits of each alternative form of response, assess the likely consequences and impact upon the viability of the polity and the task of national development, and critically evaluate the existing as well as potential levels of governmental capability, both routinized and incremental. The kind of response that is appropriate in one situation may not be proper in another. And while a particular set of circumstances may well call for a particular type of response, far more important is the fact that the particular set of circumstances can be shaped by political leadership. This is the meaning of Jennings' observation: "Situation can be shaped by the force of the great leader to the same extent that the weak leader can be shaped by the force of situation."[18] This manipulative dimension of political leadership is critically relevant to the condition of many a developing nation. The political instability that characterizes such a nation is in part the result of the critical lack of an adequate level of routinized governmental capability. The routinization and institutionalization of governmental capability generates the regularization of political relationships among participants and helps establish a high degree of predictability of behavior of both government and society. Individuals and groups under such circumstances have a fairly accurate idea as to both the upper and lower limits of demands and claims they think they can press upon government with reasonable expectations of satisfaction. At the same time, since the behavior of society is also largely predictable, government (hence political leadership) is able to prevent itself from being inundated by an excessive volume and variety of demands and claims that might imperil its own stability and capability. This condition, however, most of the developing nations have yet to achieve.

How, then, can the political leadership of a developing nation protect itself from being overwhelmed and overburdened with more environmental change and fluctuation than its capability would admit of? In other words, how can political leadership contrive to avoid a situation in which it might find none of its alternative responses alleviative of either short-run or long-range danger to the viability of the polity and the evolutionary process of development, or in which it might find itself unprepared? Depending upon the level of situational assets and the way relative costs and benefits of alternative types of response are computed, there are two major ways in which political leadership may be able to avoid such a dangerous impasse. First, political leadership should possess adequate political intelligence and perception to predict and anticipate possible environmental contingencies in terms of the kinds and volume of potential demands as results of its current behavior and policy.[19] This leadership ability is of a special kind which does not lend itself to routinization or institutionalization. Its importance, however, is vital because by anticipating and predicting a particular type of environmental change, political leadership will be able to make appropriate preparations for the particular type of response it seeks to employ, such as intensified mobilization of a certain dimension of governmental capability (for example, symbol manipulation, the strengthening of law enforcement, fiscal reform, modification of recruitment patterns, or a shift in emphasis on certain policy matters). Political leadership, then, will not be caught unprepared, and it will be able to respond with dispatch and vigor. Second, if environmental contingencies that can be anticipated are judged to be of the kind to which none of the alternative types of leadership response lends itself without seriously straining or undermining the available level of governmental capability as well as the pace and pattern of national development, political leadership may be able to take appropriate measures to prevent their emergence, again by a variety of means such as selective emphasis in its communication with participants in the political process and in certain aspects of its manifest socialization process.

This leadership attribute is of vital importance in the process of national development inasmuch as change, which is the conditon for development of society and polity, must be carefully engineered and regulated; that is, the kind, volume, and timing of change must be controlled by political leadership. The extent to which political leadership may be successful in this regard depends upon the accuracy of its anticipations and upon the skill with which it takes necessary preventive or preparatory measures. At any rate, political leadership, if fully cognizant of the nature of its role in national development and if equipped with appropriate intelligence and skill as well as commitment, is capable of shaping the future circumstances for its action as well as of preparing itself for deliberate or spontaneous environmental contingencies. It is in this sense that "the inputs of the environment are really just the outputs of the political system."[20] Demands from various groups in society and other forms of environmental change and contingency can, therefore, be controlled and determined by political leadership. It is for this reason that the more capable political leadership is in intelligence and skill, the less likely it is to encounter the kind of situation that it is ill-equipped or unprepared to handle and that will cause detrimental effects on government as well as on the process of national development.

Another important consideration concerning the issue of leadership response to environmental change follows from the above discussion. Whatever type of response political leadership may choose to employ in a given situation does not by itself constitute the whole of leadership response. Response, like any policy or decision, is the final authoritative form of leadership behavior in the face of a particular type of problem. There is always the consideration of its acceptability, legitimacy, and propriety. No type of response, in itself, is capable of automatically eliciting these three attributes. It must be rendered acceptable and legitimate to as large a portion of society as possible because government, in order to remain stable and capable of governing, must always try to maximize support for and minimize resistance against its policy. This requirement suggests that in order for political leadership to resort to one or another type of response (which, in other words, is a policy, an instance of decision-making), it must, both before and during the execution of the type of response chosen, seek to energize its supporters, convert neutrals into supporters, and reduce or neutralize opposition. To put the same idea a bit differently, leadership response to environmental change is a policy to be implemented like any other policy. In fact, policies during the process of national development are all responses to change and the requirements of change. The politics of national development differs significantly from the politics in an advanced modern polity in that policies (responses to change and to the requirements of change) are extremely difficult to implement. One of the essential tasks of political leadership is to implement those difficult policies so that society may change and progress. Another vital task, inseparable from the first, then, is in each instance of response to create a virtually new condition which will permit the implementation of necessary developmental policies and responses. In a developing society, by and large, no significant policy can be effectively implemented unless the environment (society) is rendered receptive to it. In short, the existing condition is full of obstacles against the execution of leadership policy. The level of situational assets is inadequate for its smooth implementation and ready acceptance. There is a critical handicap, so to speak, against the process of national development, and this handicap, in each instance of response decision-making, must be compensated for by a special kind of leadership behavior and policy. In this inquiry the process is called "compensatory mobilization," and it forms the subject of the next chapter.

NOTES

1. As to why these five nations displayed markedly different patterns, see the discussion "A Typology of Political Leadership" later in the chapter.
2. This review of Argentina draws heavily upon the following works: Thomas F. McGann, *Argentina: The Divided Land* (Princeton: Van Nostrand, 1966); Arthur P. Whitaker, *Argentina* (Englewood Cliffs, N.J.: Prentice-Hall, 1964); Peter G. Snow, "Argentina," in Ben G. Burnett and Kenneth F. Johnson (eds.), *Political Forces in Latin America* (Belmont, Calif.: Wadsworth, 1968); and Hubert Herring, *A History of Latin America* (New York: Knopf, 1961).
3. Robert C. North, *Kuomintang and Chinese Communist Elites* (Stanford: Stanford University Press, 1952). See also chapters on Soviet and Chinese elites in Harold Lasswell and Daniel Lerner (eds.), *World Revolutionary Elites: Studies in Coercive Ideological Movements* (Cambridge, Mass.: M.I.T. Press, 1965).
4. Karl W. Deutsch and Lewis Edinger, *Germany Rejoins the Powers* (Stanford: Stanford University Press, 1959).

5. Bernard Silberman, *Ministers of Modernization* (Tucson: University of Arizona Press, 1964).

6. Gunnar Myrdal, *Asian Drama: An Inquiry into the Poverty of Nations* (New York: Pantheon, 1968), Vol. I, Chap. 2.

7. Eugene E. Jennings, *An Anatomy of Leadership* (New York: Harper & Row, 1960), p. 15.

8. Bertrand de Jouvenel, *Sovereignty: An Inquiry into the Political Good* (Chicago: University of Chicago Press, 1957), pp. 21–22, 50–53, 299–300. Also consider the legislator and magistrate in Jean-Jacques Rousseau, *The Social Contract*, Bk. II, Chap. 7.

9. Hannah Arendt, *On Revolution* (New York: Viking, 1965), p. 225.

10. Niccolo Machiavelli, *The Prince*, in a Modern Library edition of *The Prince and the Discourses* (New York, 1950), Chap. VI, p. 21.

11. Robert Conquest, *The Great Terror* (New York: Macmillan, 1968).

12. *Ibid.*, Appendix A. For a general discussion on the short-run and long-range detriments of repression, see David E. Apter, *The Politics of Modernization* (Chicago: University of Chicago Press, 1965), p. 386; David Easton, *A Systems Analysis of Political Life* (New York: Wiley, 1965), p. 286; and William McCord, *The Springtime of Freedom* (New York: Oxford University Press, 1964), pp. 241–244.

13. Alex Nove, *An Economic History of the U.S.S.R.* (London: Penguin, 1969), p. 236.

14. *Ibid.* Nove also notes similar phenomena in Russia during the period of Kulak repression in the early 1930's.

15. Warren F. Ilchman and Norman Thomas Uphoff, *The Political Economy of Change* (Berkeley and Los Angeles: University of California Press, 1969), p. 32.

16. Gabriel Almond and G. Bingham Powell, Jr., *Comparative Politics: A Developmental Approach* (Boston and Toronto: Little, Brown, 1966), p. 201.

17. *Ibid.*, pp. 205–207.

18. Jennings, *An Anatomy of Leadership*, p. 15.

19. The importance of anticipation and prediction for innovative and creative leadership behavior is given a stimulating discussion, albeit in a different context, by Peter Drucker in *The Age of Discontinuity* (New York: Harper & Row, 1969), Chap. 3.

20. David Easton, *A Framework for Political Analysis* (Englewood Cliffs, N.J.: Prentice-Hall, 1965), p. 111.

IV

The Strategy of Compensatory Mobilization

The task of national development includes not only the development of a nation but also the creation of conditions for such development. It is one thing to say that a nation *must* develop; it is quite another to say that the nation *can* develop. To formulate a developmental policy is easy (social scientists do that in their offices!); to implement the policy is at best extremely difficult, often impossible. Implementation is difficult or impossible not because it is inherently defective or irrational but because the environment is incompatible with the policy. The policy must be implemented, however, if development is to be promoted. The most difficult task for political leadership, then, is the job of rendering the incompatible environment compatible, at least to the extent that it will allow the implementation of the policy concerned. It is precisely this task that calls for an "ability to turn situational incompatibilities into assets." No nation, no political leadership lacks an abundance of ideas and policies that it wishes to implement; few nations, few political leaderships are blessed with the kind of environment compatible with such wishes. The remainder of the present volume, therefore, will concern itself with this problem of rendering the political environment compatible with the task of national development.

CURATIVE VERSUS PALLIATIVE POLICIES

The process of national development and modernization is essentially the process of mobilizing human, material, and technological resources to increase the governmental capability to carry out a series of corporate enterprises and programs of action and to propel society on the path toward the goal of national development. But such a process inherent in the task of modernization by necessity encounters serious obstacles in the form of inadequate resources, social, political, and psychological resistance to change, and the concomitant lag in the level of institutionalization of the polity, regularization of political processes, and routinization of government capability. These obstacles constitute handicaps which, if the process of national development is to commence and continue, must be overcome; they are, in other words, disadvantages that should be compensated for. Since indiscreet mutual interactions among various social, cultural, economic, and political groups in society and between forces favoring modernity and those resisting it cannot do the job of compensating for the handicaps, it is political leadership alone that can do the job. And this job is termed compensatory mobilization. It is mobilization, or, to borrow Deutsch's idea, social mobilization through which social, political, psychological, and economic resistance to the implementation of developmental policies will be broken or reduced, so that the environment for political leadership may cease to be critically incompatible with leadership policies.[1] In this sense: "Mobilization is essentially (1) attitudinal—a commitment to action, and (2) a means of translating this commitment into action or observed behavior." Hence it involves "the notion of substantial changes in defining new referents for different sections of the population, as well as to the success of an elite in forcing acceptance of its new reference groups, both normative and comparative."[2] Mobilization, in this chapter, is compensatory because its primary and direct purpose is to compensate for the lack of compatibility on the part of the environment by temporarily creating the kind of condition that allows for the implementation of necessary developmental policies. Permanent change, which is an important part of the process of national development, can be brought about only through successful implementations of those developmental policies themselves. In short, developmental policies to be implemented are generically different from policies of compensatory mobilization, as will be clarified presently.

For purposes of convenience, it may be helpful to delineate two major types of policies and programs that are necessarily involved in successful national development. One such general type of policies may be termed *curative*. Policies and programs of this type are developmental policies proper; they are designed for the specific purpose of producing change in value and behavior and in the manner of governance, therefore increasing and expanding all three dimensions of governmental capability. They are designed to institutionalize the polity, regularize political relationships and processes, and routinize a hopefully increasing level of governmental capability. In short, they are policies for national development itself. Policies in the curative category, therefore, pertain to:

1. The establishment of new political, social, and economic institutions: such as industrial projects, subsidies to business, agriculture, and industry, land reform, formation of labor and business organizations and associations, political parties, modern bureaucracy, a modern school system.

2. The adaption of existing institutions and organizations for internal and external change and the increase in their efficiency: such as expansion of suffrage, rationalization of recruitment criteria for political, economic, social, cultural, and professional roles and functions, fiscal reform, organizational reform of existing institutions, adoption of new scientific and organizational technology, and training of technical, professional and managerial personnel.

3. Increased horizontal and vertical mobility, social and economic as well as occupational and geographical: such as reclamation of unused land for settlement and development, geographically and socially more extensive labor recruitment and development for expanding industrial and other corporate activities, improvement and expansion of educational opportunities, and expansion in communication and transportation.

These policies and measures, singly and cumulatively, if implemented, will have the effect of increasing and consolidating the governmental capability and accelerating the process of national development. They are curative in effect because they are specifically designed to facilitate change and adaptation to change—to replace the no longer adequate or healthy parts of the polity and society with more appropriate and viable ones or to modify and improve the existing ones.

Since curative policies (that is, developmental policies proper) are at best difficult to implement (and if they were not, there would be little problem of national development), there ought to be a second type of policy that makes it possible to implement them. These are policies, not for national development and modernization itself, but rather "policies for policies" of development and modernization. They are policies, in other words, for turning situational incompatibilities into assets. This second type of policy is called *palliative*. The fundamental purpose of this category of policies is to elicit and heighten favorable popular emotion and feelings (or to depress unfavorable or negative feelings) to the point of readiness, willing or involuntary, to surrender traditional commitments and loyalties and individual preferences so that members of society may, again willingly or otherwise, accept the curative policies which they would otherwise resist or reject. Policies in the curative category all involve change both immediate at initiation and long-range in cumulative effect. As such, they are likely to be explicit in purpose and content. Hence, they are more often than not likely to elicit manifest opposition as well as diffuse resistance. To use a medical analogy, the palliative is to be applied so as to anesthetize individual and societal sensitivities or to incapacitate their otherwise negative and violent reaction against the implementation of curative measures, as in surgery. In a sense, it is to ease the transition from the negative to the positive condition, from illness to health. Among general policies of the palliative category may be found:

1. The creation or exploitation of charisma, personal or organizational.
2. The concoction or exploitation of crises, internal or external, but often combined.
3. The use of a scapegoat and repression, selective or indiscriminate.
4. The invention or exploitation of a messianic ideology or myth, or what David Apter calls "political religion."
5. Selective bribery, material or symbolic.
6. The manipulation of traditional values, symbols, and institutions.

These policies may be used singly or in a variety of combinations, although distinctions to be drawn among them are, in actuality, not very clear. In each of these general types, there is wide variation. Use of this category of policies constitutes compensatory mobilization. Let us now take a brief look at each of the major types of palliatives.

CHARISMA

Personal or organizational, charisma is one of the frequently noted phenomena of a troublesome, uncertain, and unstable situation. Throughout history crises have often bred charisma. Today, with most of the world in the process of unprecedented change, hence crisis, we witness the most pervasive proliferation of charismatic leaders and organizations. In a sense, we can divide most of the developing nations into two groups: those ruled by popular, charismatic leaders or organizations or parties; and those ruled by politically mediocre, administratively inefficient leaderships. Both groups of nations are basically unstable, plagued more often than not by deep internal cleavages that render effective government difficult, and almost always handicapped by low levels of routinized governmental capability. The first group, however, presents a semblance of internal unity and dynamism because charisma generates a higher degree of leadership increment to the low level of routinized governmental capability. In the second group, internal division is undisguised and the demonstrated levels of governmental capability low in the absence of significant leadership increment. In fact, in nations of the second group, the routinized level of governmental capability may have been eroded as a result of unwise, incompetent political leadership. The first group of nations may be capable of development and modernization; the second is not. The membership in each of the two groups of nations is not static. Charisma, personal or organizational, can often perform the function of mediating or submerging conflict among competing forces and groups by generating among them a unity of dedication to the charismatic leader or movement. A society whose internal cleavages are temporarily overshadowed by such a leader or movement will, however, revert to the original condition of instability and fragmentation once the leader or the movement disappears or loses charisma, unless, in the meantime, the level of routinized governmental capability has been significantly raised and the issue of basic cleavages has been adequately dealt with.

India, for example, after the death of its charismatic leader, Jawaharlal Nehru, manifested increasing signs of debilitating instability and further fragmentation. In the last general election, Mrs. Gandhi seems to have achieved her first nationwide support and a working majority in the Lok Sabha, but whether or not she and her government will make really effective use of their enhanced position of dominance (that is, generate a high degree of leadership increment and, with it, raise the real government capability) remains to be seen. In Pakistan, between 1958 and 1968, when Field Marshal Mohammed Ayub Khan apparently retained his authoritarian charisma, there had existed an unprecedented degree of internal stability, and a considerable extent of national development, especially in terms of economic progress, had been achieved. Once Ayub lost his appeal, however, the nation witnessed a quick return to the situation of political chaos that had characterized the nation before 1958, and this has finally led to the open, bloody rupture of deep regional hostilities that had been smoldering since 1947 between the two geographical halves of the nation. The case of China is also interesting and illuminating. The Communist revolutionary government that had achieved the horrendous task of political and administrative unification of that huge country was to further political integration of the country by perpetuating the basic structure and method of power that had been established during the early years of its existence. The organizational charisma of the Chinese Communist Party, however, had declined toward the middle of the 1960's, and the revolutionary ardor that had held the rank and file together dissipated. The so-called Great Proletarian Cultural Revolution was initiated or at least encouraged by Mao Tse-tung and his followers in order to combat the surfacing of latent political ideological divisions as well as some of the traditional social and regional cleavages. In this process, Mao's personal charisma came again to be mobilized as the core of the appeal of the Revolution and Movement.[3] The extent to which these efforts of the Chinese Communist leadership may prove to be successful, in either the short or the long run, remains to be seen, however. There are numerous other nations which have exhibited, at one time or another, the same kind of relationship between charisma and political instability.

Charismatic leaders as well as charismatic parties and movements emerge in many nations not so much because they are power-hungry or glory-seeking or even revolutionary as because particular contingencies of circumstances call for them. In short, they are apt to appear as a response to conditions of deep instability and pervasive chaos from which a semblance of unity and order must be generated so that the task of national development, even national survival, may be undertaken. Charisma, in an important sense, is metapolitical. Politics as method or process of conflict management has failed; hence the need for metapolitical means. At any rate, the existence of a charismatic leader or party generally suggests underlying instability and cleavages that are temporarily submerged. This statement does not mean, however, that every unstable society has a charismatic leader or movement. The emergence of charisma is essentially a voluntary act of will.[4] More will be said about the role of charisma later, in the discussion of what is termed the *pluralistic development of affect*.

CRISIS

The concoction of crisis or the exploitation of an existing crisis is another time-honored method of quickly generating unity where no unity exists and support where no support is available. Such a crisis as would elicit domestic unity and support for political leadership may be either external or internal; often it is a combination of both. A virulent aggressive foreign policy often conceals and reflects the effort of political leadership to arouse internal unity so that it may govern more effectively, so that it may be obeyed. Certain xenophobic attitudes, such as anti-Americanism, anti-Western posture, anti-imperialism, or anti-Communism, as espoused by political leadership, often suggest same kinds of domestic instability as well as the desire on the part of political leadership to create and increase support for itself. Frequently, the existence or concoction of crisis works effectively for political leadership.

Many Arab nations today, for example, would be experiencing serious, perhaps disastrously violent internal upheavals (as a matter of fact, some of them have been experiencing domestic crises) were it not for their common quarrel with Israel. Sukarno's leadership in Indonesia might not have lasted as long as it did had it not been for his virulent anti-American and anti-Malaysian foreign policy. The Sino-Soviet border incidents of 1969 may well have indicated the need of either the Chinese leadership or the Kremlin, or possibly both, to generate either stability or more support from the people for certain policies that are difficult to implement. The Soviet Union was (and still is) suffering from a number of domestic problems that have the effect of alienating people from its political leadership, including the serious failure in agricultural policy, the issue of intellectual and literary dissent, rising consumer expectations, and certain symptoms of crypto-Stalinism. China during, and as a result of, the Cultural Revolution, revealed some of its serious internal problems. Rampages of the Red Guardsmen and the subsequent condition of near-anarchy in many parts of the country seriously disrupted normal processes of government, and the foundation of the polity was critically undermined. Perhaps more than the Kremlin, one might argue, the Peking leadership was in dire need of compensatory mobilization to restore domestic stability and governmental authority. "Common defense," observes a student of political elites, "is . . . a compelling force toward solidarity."[5]

Crises to be concocted or exploited may be internal, although such crises often spill over into the realm of external relations. The specter of counterrevolutionary activities or subversive movements is frequently invoked by a new revolutionary government or corrupt reactionary regime, though it is usually linked ultimately to some diabolical machination directed from abroad. Thus, practically every new revolutionary regime establishes some kind of *Comité du Salut Publique* both to terrorize the actual and potential opponents into obedience and to cause highly emotive and unreflective support from others for the new government. A corrupt reactionary regime threatened by an immanent overthrow resorts to Communist-hunting and labels all opponents Communist subversives. This strategy, however, is not the sole monopoly of new and unstable governments or corrupt, reactionary regimes. It can be, and often is, used by well-established, presumably stable regimes when they encounter serious resistance and challenge against them or against policies they want to pursue. Not even the United States has been altogether innocent in this regard. Most Americans still remember the era of McCarthyism. Even today, we are ceaselessly told of Communist subversion, influence, or penetration concerning a variety of problems facing the nation, from the civil-rights movement to campus unrest. These are internal "scare" tactics, used in order to induce people to fall into the particular lines of attitude and behavior desired by those who use the tactics. Again, there is some positive relationship between the use of this type of palliative and domestic dissensus and instability.

SCAPEGOAT AND REPRESSION

This technique is somewhat similar to the concoction of crises, especially internal crises, but differs from it in that the target is some socially or economically identifiable group of people in society. The Nazi policy of singling out the Jewish members of the German people is the most outstanding example of this policy in recent history. All the ills of post-Versailles Germany as well as the defeat of the nation in World War I were either directly or indirectly, but always explicitly attributed to the Jews, with the view to uniting the people behind the regime that otherwise lacked such unity, by uniting them against the victims. The massive rearmament, extensive reorganization of national economy, and total regimentation of society that the Nazi regime accomplished in a short span of time after 1933 would most likely have been at best extremely difficult without that particular palliative policy. In terms of extravagance, extensiveness, systematization, and brutality the Nazi policy certainly was unique, but this should not obscure the fact that there are many other historical examples of the same kind of policy in recent history, not to mention ancient and medieval history. The Czarist Russian regime regularly resorted to the pogrom against the Jewish populace. Similar practices were never completely absent elsewhere in Eastern Europe before the present century. The Ottoman Empire often used the same type of policy against Armenians and other non-Islamic groups within its territory. More recently, Sukarno's Indonesia carried out a policy of systematic expropriation and expulsion against the Dutch in the country and later a program of deprivation and discrimination against the Chinese in its territory.

Ethnicity is not the only criterion for the selection of scapegoat. The Kulaks were singled out for systematic victimization in Stalinist Russia in the early 1930's. In China in the mid-1950's former landlords were the object of wholesale persecution as enemies of the people. Officials of the deposed government often constitute such a scapegoat for the new and unstable regime in many a nation, regardless of whether or not they are really guilty of some serious wrongdoing during their tenure, such as corruption.[6] A certain clique or faction within the government may sometimes become the scapegoat. It can be argued, for example, that Liu Shao-chi and his followers within the Chinese Communist Party and within the Peking government have become the scapegoats for a variety of troubles in Chinese politics and economy. In all these cases, unity against the scapegoat signifies unity for the government; support for the government that wants to implement its policies and programs can be generated through uniting people against some group of people.

IDEOLOGY AND MYTH

The invention and exploitation of a messianic ideology or political myth is perhaps the most notable contemporary palliative, though it is far from being novel. From Moses' exhortations to the Israelites to the doctrine of apartheid in the Union of South Africa, history contains a number of messianic ideologies and political myths. It has also been suggested by many historians that the period since the Renaissance has been an age of ideologies. No period of history, however, seems to have been so saturated with such emotive political ideologies and myths as the era since World War II.

One reason for this phenomenon is clear: the gap, wide and often widening, between what is desired and what in fact is, between expectation and actuality. Political ideology, however, is today not merely the function of this gap. It has become a compelling weapon or instrument that political leadership employs to hypnotize people into doing what they would normally not do. Ideology and myth not only project goals to be pursued but also provide a feverish emotive context for their pursuit.[7] Sigmund suggests that ideologies which proliferate among developing nations "elicit emotional commitment by the leadership and their followers [and] are directed toward action—the development of a new society in a certain direction in conformity with certain goals."[8] The core of these ideologies is emotional and pertains to a particular type of psychic orientation and unreflective predilection to be generated among masses of people,—in short, to create a special kind of mentality —a blind faith which lends masses to easy and extensive manipulation by political leadership.[9]

The high level of politicization in the contemporary world has inevitably come to inject into the political arena what had hitherto been latent, inarticulate, nonpolitical demands and expectations. The gap between expectation and actuality, between input and output, so to speak, generates disaffection, deviant behavior, hence instability. The wider the gap, the greater the instability. In a modern historical sense, there is a positive correlation between this gap and ideological intensity, that is, the wider the gap, the greater the ideological intensity. In terms of political-leadership behavior, however, there is a whole new dimension to the meaning of ideological intensity. Traditionally, ideology was the major weapon of the opposition to the existing regime and leadership and society. This is still true today. But the novel political phenomenon in developing nations is that ideology has become also the consciously and deliberately cultivated weapon of the existing regimes.[10] In many of these new nations, the greater the political instability with which the political leadership struggles or thinks it must struggle (that is, the greater the actual and perceived resistance and defiance against the existing leadership), the greater the ideological intensity of political leadership, not to mention, in many cases, the intensity of its opposition. The primary reason for this fact is that political leadership needs to generate support for itself, the support that is perceived to be otherwise nonexistent or in short supply, and to elicit domestic unity so that it may be able to govern effectively. "For the leadership elite," therefore, "ideology compensates for the lack of other types of social cohesion in the new states ... and offset[s] disintegrative tendencies within the society as a whole."[11] Without some such ideology or myth that is capable of fanning popular emotion and arousing unreflective support for political leadership, society would be unable to achieve the unity which allows for the implementation of developmental policies and programs.

The specific content of ideologies and myths is diverse, each reflecting the pattern of political leadership's perception of its needs, society's historical experience, social and political tradition, among other features. The ideologies are sometimes designed to arouse ethnocentric pride or arrogance, to play upon xenophobia or the erstwhile sense of suffering and injustice under colonial rule, or even to engender nobler aspirations for justice and liberty. (In many such cases the content and orientation of ideology may increasingly partake of the features of another method of compensatory mobilization, namely, "traditional symbols and values," to be discussed shortly.) These are but some of the examples, but the point is that, insofar as political leadership is concerned, the content of ideology, functionally speaking, has little to do with what it apparently suggests to those to whom it is directed, but instead is designed to elicit unity in society and support for what political leadership intends to do by way of formulating and implementing certain developmental policies and programs which may or may not have any correspondence with the ideology.

SELECTIVE BRIBERY

As a method of compensatory mobilization, selective bribery can be efficacious if used wisely and discreetly. Its use is perhaps not as apparent or as well known as some of the other palliative methods. It can nevertheless be noticed historically, and patterns of its use are relatively recognizable.

During the process of transition from traditional society to modern society, especially at the early stages of the process, one of the most crucial problems confronting political leadership is the issue of the traditional or displaced elite. This problem has clearly to do with the issue of dominance over subnational elites, discussed in the preceding chapter. By and large, the type of political leadership committed to development and modernization is fundamentally different from the traditional elite in terms of perception of the needs of society, sociopolitical orientation, and recognition of the inadequacy of traditional methods and rules. This is not to say, however, that members of the new leadership are from altogether different social backgrounds, though that may sometimes be the case. As in Meiji Japan, the new leadership may arise from the traditional ruling class. The only really important distinction between the new leadership and the old elite consists in the difference between their commitments. The old is naturally committed to the preservation of traditional rule and sociopolitical relationships; the new, on the other hand, is committed to change, development, and modernization. Hence the inevitable conflict between the two.

There are, broadly speaking, two alternatives for the new political leadership in coping with the problem: liquidation and integration. These are, to be sure, archtypical solutions; they are both, in actuality, difficult, if possible at all, to carry out. Liquidation requires an overwhelming preponderance of coercive power on the part of the new political leadership, which, more often than not, is perhaps ardently to be desired but not seriously to be expected. Yet, modern history presents a few instances in which political leadership opted for this violent alternative. The Jacobin leadership of the French Revolution was perhaps the first outstanding example in this regard, whose determination to liquidate the aristocracy of the ancien régime was graphically symbolized in the guillotine. It is difficult to discern any such large-scale example in the nineteenth century, but in the present century, there are the cases of the Bolshevik leadership in Russia after 1917, various Communist leaderships in Eastern Europe in the wake of World War II, the Chinese Communist Party after 1949, perhaps to lesser extents the Revolutionary Command in Egypt after 1953, and, since then, a variety of revolutionary regimes in such nations as Iraq, Syria, Cuba, and Algeria. All these cases of liquidation of the traditional ruling class, successful or otherwise, belong to the policy of scapegoat-repression. This violent alternative is resorted to in the hope of eliminating what is considered by political leadership to be the major obstacle to the task of national development as well as of arousing unreflective, emotive support for itself. As a method of dealing with the old or displaced elites, however, liquidation can work only if the new regime possesses unchallengeable power of coercion as well as unflinching and ruthless determination to carry it out. Moreover, this policy can produce a variety of negative consequences which the new leadership may or may not anticipate. The traditional ruling class, its existence now blatantly threatened, may, in desperation, strike back with armed revolt, as in Russia after 1917, throwing the entire society into a costly, devastating civil war. Many members of the traditional class may flee the country to engage in subversive activities from abroad or to gather forces for counterrevolution, as did members of the French aristocracy after 1789. In either case, there is produced an added source of instability and insecurity for the new political leadership which is in turn compelled to divert much of its scarce resources to the added task of coping with it. In the end, even if the new political leadership survives, the cost, both tangible and intangible, of coping with consequences of its attempt to liquidate the displaced ruling class and its allies may well exceed the benefit arising out of their ultimate defeat.

The other archtypical alternative, namely, integration, as the means of resolving the problem of the displaced ruling class is at least equally difficult and dangerous, but in the long run far more significant and valuable for purposes of national development and modernization. (The two methods are ideal types. In actuality, the methods used are varying mixtures of the two.) Except in the most backward traditional society, the relative size and residual influence of the old ruling class, for example, the aristocracy, landed oligarchy, or bourgeoisie, are considerable. This fact makes it extremely difficult for political leadership to eliminate or subjugate the class to the new scheme of things. Members of the class as well as the class itself still command widespread traditional respect and support, however parochial that may be, from large portions of society, and its harsh treatment by the new regime may well provoke antipathy and resistance among the tradition-minded populace. In addition, the traditional ruling class or displaced elite is the one that is generally best educated and possesses a variety of skills and talents that are essential to the task of national development. In some instances, it may be the only literate class in society. Apart from the obvious difficulty, even impossibility, of liquidating or forcibly subjugating the former ruling class, therefore, a task that would inevitably necessitate diversion of large amounts of human and material resources from productive endeavors, there is this need to mobilize and utilize the skills and talents of members of the traditional ruling class for the development and modernization of society. Under the circumstances, the only meaningful alternative is to induce the erstwhile ruling class to support the new regime and to integrate it in the whole scheme of development and modernization.[12]

Integration, however, calls for a special type of policy-making. By definition, the displaced ruling class is dissatisfied with the new regime and regards its members as usurpers, hence illegitimate. The displaced elite, furthermore, is opposed to what the new political leadership is trying to promote, since the scheme of the new regime will inevitably further reduce the status and power of tradition. Whatever the regime does, therefore, elicits only suspicion, resentment, hostility, and resistance from this class. In order for the new regime to win the support of this class, it must elicit some identity of interest between itself and the disaffected class. This is the first prerequisite for meaningful integration of the traditional class into the process of development and modernization. But the question is: How can such identity of interest be elicited from the resentful and hostile class of politically experienced, still latently influential people? Ultimately, manifest socialization may do the job, but that takes decades, even generations, to be accomplished. The need for support, however, is immediate. This is where bribery becomes a politically relevant tactic.

One example of this type of compensatory mobilization may be seen in the treatment Meiji Japan's modernizing leadership accorded the *daimyo* and *samurai*.[13] The *daimyo*, former feudal lords, were given both lucrative financial rewards and ranks of nobility, and their vassals, the *samurai*, were provided with pensions and a number of other preferential treatments. The substance of bribery as well as the manner in which it was offered was such that it gradually but surely persuaded the traditional ruling class that their fortune was inextricably tied to the fortune of the modernizing political leadership and the development of their nation. With this sense of identity of interest engendered, resistance from the traditional ruling class declined and its support for the new regime steadily increased, thus enabling the regime to carry out a series of curative developmental policies which could not have been implemented if resistance from the traditional ruling class had persisted. Once the displaced ruling class perceived an identity of interest between itself and the new regime and came to support the general direction of policies and programs of the modernizing leadership, it became possible for the regime to enlist and mobilize the skills and talents of members of this class for purposes of development and modernization. It was largely from this class, which would otherwise have remained hostile and opposed to modernizing programs, that such developmental functionaries as school teachers, bureaucrats, policemen, doctors, managers, entrepreneurs, and financiers came during the Meiji era. Without the positive participation of former *samurai*, Japan's national development since 1868 would certainly have been at best ponderous and spasmodic, and at worst impossible.[14]

Targets of selective bribery may be other than the traditional ruling class. If political leadership feels that implementation of land reform, for example, will encounter serious and determined resistance, from, say, the church for one reason or another, it may find it wise to induce the religious institution to support, or at least refrain from interfering with, land reform by offering it some special privilege, material or symbolic. Likewise with the military. The military in many a developing nation is frequently conservative in outlook and regards such modern institutional innovations as the organization of labor unions and political parties with suspicion, if not with outright distaste and hostility.[15] In the face of opposition from the military, political leadership may choose to bribe the military with new weapons, the promotion of influential officers to generalships, or larger military appropriations than would otherwise be expected. Other groups, such as the business community, the landowning class, and labor, may become the object of selective bribery from time to time, depending upon the type of curative developmental policies political leadership wishes to implement, the extent and strength of resistance against them, and the perception and capabilities of political leadership itself.

It must be noted, however, that selective bribery, like any other type of palliative, is not the characteristic tactic of political leadership in developing nations alone. The political leadership of an advanced, industrialized democratic society uses this tactic when occasions call for it. The President of the United States, for example, faced with opposition from certain powerful members of Congress to a program he has proposed, may choose to placate top leaders of opposition by ordering the Defense Department to grant a certain defense contract to constituencies of those opposition leaders, by enlisting them on certain internationally or nationally prestigious missions or commissions, or by otherwise demonstrating effusive respect and admiration for their statesmanship. In all these instances, in developing and developed nations alike, the purpose is to elicit support where there is none and to eliminate or reduce resistance that makes the implementation of certain policies difficult or impossible.[16]

TRADITIONAL SYMBOLS AND VALUES

Politics, however it may be defined, can be regarded as one-third force and two-thirds symbols. No polity can survive without means of ultimate sanction against those who dare to challenge and defy it. At the same time, no polity can last long unless it is able to justify its existence—legitimize itself—in the eyes of those whom it governs. (Ideology is one means for such legitimation.) Force cannot do this job. Force punishes but cannot legitimize. Legitimacy is the function of symbols. The greater and more durable the efficacy of such symbols, the more stable the polity concerned. But this is precisely the reason why new nations are unstable, not so much because they lack the means of coercion, as because they lack efficacious symbols by which to justify and legitimize their polities. In other words, new leaderships and polities lack adequate support and adherence from people, not to mention support for specific developmental policies that need to be implemented. What sort of symbols, then, should be mobilized and manipulated to elicit support, so that the new polity, its leadership, and its policies may come to be regarded as proper and necessary?

It is axiomatic that masses in a developing society are tradition-bound in their attitudes, predilections, and values even though they may desire the comfortable, affluent life of modern society. In order to justify and legitimize developmental policies and programs that in their very nature and consequences are contrary to forces of tradition and parochialism, they must be rendered palatable to the masses. This is where the use of language and values and symbols of tradition becomes of great importance. Modernizing policies and programs have to be justified by tradition; they must be sugarcoated, so to speak, with the sweet and accustomed taste of values and symbols with which the masses have a ready feeling of identification, security, and comfort.[17] We shall have an occasion shortly to discuss this matter in detail, but suffice it at this moment to refer again to the experience of Meiji Japan's modernization. The task of national development in that feudal, tradition-bound society was carried out with amazing dispatch and efficiency in part because its modernizing leadership, instead of adopting the Western language and symbols of bourgeois revolution, political equality, and rationalism which was totally alien to the Japanese people, made clever use of traditional indigenous symbols and values for legitimizing itself and its policies in a manner that was evocative of pride in Japan's unique background and heritage. (In contrast, the opposition movement—so-called *jiju minken undo*—resorted, unwisely as it turned out, hence ineffectively, to the use of the language of Western parliamentary democracy, civil liberties, and popular sovereignty.) It was thus that tradition was rendered supportive of modernity, instead of remaining hostile and resistant to modernity. In an important sense, it was traditional symbols and values that made Japan's rapid modernization possible.

Compensatory mobilization constitutes political leadership's effort to overcome obvious handicaps on the path of national development by means of creating the kind of condition, which is neither germane to nor inherent in the existing situation (the level of situational assets, or the situational score in Chapter III), which permits the implementation of curative developmental policies. This process is the same, in essence, as generating a high level of leadership increment to the existing low level of regularized governmental capability which, because of its inadequacy, is incapable of implementing necessary programs and enterprises for development and modernization. The area of leadership increment to government capability (A-B) in Figure 1 in the previous chapter, therefore, represents the level of the need for compensatory mobilization as well. The greater the handicap encountered on the path of national development, therefore, the greater the need for compensatory mobilization. Compensatory mobilization is the function of political leadership. The relationship among these key dimensions and the developmental spectrum of society may be seen in Table 16.

Compensatory mobilization as leadership strategy, however, does not guarantee its own success. If properly employed, it can produce the effect desired, namely, an increase in the level of demonstrated governmental capability (as opposed to the routinized level of such capability), hence the generation or acceleration of developmental processes. But if employed unwisely without proper consideration and caution, it will subvert, disrupt, and distort the process of development more than its

Table 16. Developmental Dimensions and Developmental Spectrum.

Dimension	Traditional	Transitional	Modern
Situational feature	stable	unstable	stable
Situational score	low	medium	high
Need for compensatory mobilization	low	high	low
Level of institutionalization of polity	high	low	high
Regularization of political relationships	high	low	high
Need for leadership increment to governmental capability	low	high	low

absence would. Such danger of compensatory mobilization will be discussed in some detail in Chapter V.

THE PLURALISTIC DEVELOPMENT OF AFFECT

National development is, in an important sense, predicated upon change in values and behavior patterns. Values and behavior patterns are part of what is generally called "political culture." National development, then, calls for some change in the prevailing political culture of society. Political culture, however, is neither static in meaning nor constant in its response to different stimuli. Insofar as it is the creation of man and society, it is amenable to manipulation by man. It can, in short, be modified. A student of political culture observes:

The changeability of basic political beliefs is indeed a crucial question to the elites of the developing nations. It is customary to think that cultural dimensions are unchanging factors that form the setting within which politics is carried on; that culture conditions politics, but not vice versa. Certainly this was the main argument of much of the national character literature. But the situation is sharply different today. Basic beliefs have not become the object of direct concern and attempted manipulation by the political elites in many nations.[18]

The question, then, is: How can political culture be manipulated? Obviously there are ways and strategies for changing politically relevant values, beliefs, and behavior patterns—ways and strategies that could be abstracted from history. In this section of the present chapter, however, the problem will be examined as one of the most crucial dimensions of the developmental stage that calls for compensatory mobilization. The dimension at issue here is transition in attitude, values, and patterns of behavior from traditional to modern.

The transition in this regard, for which compensatory mobilization may become the major instrument, need not, and often does not, extinguish all of the old attitudes, values, and patterns of behavior. The core of such transition is the development of plural affective orientation, or what Lerner called "psychic mobility," and not a complete switch from one set of attitudes, values, and behavior patterns to another.[19] An example of this transition may be briefly reviewed. One of the critical problems in the process of development and modernization is the need to engender in members of society a positive modal affect toward modern methods, institutions, and goals. This need does not warrant that attachment to the old be completely eradicated, although leaderships of some societies mistakenly feel it does. For example, in a more or less typical developing society, there is persistence of the individual's traditional loyalty toward his immediate communal, tribal, or regional group while there is critical need for loyalty toward his new nation-state and polity. The development of loyalty toward the nation-state or the idea of common citizenship, however, does not and need not cause severance of his affective ties with his traditional universe. Especially since the new polity and new ways are not sufficiently institutionalized and not adequately internalized in the mind and heart of the citizen, the retention of traditional ties is not only desirable but also necessary to provide a psychological cushion against potential psychic dislocation and to insure a certain degree of autochthonic continuity of the social and cultural fabric that is essential for the stable, evolutionary growth of society on the path toward modernity. What is required for the process of national development, then, is that the individual citizen develop a positive affective orientation toward his nation, its modern institutions and goals, while retaining his customary loyalty toward his family, village, and other objects of traditional loyalty and affective orientation. With a growing pace of national development, some of his traditional loyalties may well lose their relevance to the individual citizen.[20]

This process can take place spontaneously for some people without any conscious attempt on the part of political leadership. Suppose, for example, a rural person migrates to an urban center and becomes a factory hand—a not untypical situation in which he will, first only on the job but eventually off the job as well, associate with members of different regional, ethnic, and cultural backgrounds and at the same time learn and acquire more universalistic attitudes, values, and patterns of behavior. This process may take a long or short period of time, depending upon the nature and intensity of the circumstances and of the association. At any rate, if the process is not disrupted by the person's early return to his village or by unemployment or by some other cause, it will presumably enable him spontaneously to develop an increasingly wider range of objects for positive affect. Among these new objects may be certain values and goals as well as roles and institutions which, cumulatively, constitute the polity and the new society. For the individual, the political aspect of national development, in an important sense, signifies an expansion in the range of his affective orientations as well as an appropriate shift in and restructuring of objects of affect in order of political and societal importance and priority. This phenomenon may be called *affective pluralism* and the process of its emergence the *pluralistic development of affect*.

The pluralistic development of affect, however, is and frequently should be manipulated by political leadership; that is, it often results from certain types of compensatory mobilization. Spontaneous affective pluralism takes a long time to develop, but the urgency of the task of national development today necessitates a much more rapid development of affective pluralism. And this is where the role of political leadership again becomes crucial. Two general but nonetheless distinct patterns of political-leadership contrivance to elicit the rapid development of affective pluralism are explored below.

One archtypical pattern is the use of personal or organizational charisma, especially personal. Charismatic personal leadership often serves the function of easing the psychic pain and sociocultural dislocation that frequently accompany the period of transition from tradition to modernity. In a typical traditional society, political relationships are basically personalistic and visual: actors are related to one another according to a personalized and visible frame of reference. Even though the political process may be objectively identified by political scientists as suprapersonal or impersonal as an abstract category of analysis, it is inseparable from the person or persons who partake of such object or process. This is the main reason for the primacy of personal loyalty in the politics of traditional society as the basis of political relationship. Within this context, political decisions, too, are perceived as having concrete, immediate, and personal meanings and impact upon the normal life of the individual within the political community. There is, therefore, that sense of close intimacy in terms of both the relationship among actors and the relevance of political decision-making and decisions made. Such traditional affective orientation thus nurtured and long maintained cannot readily be transferred to such impersonal and invisible abstractions as the rule of law, common citizenship, or the constitution. But the emergence of affective orientations toward these abstractions is exactly what a modern nation-state and polity demands of its citizens. In a modern state, members of the community are related to one another not through visual mutual contact nor through a network of personal loyalties, but through a common sharing in the abstract notion of common citizenship and nation and through common respect for and adherence to the invisible network of impersonal laws and regulations. Thus, where political relationships and political decision-making no longer have that concrete and concretely human meaning and immediate impact on the normal life and feelings of the ordinary individual, hence losing that sense of personal intimacy that is one of the most outstanding characteristics of traditional society, the result is serious psychological dislocation, subsequent anomie, and concomitantly various types of antisocial and deviant behavior on the part of the individual ranging from withdrawal to violence. Man, in short, has been uprooted.

In order to facilitate the mobilization of society for national development, therefore, political leadership must try to avoid this kind of psychically, hence socially and politically disturbing situation while at the same time attempting to promote the proper patterns of pluralistic development of affect so that the task of national development may be carried out. This is where charisma, especially of the personal type, becomes valuable.

One reason why it is highly unlikely that a sense of national identity can be rapidly formed is that the process involves a fundamental alteration in the loyalties of those people whose primary attachment was previously given to subnational groups. If the attempt is made to create a national identity in a short space of time, there appear to be only two loci around which it could develop: a set of emotionally charged symbols or a charismatic leader.[21]

Charisma, in an important sense, is an irrational or nonrational quality that has historically performed the function of filling a psychic vacuum created by deep feelings of fear, anomie, or insecurity in situations of confusion, discontinuity, and distress. In one sense, it has invariably been associated with the person who "possesses" it rather than with the institution, office, or role that he represents. The strength and virtue that emanate from charisma inhere in the person himself, and not in the office he holds.

Charismatic authority differs from the other two types [of authority, that is, Weberian traditional and modern] in two fundamental respects. Traditional and legal-rational authority are institutionalized in belief systems and are therefore vested in the role rather than in the person. In contrast, the locus of charismatic authority is in the capacity of a particular person to arouse and maintain belief in himself and his mission as the source of authority.[22]

It is for this reason that the Napoleonic Empire, with all its sudden grandeur and apocalyptic demise, would have been unthinkable without Bonaparte. The phenomenal success of the Chinese Communist Party in unifying the gigantic nation could not have been so spectacular without Mao. Likewise, the mercurial growth of Nazi Germany would have been impossible without the charismatic lunacy of Hitler; and the New Deal would not have been so successful and historic had it not been for the unmistakably personal, superbly confidence-inspiring aura of F.D.R. Each of these charismatic leaders emerged in a time of crisis, in a situation of confusion and insecurity, and helped to create a new situation, a new polity, a new society. Each, in his own way, served as "the model of the new human being required by the newly evolving pattern of life" and succeeded "in encouraging, by his very example, a rapid transformation of existing attitudes."[23] This type of intensely person-centered charisma is especially useful in mitigating the kind of psychic dislocation likely to arise from a sudden change in the nature of politics from visual and personalistic to abstract and impersonal which, in the end, constitutes political development. As Lipset observes:

Personal charisma requires neither time nor a rational set of rules, and is highly flexible. A charismatic leader plays several roles. He is first of all the symbol of the new nation, its hero who embodies in his person its values and aspirations. But more than merely symbolizing the new nation, he legitimizes the state, the new secular government, by endowing it with his "gift of grace."[24]

Charisma, comments Easton, "helps in the transfer of legitimating sentiments from one regime and its authorities to another and to the stabilization of attachments once the transfer has taken place."[25] By rendering visible and emotively personal the new regime and polity, which in reality is designed to become abstract and impersonal, the charismatic leader is able to help citizens develop a positive affect toward the new polity and nation which he now represents and personifies.[26] In so doing, charisma also transcends the internal cleavages in a developing society and thus is able to perform the function of "establishing political order in the face of social and cultural heterogeneity."[27]

Charisma may be associated with certain organizations or movements or institutions. One historically prominent example of institutional charisma is the Papacy. Also, the monarchical throne was once regarded as possessing some kind of charisma—a gift of grace, an unquestionable, unassailable, awe-inspiring quality. In more primitive societies, there are cruder and simpler symbols or institutions of charisma, possession of which gives a person some supernatural qualities which inhere not in him but in the symbol or institution he represents or occupies—the conch, for example, in William Golding's celebrated novel, *Lord of the Flies*. In some developing nations, a revolutionary mass party or movement often elicits the same kind of response among people as that of primitive tribesmen toward the mask worn by a witch doctor. The power of charisma is the same in all these cases—the Papacy, the royal throne, the conch, the witch doctor's mask, or the revolutionary movement—namely, the power to induce people to behave in a way they would not in the absence of such charismatic symbols or institutions or, as Lacouture notes, to make "something out of nothing."[28] The messianic and intoxicating emotional fervor that the Chinese Communist Party inspires or is said to inspire among the millions of Chinese is a manifestation of the potency of a highly charismatic movement or organization, which apparently induces the traditionally familist Chinese to behave in ways that would have been unthinkable before 1949. Almond and Verba suggest that, in Mexico, the Partido Revolucionario Institucional (PRI) and *presidencialismo* are charismatic to the extent that they elicit strong "system affect" and general popular support for the government, even though these attitudes are underlain by contradictory and paradoxical elements of rejection of bureaucratic authority and dissatisfaction with system performance.[29] In these cases, affective orientations toward new polities and institutions are developed, and legitimacy and authority of the new regimes strengthened, by means of engaging emotional and psychic dimensions of people and society in support of the charismatic movement or party. Thus, charisma, be it personal or organizational, can create "an important transitional phenomenon which can further political integration."[30] Max Weber's classical typology of authority is still useful and relevant: charismatic authority, in an important sense, is a transitional function between the traditional visual and personalist authority and politics and the rational, impersonal, abstract authority and politics. It is a necessary bridge between the two types of political universe.

A second pattern of political-leadership manipulation, or compensatory mobilization, which is conducive to the pluralistic development of affect is the mobilization and manipulation of traditional symbols—verbal, visual, and institutional, (Nordlinger's symbols).

It is axiomatic that language shapes politics at least as much as politics shapes language.[31] Language is the means not only for communicating facts and ideas, but also for justifying and legitimizing actions and programs. It is, moreover, a powerful means of changing and modifying perceptions, values, facts, ideas, and beliefs. Language, therefore, is a potent instrument for shaping the political universe, for selecting and positing real and imaginary events, for giving connotations and denotations to ideas and events, for establishing necessary and internal relations between presumed essence and empty names, and thus for mythifying the political universe and political life as legitimate.[32] The language used for this purpose, especially in the transitional period characterized by actual or imminent psychic dislocation must be of a special kind. It must be capable of readily eliciting a positive response from masses who are still psychically bound to tradition. That is to say, it must be able to impart direct consonance and relevance to citizens' personal experiences and needs. Therefore, traditional language is most readily capable in this regard. Traditional language can be turned into a potent instrument for forming the kinds of values, beliefs, habits, and behavior among citizens that induces the promotion and acceptance of new values and beliefs, the institutionalization of a new polity, and a new set of political relationships. A parliamentary democracy, for example, can be justified or rationalized in many ways. It can be justified by reference to normative philosophical considerations, à la Locke or Jefferson. It can be rationalized in terms of the sophisticated tripartite idea of conflict, bargaining, and compromise. And it is easy to make parliamentary democracy sound attractive by simply saying that it is the form of government of the most modern and wealthy nations and that all other nations, if they want to be modern and prosperous, should emulate it.

The way a given idea or action or institution justifies itself, however, is unique to circumstances. Else, justification cannot be accepted as just. In a typical tradition-bound society, none of the justifications mentioned above will be capable of genuine legitimation. Natural right, while objectively a universal human property (at least in the eyes of a Westerner or Western-educated person), is, at least in terms of its articulation and elucidation, essentially Western in its semantics and philosophical predilection, hence an alien concept to the people in the developing nation. Conflict, bargaining, and compromise as the central decision-making method of democracy are equally novel in a predemocratic or nondemocratic context in which society as well as human relationships are hierarchically structured and stratified. Hierarchy signifies eschewal of conflict, bargaining, and compromise in the allocation of values. The argument that democracy is the government of modernity and material abundance may initially elicit some popular interest, but as soon as it becomes evident that such a form of government does not quickly produce modernity and abundance, it will suffer rejection. On the other hand, if democracy (or, for that matter, any new polity or regime) is justified and explained in terms that are within the traditional frame of reference for justice, propriety, and communal harmony (for example, that the new government or formula respects the role of the family, relies on cooperative endeavor rather than competitive struggle among groups of people, and therefore is not only consistent with but also strengthens the virtues of community heritage), that is, if the new is couched in the language of tradition it will appear far more palatable, appealing, and therefore legitimate. Furthermore, the use of traditional language avoids offending values and interests which people hold dear, even though ultimately the polity to be established is committed to eradicating those values. Likewise with any developmental policy or program. Traditional language is what people are familiar with and hence comfortable with. Alien language is strange, uncomfortable, hence ultimately alienating and generative of negative, distorted, or misdirected sentiments. This statement does not mean that no foreign ideas or ideologies can be effectively propagated and accepted. The important thing is that they must be made to appear indigenous or at least consonant with native tradition, or put in the kind of semantic and political context in which indigenous psychic and cultural referents still remain salient to individuals and groups. Novelty as such is not a sound basis for acceptance, let alone permanence.

Traditional visual symbols, too, can and should be mobilized for the purpose of engendering the kinds of feelings and attitudes consistent with the development of modern values, attitudes, and behavior patterns. Among these visual symbols are costumes, rituals, and settings for political occasions. If these and other visual symbols are manipulated to appear referential to those values and beliefs to which people are accustomed and with which they have a feeling of identity, then they can become evocative of the kind of sentiment that, while subjectively blind to the real substance behind the facade of traditionality, may be objectively supportive of it.[33]

Traditional institutions and organizations can also be utilized to serve the interest of progress and development. In this respect, Lipset makes a very suggestive observation:

[N]ew nations which retain local rulers—for example dukes, counts, chiefs, clan head, etc.—and create a larger national system of authority based on them, may be more stable than those which seek to destroy such local centers of authority.[34]

Stability gained in this fashion is at least in part owing to the fact that the masses are accustomed to seeing certain roles performed by traditional personages or role holders. What is important to them, however, is the performance of role, rather than that a particular kind of individual perform the role. This point is made clear by Oksenberg when he discusses the relationship between Mao Tse-tung and the Chinese masses:

... perhaps most of the population in rural areas at least, where tradition still seemed strong even in the late 1960's, expected their leader to play a role similar to the emperor in traditional China—that of a wise and benevolent ruler who, while far removed from them, was responsible for ordering their universe. ... Mao's conduct in office—his regal aloofness, his blend of reigning and ruling—suggests a studied response to, and manipulation of, a widely held desire for him to personify the unity and hopes of the nation.[35]

All too often, the political leadership of a new nation attempts blatantly to discredit and destroy not only traditional bases of social influence and political power but also traditional institutions and organizations and roles in order to establish a strong, centralized regime. In doing so, political leadership is really depriving itself of means and instruments that are readily available to it for its purpose of promoting modernization and development in general and of consolidating the new polity in particular. Furthermore, it often attempts to discredit and destroy those institutions and organizations even before its actual power and authority, hence its governmental capability, lacks an adequate level of compelling strength and while its legitimacy is far from full acceptance by society at large. Many a political leadership publicly attacks those traditional institutions as well as traditional values and beliefs as backward, reactionary, and feudal, and tries to legitimize itself with an alien language of progress, change, and modernity. This approach is especially true with revolutionary political leaderships. Lewis cogently observes:

While the older states retained a degree of social cohesion which helped cushion some of the worst shocks in the industrialization process, many revolutionary elites have not only undertaken to modernize in a rapid and disruptive manner, but have consciously repudiated the premodern social relationships which might help sustain minimal social cohesion. In these cases, their leadership strategies have doubly compounded the difficulties in achieving orderly, sustained growth. ... In short, the revolutionary elites do not utilize previously existing or spontaneously emergent social institutions and personal motivations to sustain modernization. Instead they exacerbate disorder and destroy potential support; they thereby "sow the seeds of their own destruction."[36]

Retention of some, if not all, of the traditional bases of influence and power, institutions and incumbents, at least until the new regime has acquired an adequate level of power, legitimacy, and general governmental capability may well be of positive value to the task of national development because the traditional bases can be manipulated to perform the function of an intermediary between the new regime and the tradition-bound masses, thereby (1) rendering the new regime relatively easier to accept, and (2) for the same reason, making it relatively easier and economical for the new regime to govern society more effectively with less disruption and instability, especially when it still lacks an adequate level of command and authority.[37] Furthermore, such an approach on the part of political leadership helps to alleviate and deflect social, psychological, and political disruption and divisiveness that generally result from efforts to modernize and develop. Not only does it provide a necessary cushion against acute dangers of anomie, discontinuity, and deviant behavior, but it also yields a set of institutional and social mechanisms which translate modern ideas, methods, and goals into terms that are acceptable to tradition-bound masses.[38]

Thus, elements of tradition, such as language, visual symbols and values, institutions and their incumbents, can and often must be mobilized in the service of national development and modernization in general and in the elicitation of positive affective orientations toward new values, institutions, and goals in particular. They all represent forces of tradition, but they can be transmuted into a potent vehicle for generating forces of modernity.

THE NEED FOR GENUINE MUTUALITY OF INTEREST

It is in the nature of compensatory mobilization that it is positively contributive to national development only if political leadership increases the level of general governmental capability to the extent that society will remain committed to the new polity even when the charismatic leadership declines or the potency of traditional symbols and institutions now mobilized dissipates. Unless this is done, the death of a charismatic leader or the decline in emotive capacity of traditional symbols and institutions will precipitate a return to the original, inherent conflict between modernity and tradition, thereby causing regression or decay of the polity and of national development. Clearly, then, the pluralistic development of affect, if it is to be viable and permanent, must be accompanied and buttressed by some other quality in the relationship between the new polity and society, between the government and the governed, that is, by a positive evaluative orientation on the part of society toward its polity, its leadership, and its goals.

To be sure, man is not altogether rational, Aristotle's contention notwithstanding, and his reluctance to accept what is objectively and rationally obvious and beneficial may be tenacious. But another aspect of human nature is equally powerful. Since the emergence of the revolution of rising expectations, man has become increasingly acquisitive and covetous of material as well as psychic gratifications. To this extent, if no other, man is rational. Rational behavior is predicated upon a perception of the range of possibilities in terms of the relationship between effort and payoff, between support and reward, between input and output. In this sense, man has generally behaved rationally within the context of the range of possibilities that he perceives, whether he is an illiterate peasant or a university professor.[39] If this observation constitutes a reasonable assumption about basic human behavior, then it seems that positive affective orientations toward the new polity will be solidified if the polity is perceived as able to confer the benefits that traditional ways of doing things no longer can, because people come to recognize that their well-being is bound up with the new polity. It is here that the need for constantly increasing levels of welfare in the allocation of values becomes clear. In short, the pluralistic development of affect is further stimulated and the emergent affective pluralism fortified and increasingly habituated by the perceived identity of interest between the government and the governed. Positive affect, in other words, is to be reinforced by positive evaluation.[40] Ultimately, this is the only way for genuine and viable integration of society and for harmony between government and governed. Only on this basis can affective pluralism acquire the necessary quality of resilience and permanence. Any other basis for positive affect and national identity is intrinsically fragile. The exploitation of charisma and the manipulation of traditional symbols and institutions are applications of compensatory mobilization; as such, they are temporary in efficacy. They are ad-hoc, stopgap measures that are short-run in their effect and not the substance of a foundation for the viable stability and dynamic development of society. It is incumbent upon political leadership, therefore, to increase the governmental capability in the meantime at least to the extent that is resistant to serious disruption and that is capable of sustaining people's identification, however grudging, of their life interest with the maintenance and progress of the new polity.

The detailed discussion above has concerned only two paradigmatic patterns of compensatory mobilization for stimulating the pluralistic development of affect and for engendering a concrete identity of interest between government and governed in a new nation. There seems to be some congruent, mutually complementary relationship between the two patterns of compensatory mobilization. Successful national development, it may be argued, calls for some combination of these two patterns. Perhaps one outstanding example in this regard is the conduct of the modernizing political leadership of early Meiji Japan.

Japan in 1868 was deeply fragmented in terms of power distribution and political and regional rivalries despite the seeming unity against the deposed Tokugawa shogunate. Its modernizing leadership was therefore faced with powerful, pervasive, deeply entrenched traditional forces (for example, the *daimyo*, the *samurai*, the agrarian sector) that were either openly or latently opposed to its purposes and policies. The Restoration, despite the popular view prevalent among students of Japanese history and politics, by no means signified support for modernization and development. The new imperial government, formed upon the formal Restoration of the throne as instrument of governance and of reign, was inevitably unstable, uncertain, and most precarious. Effective political power was still dispersed among about 260 *daimyo*, and the new government could exist only at the indulgence of these feudatories. Furthermore, because of its regional and intellectual background and the manner of its emergence, the modernizing elite's position was extremely precarious, its legitimacy highly dubious, and its authority virtually nil. The odds were definitely and overwhelmingly against not only modernization but also the modernizing elite. We now know the story of phenomenal success achieved by the initially weak, insecure leadership in acquiring and consolidating power, rapidly breaking up the effective influence of the traditional ruling class, and unifying the whole nation under its authority. There were many reasons for this objectively most unlikely and unanticipated success, and they all pertain to the nature and role of political leadership in the process of national development. One of them was undoubtedly the skill and intelligence with which the modernizing leadership mobilized and combined those two patterns of compensatory mobilization for the pluralistic development of affect among citizens in general and among members of the powerful traditional ruling class in particular, and buttressed it with careful policies for eliciting a positive identity of interest between society and the new polity. For example, the tradition of visual, personalist politics was retained by making the Emperor a paternalistic, benevolent man-god, full of charisma, who addressed the citizens as "my loyal subjects," and by conforming the new emperor-subject relationship to the traditional

Confucian model of intrafamilial relationship between father and children, while, in actuality, he was in the process of becoming the figurehead of an impersonal, bureaucratic modern state. The language used in describing and legitimizing the new politics and the new polity was basically traditional, evocative of and deferential to the nation's proud past and the uniqueness of the Japanese people and their culture, and largely eschewing radical, liberal, constitutionalist vocabularies of modern polities of the West. Visual symbols of native tradition and past glory were fully exploited, with the Emperor and high dignitaries attired on formal occasions in traditional costumes and regalias in the setting of ancient rituals of authority and majesty. Traditional and archaic social stratification was formally and legally abolished, but the visual and symbolic signs of rank differences and class distinctions were deliberately retained through the creation of the ranks of nobility for former feudal chieftains and through the preferential treatment accorded to former *samurai* in all fields of activities. And, perhaps more important in terms of integrating the displaced ruling class and mobilizing that class for national development, concrete policies were formulated and implemented for purposes of eliciting an undeniable identity of basic interest between the erstwhile ruling class and the new order of things and the new regime, thus not only mitigating danger and resistance from the class concerned but also effectively mobilizing the talents and abilities of members of the class which were critically needed for the task of national development. Without the skillful compensatory mobilization for the pluralistic development of affect, the story of Japan's modern development would have been considerably different.

Politics being what it is, there is no easy blueprint for the use and effectiveness of compensatory mobilization, including those two patterns for eliciting a pluralistic affect and promoting development and modernization. Circumstances differ from one situation to another, from society to society. The utility, effectiveness, and ultimate benefit of compensatory mobilization depend primarily upon the intelligence and skill of political leadership.

NOTES

1. Karl W. Deutsch, "Social Mobilization and Political Development," *American Political Science Review*, LV (September 1961). Social mobilization is "the process in which major clusters of old social, economic and psychological commitments are eroded or broken and people become available for new patterns of socialization and behavior" (p. 494).

2. J. P. Nettl, *Political Mobilization: A Sociological Analysis of Methods and Concepts* (New York: Basic Books, 1967), pp. 32–33.

3. For some of the ways in which Mao's charisma is constantly enhanced and energized at the grass-roots level, see, for example, Stephen Fitzgerald, "China Visited: A View of the Cultural Revolution," in Bruce Douglass and Ross Terrill (eds.), *China and Ourselves* (Boston: Beacon Press, 1970), esp. pp. 18–21.

4. "We must not fall into the error of believing that leaders whom we regard as 'charismatic' are individuals whose exceptional qualities come to be spontaneously recognized by their populations. They are often persons who succeed more than others in exploiting the situation around them.... In a way, they are not 'picked' by their people; it is the other way around." K. J. Ratnam as quoted in W. Howard Wriggins, *The Ruler's Imperative: Strategies for Political Survival in Asia and Africa* (New York: Columbia University Press, 1969), p. 94.

5. Lester G. Seligman, *Leadership in a New Nation* (New York: Atherton, 1964), p. 3.

6. "... in a revolutionary situation the accusation of corruption is raised because it has always proved to be an effective weapon." W. F. Wertheim, "Sociological Aspects of Corruption in Southeast Asia," in Reinhard Bendix (ed.), *State and Society: A Reader in Comparative Political Sociology* (Boston: Little, Brown, 1968), p. 562.

7. Ideology, therefore, becomes "the principal political manifestation of social change." Manfred Halpern, *The Politics of Social Change in the Middle East and North Africa* (Princeton: Princeton University Press, 1963), p. 197. Also consider the concept of "the charter myth" in Barrington Moore, Jr., *Political Power and Social Theory* (New York: Harper & Row, 1965), pp. 10–16.

8. Paul Sigmund, Jr., *The Ideologies of the Developing Nations* (New York and London: Praeger, 1963), p. 4. See also Harold Lasswell, "The Language of Power" in Lasswell, Nathan Leites, and Associates, *Language of Politics* (New York: Steward, 1949), p. 10; and Reo M. Christenson et al., *Ideologies and Modern Politics* (New York: Dodd, Mead, 1971), pp. 14–18.

9. For an excellent recent discussion of the political role of such ideology, see Giovanni Sartori, "Politics, Ideology, and Belief Systems," *American Political Science Review*, LXIII (June 1969).

10. Perhaps the most intensive and comprehensive way in which ideology penetrates all aspects of societal life is seen in China today. The citizenry is completely reorganized and grouped so as to insure a maximum penetration of official ideology and a maximum popular response and support to it. See, for example, James R. Townsend, *Political Participation in Communist China* (Berkeley and Los Angeles: University of California Press, 1969), esp. Chaps. 6 and 7.

11. John W. Lewis, "The Social Limits of Politically Induced Change," in Chandler Morse et al., *Modernization by Design: Social Change in the Twentieth Century* (Ithaca and London: Cornell University Press, 1969), p. 13.

12. On the problem of integrating the traditional ruling class as well as emergent classes, see, for example, Seymour Martin Lipset's discussion of the crisis of legitimacy in his "Social Requisites of Democracy: Economic De-

velopment and Political Legitimacy," *American Political Science Review*, LIII (March 1959).

13. For Meiji Japan's treatment of the former ruling class, see Taketsugu Tsurutani, *Tension, Consensus and Political Leadership: A New Look into the Nature and Process of Modernization* (unpublished Ph.D. dissertation, University of Wisconsin, 1966), Part II, Chaps. 15 and 16.

14. National unification of India after independence in 1947 was achieved at least in part because of certain conspicuous elements of selective bribery. Not only did the Constitution reserve considerable and in certain policy areas exclusive, power to the states (for example, the power to tax agricultural incomes), but also special financial as well as symbolic dispensations were granted traditional territorial rules (that is, lucrative pensions and the retention of traditional princely rights to fly their own flags, to maintain civil and military staffs, and so on).

15. For characteristics of the military that are relevant to our present consideration, see, among others, Edward Shils, "The Military in the Political Development of the New States," in John J. Johnson (ed.), *The Role of the Military in Underdeveloped Countries* (Princeton: Princeton University Press, 1963), esp. p. 31, and contrast Shils' discussion with Eric A. Nordlinger, "Soldiers in Mufti: The Impact of Military Rule Upon Economic and Social Change in the Non-Western States," *American Political Science Review*, LXIV (December 1970), 1131-1132.

16. Bribery, selective or not, connotes "corruption" and is still likely to evoke some frowns on the part of Western students of comparative politics. Much like "violence," however, "corruption" can (but not necessarily does) perform certain functions in developing countries at different levels of polity and society and in different but specific contexts. Quite unlike "violence," however, it has not been subjected to systematic inquiry. Two of the few studies that come to mind are David H. Bayley, "The Effects of Corruption in a Developing Nation," *Western Political Quarterly*, XIX (December 1966), and J. S. Nye, "Corruption and Political Development: A Cost-Benefit Analysis," *American Political Science Review*, LXI (June 1967).

17. Political leadership should, therefore, "sell a new idea by describing it as an old one." Marius B. Jansen, "Japan Looks Back," *Foreign Affairs*, XLVII (October 1968), 40.

18. Sidney Verba, "Comparative Political Culture" in Lucian W. Pye and Sidney Verba (eds.),*Political Culture and Political Development* (Princeton: Princeton University Press, 1965), p. 520. Also see Ralf Dahrendorf, *Class and Class Conflict in Industrial Society* (Stanford: Stanford University Press, 1959), pp. 233-234.

19. Daniel Lerner, *The Passing of Traditional Society* (Glencoe, Ill.: Free Press, 1958), pp. 51-52.

20. For an interesting example of case studies of the relationship between citizenship and social variables, see Joseph W. Elder, "National Loyalties in a Newly Independent Nation," in David E. Apter (ed.), *Ideology and Discontent* (New York: Free Press, 1964).

21. Eric A. Nordlinger, "Political Development: Time Sequences and Rates of Change," *World Politics*, XX (April 1968), 503. For the role of charisma as one of the few methods by which to solve the problem of psychic dislocation

during the transitional period, see also Lucian W. Pye, *Politics, Personality, and Nation Building* (New Haven: Yale University Press, 1962), p. 288.

22. Ann Ruth Willner, *Charismatic Political Leadership: A Theory*, Research Monograph No. 32, Princeton University Center for International Studies, 1968, p. 2.

23. Manfred Halpern, *The Politics of Social Change in the Middle East and North Africa* (Princeton: Princeton University Press, 1963), p. 284. Also consider Henri Laugier's concept of "being" as an imperative for new nations in Jean Lacouture, *The Demigods: Charismatic Leadership in the Third World* (New York: Knopf, 1970), p. 7.

24. Seymour Martin Lipset, *The First New Nation: The United States in Historical and Comparative Perspective* (New York: Basic Books, 1963), p. 18. See also Lacouture, *The Demigods*, pp. 51–52.

25. David Easton, *A Systems Analysis of Political Life* (New York: Wiley, 1965), p. 304.

26. For an interesting discussion of charisma in this respect, see Claude Ake, *A Theory of Political Integration* (Homewood, Ill.: Dorsey Press, 1967), Chap. 4, "Charismatic Legitimation."

27. Guenther Roth, "Personal Rulership, Patrimonialism, and Empire-Building," in Bendix (ed.), *State and Society*, p. 589.

28. Lacouture, *The Demigods*, p. 20.

29. Gabriel Almond and Sidney Verba, *The Civic Culture: Political Attitudes and Democracy in Five Nations* (Boston and Toronto: Little, Brown, 1965), pp. 310–312. For charismatic political parties, see Irving Louis Horowitz, *Three Worlds of Development: The Theory and Practice of International Stratification*. New York: Oxford University Press, 1966, pp. 225–253.

30. Ake, *A Theory of Political Integration*, p. 52.

31. Dankwart A. Rustow, *A World of Nations* (Washington: Brookings Institution, 1967), p. 47.

32. Ernst Cassirer, *Language and Myth* (New York: Dover, 1946, trans. by Susanne K. Langer). See also Jacques Ellul, *The Political Illusion* (New York: Knopf, 1967), Chap. 3.

33. For relevance and potency in the manipulation of verbal and visual symbols in politics, the best work thus far is Murray Edelman, *The Symbolic Uses of Politics* (Urbana: University of Illinois Press, 1964), esp. Chaps. 5–7. See also Charles E. Merriam, *Systematic Politics* (Chicago: University of Chicago Press, 1945), pp. 81–93.

34. Lipset, *The First New Nation*, p. 17.

35. Michel C. Oksenberg, "Policy Making Under Mao Tse-tung, 1949–1968," *Comparative Politics*, III (April 1971), 325.

36. Lewis, "The Social Limits of Politically Induced Change," in Morse et al., *Modernization by Design*, pp. 9–10.

37. What this contention suggests is that in a fragmented society where power is widely dispersed, one of the first tasks for national development is the mobilization and coalescence of elites of diverse regional, political, or other groups. Once these subnational elites have coalesced in support for the new regime and some kind of minimal consensus emerges between them and political leadership, the mobilization of societal resources for development and modernization will be greatly facilitated. This description at least in part, pertains

to selective bribery as compensatory mobilization, but differs from it in that the direct object of manipulating traditional institutions and their incumbents is the masses at large, and not those institutions and incumbents.

38. For an interesting study of the use of tradition for modernity, see Lloyd, I. Rudolph and Suzanne H. Rudolph, *The Modernity of Tradition* (Chicago: University of Chicago Press, 1967).

39. "Unless the village system as it stands is seen as rational and intelligent within its circumstances, there is the gravest danger of impatient within its circumstances, there is the gravest danger of impatient action which will bring on this violence of despair. The peasant may be uneducated: but he is an adult, he is experienced, and he has as high a degree of intelligence as any of us. He has time to think and calculate, and, within the limits of vision, his reckoning is right." Guy Hunter, *Modernizing Peasant Societies* (New York and London: Oxford University Press, 1969), p. 52.

40. An excellent proposition concerning the process by which positive affective and evaluative orientations toward a new form of polity and society are generated and consolidated is found in Richard M. Merelman, "Learning and Legitimacy," *American Political Science Review*, LX (September 1966). Merelman's argument derives from learning theory in psychology and explores the manipulative dimensions that inhere in the process of learning—which, in the political universe, is the policy-making process.

V

The Dangers of Compensatory Mobilization

Stability and change, as Machiavelli noted long ago, are far easier to generate then to institutionalize. Haiti, for example, was stable according to certain kinds of criteria under "Papa Doc" Duvalier; Spain is stable under Generalissimo Franco. So is the Union of South Africa. So is Rhodesia. Stability, in this sense, is best achieved by tyranny. Since such stability is the function of coercion, however, it is not institutionalized. India under Nehru, one might say, was stable; France under de Gaulle was likewise stable. So, perhaps, was Egypt under Nasser. Stability in these countries, however, was the function of charismatic leadership. It was, therefore, not institutionalized. Eliminate charisma or coercion, and instability is the most likely result. So it is with change. From time to time, phenomena of change take place in certain developing nations; for example, parties are organized, a modern civil service is established, there is an outpouring of popular interest in economic modernization and social change. More often than not, however, such change turns out to be superficial, unsupported by genuine commitment and viability: political parties dissolve into parochial, narrow-based cabals, hindering rather than helping progress; the civil service disintegrates into an institution of corruption, incompetence, and patronage; and the public interest in modernization reveals its true nature as greedy expectations untempered by awareness of their price. Change was not institutionalized, after all. The transiency of apparent stability and change also pertains to the transiency of compensatory mobilization. Danger of deception, of mistaking what is apparent for what is real, inheres in both. Let us take a brief look at such danger inhering in each of the five paradigmatic types of compensatory mobilization.

THE INHERENCE OF DANGER

CHARISMA

Charisma, whether personal or organizational, has two major, one might say intrinsic, dangers in it. On the one hand, its own potency creates a delusion about the quality of society, the polity, itself. During much of Nehru's stewardship, India was regarded by most as stable, not because it was but because Nehru's ability was mistakenly equated with the presumed quality of Indian polity. India was thus democracy's hope in Asia. It really was not, because while "he personified national purpose and identity," as Myrdal argues, "[h]is political strength was . . . India's weakness."[1] Or, Nehru's charisma served, as Lacouture puts it, "as an alibi for citizens' collective refusal to shoulder their own responsibilities."[2] The mere fact that charisma beclouds the eyes of observers and thus dissembles the underlying instability which it purports to transform into temporary stability suggests a strong temptation on the part of political leadership to wallow in the false sense of security induced by the palliative of charisma, to persuade itself that all is not as bad as it has feared, and to postpone the unpleasant task of implementing such curative measures as are warranted by the process of national development.[3] The fundamental relationship between curative and palliative is thus neglected, for, as Halpern argues, charisma as an instrument of compensatory mobilization "cannot assure stability but can only originate the foundation upon which stability may be established."[4] On the other hand, charisma seems to have the natural proclivity to reify itself, with the result that the virtue and capability of the charismatic leader or organization become vastly exaggerated.[5] At the same time, other leaders and would-be leaders as well as political institutions of the polity suffer from inordinately low levels of prestige and public acceptance.[6] A common consequence of this aspect of charisma is overexpectation on the part of society and, perhaps more dangerous, on the part of charismatic leadership itself, and subsequent and inevitable underperformance. Charisma, therefore, can become a critical destabilizing force rather than remaining a stabilizing, mediative force in the transitional period.[7]

Charismatic leadership increment to the governmental capability is not permanent. Unless appropriate curative measures are undertaken in the meantime, society is bound sooner or later to discover that the charismatic leadership really is incapable of the level of performance it has promised or people have been led to believe it capable of. Not only does a charismatic leader's death before his charisma has been dissipated produce the so-called crisis of succession, but his successors suffer from the overexpectations of society since they are now expected to perform as well as the deceased was regarded as capable of performing. There is also an added element of instability in this case: while the populace expects the new leaders to perform as well as the deceased charismatic leader was regarded as capable of performing, they are not accorded the same level and kind of support and respect by the populace as the dead leader was, for the predominance of charisma both as center of effective power and source of legitimacy has meanwhile produced the effect of belittling the prestige and status, even competence of those who are now leaders, and of dwarfing their role and political institutions to the point where they are unable quickly to acquire the kind of integrity and authority that is vital for effective governance.[8] This, in addition to the low level of routinized governmental capability itself, is a major cause for the drastic instability that all too frequently accompanies the decline or disappearance of a charismatic leader or organization.

CRISIS

The concoction or exploitation of external crisis has its inherent danger as a method of compensatory mobilization. In the first place, "ill-feeling toward other countries is not a safe foundation on which to build national unity,"[9] as hatred for another person cannot be the basis for one's self-respect. More important, as far as the process of orderly development and modernization is concerned, is a number of negative, destabilizing consequences of this palliative that are often difficult to obviate. One such consequence is the tendency toward overpoliticization. In an overt campaign against the external danger, real or imaginary, that threatens the polity, people are mobilized into the political arena, albeit for the sake of temporary expediency as palliative, without either having acquired or quickly acquiring the discipline and common rules for constructive political relationships and mutual interactions that are necessary for stability and civil politics. While the crisis lasts (or is manipulated to last) and the popular attention is focused on it, the domestic situation may remain manageable to political leadership; that is, political leadership may enjoy a widespread popular support. This kind of mobilization—indeed overpoliticization—at the same time, but especially after the crisis is over or the sense of crisis dissipates, generates new sources of demand on the polity and its leadership which the existing level of governmental capability is ill-equipped to cope with and which renders the implementation of developmental policies and programs extremely difficult. The likely result, then, is the emergence of an acute disequilibrium between expectations and performance, between input and output.

The natural tendency toward overpoliticization is not the only detrimental consequence of the exploitation of external crises as compensatory mobilization. As Seligman suggests, capitalizing on outside crisis gives rise to values and interests that may, in the long run, prove to be detrimental to the viable growth and development of society.[10] For example, the dominant focus on threat from the outside usually causes a potent increment to the power and influence of particular groups in society, such as the military, heavy industry, and certain ideological groups; it also leads to an exaltation of certain types of attitudes and beliefs, such as toughness, aggressiveness, uncritical acceptance, and blind obedience. External crisis, being one type of compensatory mobilization, however, cannot be kept at a high level of intensity over a very long period of time, especially when such crisis is less than real. The sense of unity and community generated by the belief in the existence of an external enemy intent upon destroying the nation at the first opportunity is destined to dissipate sooner or later. In the meantime, those groups in society that materially or symbolically benefit from the external crisis and subsequent militancy of society develop vested interests in its continuation which they will not relinquish willingly. They, in short, become powerful and influential to the extent that it becomes difficult for political leadership to control them adequately, let alone dislodge them. Those attitudes and beliefs that this particular type of compensatory mobilization has in the meantime given rise to may result in strengthening forces that are openly or latently opposed to modernization and development. Apart from the consideration of what curative developmental measures may have been undertaken at what level of effectiveness while compensatory mobilization was effective, the cumulative effect of those consequences, for which political leadership did not wittingly bargain, may be far beyond the level of governmental capability adequate to resolution. The result of this kind of compensatory mobilization is paradoxical and self-defeating, for compensatory mobilization, in the first place, was invoked precisely because of the inadequacy of the existing level of governmental capability.

SCAPEGOAT AND REPRESSION

Use of scapegoat and repression, when effective, contains its own dangers. Since specific crimes or wrongdoings are attributed to the scapegoat, public presumption cannot but be that the incumbent political leadership (or the regime) is superior in moral virtue and political integrity, let alone competence, and the elimination or punishment of the scapegoat, people are led to believe, will make their lives better. Again, this thought process gives rise to the kinds of expectations which the incumbent leadership may be unable or can ill afford to meet, at least over an extended period of time, especially in view of the low level of governmental capability. The incumbent leadership which resorts to repression may soon be found to be as defective and wanting as those who have been singled out for repression. Furthermore, the public temper that such a palliative generates may become difficult to contain or dissipate and may transform itself into antigovernment sentiment, in which case, the incumbent leadership will find itself in a situation for which it is not prepared.

IDEOLOGY AND MYTH

Ideology is perhaps the most potent instrument for massive mobilization and politicization. It is capable frequently of generating the ultimate height of feverish involvement of the masses in the political process of the polity. In a sense, it charismatizes the entire society and often transforms it into a mass movement. It can achieve the apex of societal and political mass intoxication, but because of this fact, its aftereffect, like a hangover, is positively correlated to the level of its potency.[11] Especially "when issued as unmitigated dogma, ideology paves the way for massive disillusionment."[12] The kind of letdown effect it causes, unless prevented or alleviated by some appropriate curative measures in the meantime rapidly to increase the governmental capability, can engender dejection, apathy, defeatism, and anomie that will seriously undermine the process of development and modernization. Like charisma, especially, ideology or myth in effect promises, by implication if not by explict and detailed statement, far more than it can in fact deliver. For political leadership that consciously employs this type of compensatory mobilization, there is an imminent dilemma, for "[t]oo little promised may not mobilize: too much may embitter.[13]

SELECTIVE BRIBERY

Selective bribery, in itself quite unlike the preceding four methods of compensatory mobilization, usually involves immediate expenditures of concrete material and symbolic resources by political leadership and government. In the case of material bribery, much of the financial resources of government (especially the distributive dimension of its capability) is diverted from productive endeavors that are vitally warranted, such as investment, social welfare, and education. The Meiji

Japanese government was even forced to negotiate a large loan from London in 1872 in order to meet the financial obligations incurred by its policy of selective bribery to the former feudal lords and their retainers. In bribing, moreover, no more should be given than is absolutely necessary, but the limit of such necessity may be virtually impossible to recognize. The balance sheet of selective bribery is very difficult to decipher even for political leadership. And bribery may not pay off at all. Likewise with the policy of symbolic bribery. Granting appurtenances of honor and prestige to a group of people or to a certain class in society may have the unintended effect of extending political power and influence for that group or class. Sooner or later, unless some powerful mitigative measures are taken in the meantime, this effect will constitute a new obstacle to political leadership by circumscribing its maneuverability, for the class or group thus bribed may soon become a rival source of power, thus on balance weakening, rather than strengthening, political leadership and governmental capability.

TRADITIONAL SYMBOLS AND VALUES

The manipulation of traditional symbols and institutions is just as delicate a business. The range of connotations and denotations of a particular symbol or value may be wider or narrower than political leadership is aware of, and this variability is something over which no political leadership can hope to retain effective control. For not only does the range of connotations and denotations fluctuate over time, but also connotations and denotations themselves lose their efficacy as there emerge new modes of association between symbols and policies. When there is such fluctuation and shift, traditional symbols that have thus far served the purpose of legitimizing particular developmental policies and of eliciting certain proper behavior patterns on the part of society lose their proper effect. Merelman in his discussion of legitimacy symbols calls attention to the danger of disjunction between symbols and policy and of "connotative overflow." As Merelman notes, "care must be taken to maintain the association between particular symbols and the policies they legitimize,"[14] but extreme caution and constant attention are required on the part of political leadership to continue to maintain such appropriate association over time, especially because developmental policies, as they continue to be implemented, necessarily cause perhaps slow but nonetheless inevitable change in the nature and content of the political and social environment. When the proper association between symbols and policies is disrupted, compensatory mobilization loses its effect. Whether or not change in value and behavior induced by developmental policies in the meantime becomes integrated and institutionalized before the symbol-policy association loses its utility is problematical, however. Connotative overflow has to do with a particular symbol intended to elicit an appropriate response to a given policy becoming related, "in the public mind, to other symbols which are associated with other, and from the standpoint of the policy-maker, inappropriate behaviors and policies out of favor."[15]

These two major problems of the manipulation of traditional symbols (hence values and institutions as well) suggest the need for the circumscription and contextualization of uses of traditional symbols to avoid connotative overflow and for the maintenance of a reserve of symbols or the generation of symbols to counter the loss of utility of symbols currently in use and to legitimize any new policy sequence. The relevance of this need will become apparent when we take a passing glance at one of the major problems of compensatory mobilization encountered by Meiji Japan.

SHORT-TERM ADEQUACY AND LONG-TERM INADEQUACY

The common and fundamental problem with all five paradigmatic methods of compensatory mobilization is the constant danger that they can easily lead to a situation in which political leadership finds its power and capability undermined and its ability to promote national development reduced, instead of producing the result which they are intended to produce. Compensatory mobilization can be effective but is dangerous, as drugs are both effective and dangerous. But the parallel between compensatory mobilization and drugs ends here. While, in medicine, the quantity and quality of anesthetics or any other kind of drug to be used as a palliative in a given case can be accurately measured so as to insure the desired degree and duration of effectiveness, compensatory mobilization as a method of political palliative is not amenable to accurate measurement; nor can one successful instance of compensatory mobilization be replicated with any significant degree of uniformity, as in medical anesthesia.

Reasons for this problem are that compensatory mobilization does not lend itself to quantification and qualification; it cannot be pretested; the perception of political leadership as well as of the masses constantly fluctuates without their being aware of it; the circumstances for compensatory mobilization cannot be measured with the kind of accuracy that is possible in medical diagnosis nor can its consequences be precisely predicted as in medical prognosis. Then there are what one recent writer on comparative politics calls "problems of short-term adequacy and long-term inadequacy."[16] A given instance of compensatory mobilization (that is a particular palliative used in a particular way under a particular set of circumstances) may be eminently successful in the sense that it in fact does render society amenable and adaptable to the implementation of curative developmental policies at the time of such mobilization. For example, a highly popular charismatic leader may be able to convince people to support a certain curative measure for national development, such as the institution of a land tax in money, which will enable the regime to derive a constant level of revenue for rational financial and budgetary practice, thereby increasing the level of governmental capability. The very success of this instance of compensatory mobilization, however, can cause serious long-term trouble for the polity and its leadership. The successful compensatory mobilization in this hypothetical instance was carried out at the expense of the meaningful development and growth of a viable decision-making process which may have been available, since the condition for acceptance of the curative developmental policy in this case was facilitated solely by virtue of the appeal of a nonrational, personalistic criterion of decision-making and the relationship between government and governed. Thus, a certain step, or a certain way in which the step is taken, in the direction of national development may eventually result in a step or two backward in the long run. This is the pitfall that is very easy for political leadership to overlook.

Another hypothetical instance of a successful use of compensatory mobilization producing a long-run detriment may be cited. In this case, compensatory mobilization, designed to create necessary conditions for the implementation of certain curative policies, subverts some of the viable change brought about by the developmental curative measures that have already been implemented. Suppose certain universalistic rational criteria for recruitment have been introduced and are slowly being expanded in all relevant spheres of government and society. This, certainly, is a step in the right direction. At this point, political leadership, in its eagerness for another curative measure (such as fiscal concentration on the industrial sector) and in its impatience with lack of popular support for such a measure, opts for the concoction of some stirring nationalistic ideology as a method of compensatory mobilization. Now, this method may indeed serve its purpose, namely, to generate widespread, hyperemotive adherence to leadership's policy of concentrating on the modern industrial sector. In the process, however, the very ideological intensity generated by compensatory mobilization may well undermine the maintenance of modern rational universalistic criteria for recruitment, by giving rise to the dominance of ideological commitment and support as the major criterion for recruitment, reward, and promotion. Competence and achievement will then be relegated to secondary, even peripheral consideration and, as a result, the long-run government capability and modernization may well be seriously weakened.

It cannot be overstressed that the very meaning and purpose of compensatory mobilization dictates that appropriate curative measures be undertaken while compensatory mobilization is in effect. Compensatory mobilization can produce social cohesion and support for political leadership. Such cohesion and support are as temporary as the palliative used, however. In order for such cohesion and support to become real and permanent, it is imperative that curative developmental measures be implemented so that the level of governmental capability may be raised, political relationships more regularized, and organs of the polity more institutionalized. Else, consequences of inevitable dissipation of the effect of compensatory mobilization will be critical and, in fact, may plunge society into conditions that are worse than before compensatory mobilization.

In order to escape from these conditions, some political leaderships often use one method of compensatory mobilization after another, while being unable or unwilling to carry out necessary curative developmental policies. For example, Indonesia, with the decline of constitutional government, came to be dominated by the personal charisma of Sukarno. Sukarno, however, perhaps fearing that his charisma might not last very long, soon employed belligerent postures in the international arena and appointed himself a haughty yet not altogether impartial arbiter in world politics. Not satisfied with this stance, he next inflamed the crisis over West Irian, the expulsion of Dutch nationals from Indonesia, the anti-Chinese campaign, and the policy of confrontation with Malaysia. In the meantime, little was done in terms of viable domestic development and modernization. Nkrumah of Ghana, too, resorted to a series of compensatory mobilizations without in the meantime taking vigorous developmental measures within his own country. First, it was primarily his own personal charisma as the leader of national independence; then a militant, if not physically aggressive, foreign policy; and finally a messianic ideology of Pan-Africanism, with himself as its prophet. Indeed, one can argue that any nation whose political leadership engages in one mode of compensatory mobilization after another in quick succession is suffering from a serious malaise of internal stagnation, even decay. In the absence of appropriate curative measures, society may continue to live in the euphoria of anesthetic abnormality, without having its malaise treated and cured.

COMPENSATORY MOBILIZATION AND NATIONAL DEVELOPMENT

The relationship between compensatory mobilization and national development may be summarized simply, as in Figure 2.

Palliative Policy

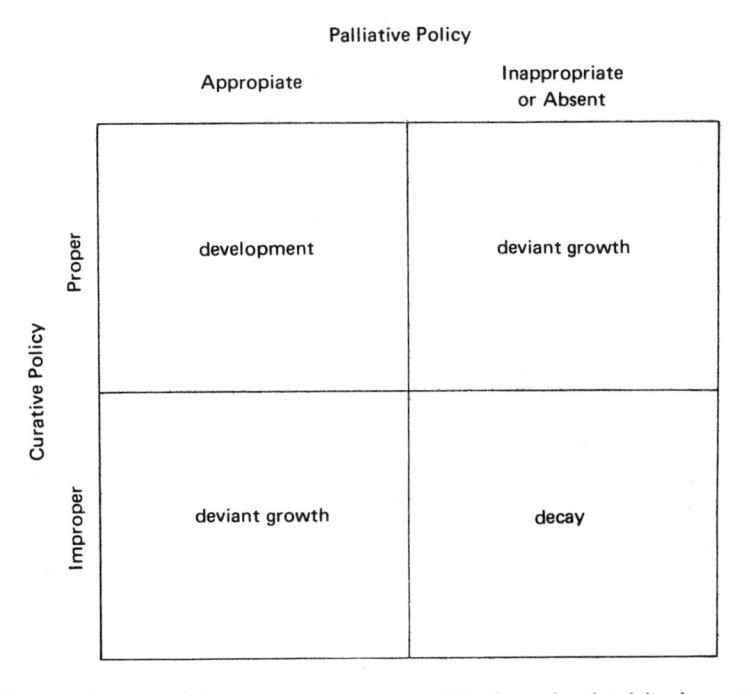

	Appropiate	Inappropriate or Absent
Proper (Curative Policy)	development	deviant growth
Improper	deviant growth	decay

Figure 2. Relationship between compensatory mobilization and national development.

A given instance of compensatory mobilization should be such that it will not inhibit, undermine, or distort the implementation of curative developmental policies that might become necessary in the near future. This concerns the dimension of the integrative relationship among not only palliatives but also curative policies as well as between compensatory mobilization and actual change. This relationship can be ascertained only through rigorous empirical investigation, but the point may be suggested here through a synoptic glimpse at an empirical case of modern Japan. The political and cultural tradition which Meiji Japan inherited from the Tokugawa period rendered it desirable that, in order for national political and administrative unification to be feasible, the personalistic and visual elements of political authority be retained in the transfer of power from the feudal system to the modern nation-state so as to avoid psychological dislocations that would result from the contextual change from personalist-visual politics to legal-abstract politics. Thus, the charisma of the Emperor was concocted and exploited fully as compensatory mobilization, and the political and administrative unification of the nation was successfully carried out in an amazingly short period of time. Once this had been accomplished, however, further political development of the nation as a modern state warranted that, especially after the promulgation of the Constitution of 1889, political authority and legitimacy thus personalized in the Emperor be rationalized and institutionally routinized by divorcing it from the personalistic charisma of the Emperor and transferring it to the Constitution and the polity, in order that the loyalty of the people, without necessarily being detached from the person of legal sovereign, might be directed also to the institutions of the constitutional polity. In short, there was a clear need for further expansion in the pluralistic development of affect, namely, the generation and strengthening of system affect.

This crucial task in the process of national development, however, proved extremely difficult because of the particular type of compensatory mobilization to which the modernizing leadership had earlier resorted in order to implement the curative measure of political and administrative unification against the resistance, overt and covert, of the traditional ruling class. At any rate, the necessary task of the pluralistic development of affect toward the constitutional polity itself was not accomplished, at least not adequately.[17] Fearing, instead, the weakening of imperial charisma and authority in whose name it had been carrying out developmental policies for the nation, the Meiji leadership deliberately tried to minimize whatever positive effects the new constitutional polity as an abstract legal entity might have upon the political process and to further the pluralistic development of affect, by perpetuating personalistic, visual relationships as the primary criterion for political and social relationships and conflict management and thereby discouraging the emergence of meaningful system affect.[18] The main reason for this pattern of conduct on the part of political leadership was apparently fear of losing its personalistic and oligarchical power to those who would enter into the polity and strive to rise through it to claim power as the legitimate goal of members of a modern constitutional polity. The Meiji political leadership, admirable in its behavior in many critical situations, thus vindicated Lord Acton's famous dictum. Far more than the alleged "legal" or structural weaknesses of the Meiji Constitution, it was this pattern of conduct of the incumbent political leadership that ultimately undermined further progress of political development in the prewar Japan.

From this as well as other experiences of Meiji Japan, several tentative hypotheses emerge. One is that a successful instance of compensatory mobilization can inhibit the adaptive capacity of the polity in the future. This is, in a somewhat different context, the same as Fagen's warning about "short-term adequacy and long-term inadequacy." Initial success, in short, might undermine the possibilities of future success. Second, it can be argued that the particular manner in which success was achieved may distort the perception and perspective of political leadership. The Meiji political leadership had been committed to the development of the nation as a modern state able to compete on an equal footing with advanced Western nations. There is reason to believe, and some students of modern Japanese politics and history contend, that its ultimate concern was Japan as a nation rather than the Emperor either as institution or person. It simply used the Emperor and throne for purposes of promoting national development. But once the leadership had achieved the phenomenal task of rapid political and administrative unification of the nation by virtue of its skillful manipulation of the imperial charisma and subsequently implemented a series of concrete developmental curative measures and programs on the strength of that particular type of compensatory mobilization, it eventually came to identify not only its successes but also its power and authority with those of the imperial charisma. In short, charisma, as a method of compensatory mobilization, had become reified, and the political leadership had become the prisoner of its own method, which had initially been meant to be only compensatory, thereby rendering itself less and less adaptive. As a result, many vital elements of institutional infrastructure necessary for a constitutional and parliamentary polity, such as political parties, pressure groups, party competition and loyal opposition, were deprived of necessary opportunities to develop and acquire integrity and autonomy in the new polity.

A similar long-range handicap may be created by certain types of curative policies as well. A case in point, again in reference to Meiji Japan, is the conscript army. One of the chief instruments as well as characteristics of a modern state is a national army recruited universally on rational criteria from all segments of society. In the process of modernization and development, the army performs both the political-socialization function and the national-security function. In the former function, the national army or military service can bring about an effect of inculcating in its recruits a sense of nationhood, patriotism, common citizenship, and acceptance of and respect for modern technological and organizational values such as efficiency, discipline, command, and responsibility as well as competence and achievement as bases for the individual's value and utility. In this respect, the military service is uniquely contributive to modernization and development. At the same time, however, it is in the nature of military training to disdain, scorn, even abhor compromise, competition, opposition, disagreement, and conflict as well as challenge to authority and command. The overriding emphasis placed upon the military and its virtues during the early Meiji era, understandable though it might be in view of Japan's past martial tradition and the age of imperialism into which modern Japan had been born, elevated the values and virtues of the military, including essentially antipolitical ones, to the pedestal of national virtues to be emulated by all citizens.[19] While such a phenomenon had the effect of consolidating and strengthening the unity of the nation and the stability of society as well as the authority and legitimacy of the polity, it at the same time rendered seriously difficult, if not impossible, the emergence and growth of those political institutions, such as parties, group activities, competition for political power, and loyal opposition, that are essential in providing dynamics for a viable polity and in rendering a polity flexible and adaptable in the face of a continuously changing political environment. As a result, political parties in prewar Japan never managed to acquire the level of integrity, autonomy, and influence that they would have needed in a constitutional parliamentary polity. The ease with which the militarists in Japan destroyed the nascent political-party system in the 1930's is not very difficult to understand. Basic human rights and civil liberties were also readily suppressed in prewar Japan not only because the government was repressive but also because the society at large held them without deep conviction and commitment.

THE DIFFERENTIAL IMPACT OF DEVELOPMENTAL POLICIES

There is one especially crucial consideration about the process of modernization and development that has thus far been deferred, and that is the issue of differential impact.[20] While national development is intended to benefit the entire society in the long run, immediate, short-run, even relatively longer-range effects of developmental processes affect differently various groups and parts of society. This differentiation is especially true with policies and programs of the curative type. Their effects as felt by different parts in society are diverse; some positive, others negative, still others perhaps neither. To the extent that more segments of society feel positive effects of such measures, the developmental process may be said to be proceeding smoothly. On the other hand, if more groups feel negative effects of the same measures, development and modernization, despite the implementation of significant curative measures, are hampered, even distorted.[21] Broadly speaking, there are two major causes for, hence results of, differential impact: perceptual and material.

In a transitional society, perceptual patterns of different groups in society are likely to be diverse and uneven. The particular range of expectations, hence of perceived possibilities of one social group (for example, the peasantry) differs from that of another group (for example, the landed oligarchy) as a result of the traditional social stratification and interclass relationships as well as of the particular vision of the future entertained by each group. Added to this difference in perception, and because of it, is the fact that almost every significant developmental policy made by political leadership is likely to be viewed far less in terms of the corporate interest of the entire community and far more in terms of parochial group and class interests than in a more developed and consensual society. This narrowness is in part owing to the insufficiency or absence of the pluralistic development of affect. Thus, a given policy—say, the organization of a conscript army recruited on the basis of rational modern criteria—may be viewed by one group, for example, the traditional aristocracy, as subversive of its social status and symptomatic of the sinister schemings of the parvenu now in power, while the lower strata of society may consider the same policy in terms of the opening of a new channel for upward mobility. Another leadership policy, for example, a dam-building project to render more land arable in an especially inhospitable region, may be viewed quite differently by those living in the region concerned and by those living elsewhere. Neither views it as beneficial to the entire nation but rather in terms of sectional or regional parochial interest. In short, a wide range of significant developmental policies and programs encounters a diversity of interpretation and reception which more or less parallels vertical and horizontal social cleavages.

The material cause of differential impact consists in different patterns of material consequences likely to be produced by developmental policies coupled with the particular pattern of skill distribution obtaining in transitional society.[22] Because of the wide range of inequities inherited from traditional society, the extent to which people are capable of benefiting from a developmental policy or program varies widely from class to class, from group to group.[23] Disparity in the level of education, literacy, exposure to modernity, and fundamental organizational ability is extremely wide between the well-to-do and the poor, between the rural and the urban sector, between one region and another. In an important sense, differential material impact is the function of this wide disparity.

Take, for example, the modernization of agriculture. Agricultural modernization is generally considered not only necessary for increased productivity and hence for national development, but also desirable to all, including, naturally, the peasantry. From the over-all perspective of national development, there is little doubt about the value of increased agricultural productivity because of what it implies for the economic well-being and increased economic capability of the entire nation as well as for the general governmental capability. In actuality, however, the consequences of such a presumably rational, eminently plausible developmental policy are mixed. The modernization of agriculture involves the use of more potent fertilizers, which usually means chemical fertilizers, as well as the adoption of modern agricultural implements. Both improvements mean an outlay of capital, however small by urban standards, on the part of the peasant, which he may not be able to afford. Modernization also means a drastic decline in the man-land ratio. The likely result is twofold: Marginal farmers soon find themselves in an insoluble financial bind because they are unable (so rendered in part by the psychological inhibition characteristic of the tradition-bound) to afford necessary quantities of fertilizers and modern implements, especially when the yield, hence income, is curtailed by bad weather or some other natural disaster.[24] Even if they can purchase necessary fertilizers and implements, they cannot compete effectively with large landholders because of the difference in the unit cost of production, which is greater for small farmers than for the large ones. Sooner or later, therefore, small, especially marginal farmers are likely to be driven into increasing indebtedness, which will ultimately force them to abandon their land. In the meantime, modern farming methods call for a smaller number of workers per unit of arable land, so that more and more of the labor force becomes superfluous and redundant. The process of eliminating superfluous labor naturally begins with hired hands, such as tenant farmers, sharecroppers, and farm laborers. Added to this number are those marginal and small farmers who are forced out of their own farms. They are now jobless and without alternate means of livelihood.

The description above constitutes the first aspect of differential material impact. The second aspect is that the former tenants, sharecroppers, farm laborers, and marginal farmers—because of the disparity in equity between the urban and rural sectors as well as between the well-to-do and the poor in terms of formal and other education, skill, and literacy—are unable to adapt themselves to the different kinds of occupations that are avilable to those with certain levels of education, literacy, a modern outlook, and skill. In a more developed society, a farm boy can go to the city and readily adapt himself to an urban job and urban life because his level of education, literacy, manual and other skills is likely to be similar if not identical to that of many of his urban counterparts. This adaptability is not present in a transitional society. So the ultimate consequence of differential impact of a presumably rational policy on agriculture is a huge increase in the *Lumpenproletariat*. And in this case, as in many others, differential material impact produces differential perceptual impact, and vice versa. In fact, they reinforce and aggravate each other. Material deprivation leads to alienation, anomie, and hostility; alienation, anomie, and hostility further magnify the perception of deprivation. The result is deviant behavior that threatens the polity and society.

The implications of differential impact, whether perceptual or material or both (the last seems most prevalent), are serious indeed. One of them is that political leadership should calculate the costs of implementing every major developmental policy and program in terms of the possible extent of such differential impact. Such costs are directly related to the vital issue of stability and of governmental capability. The greater the costs (that is, the greater the extent and magnitude of differential impact), the greater the likelihood of increased instability, hence the greater the likelihood of a digressive, even regressive development of society. Second, differential impact, especially when it is extensive and intense, may not only aggravate existing cleavages but also create new lines of fragmentation of society. One dimension of national development is the reduction and ultimate elimination of divisive hostility and rivalry among various regions, groups, and classes. Differential impact can indeed push society backward in this regard. Third, the aggravation of cleavages and the subsequent increase in hostility, alienation, and anomie create a fertile soil for radical challenge and opposition movements against political leadership. As argued in an earlier chapter, one of the fundamental tasks of political leadership in promoting national development is to maximize support and minimize resistance. The level of existing governmental capability in transitional society is relatively low, and especially crucial is the regulative dimension of such governmental capability. This is all the more important reason that political leadership should take care that opposition and resistance against it not be given opportunities for expansion and support. Differential impact may well undermine political leadership in this regard.

Differential impact, one may suggest, is the function of diversity in the levels of mobilizability and integratability of social classes and groups in the process of national development. Some classes or groups are more readily mobilized and integrated into the new scheme of things than others. And much of the instability that characterizes the process of development and modernization is the function of such difference among various groups in the rate at which they lend themselves to necessary mobilization and integration. This factor suggests, then, that political leadership (or government) needs to take appropriate measures to mitigate individual as well as cumulative effects of differential impact both for groups concerned and for society at large. In other words, every significant developmental policy that is likely to cause differential impact should be accompanied by a contingency plan or measure in order to insure that differential impact be minimized, alleviated, or, if possible, eliminated so as to guarantee a maximum feasible yield from the developmental policy. This is where local applications of compensatory mobilization might become relevant, although curative measures are certainly indispensable.

The role of "contingency" policy is mitigative; its purpose is to minimize hostility, alienation, and anomie and to increase positive affect and support for government. In the case of differential impact arising out of different perceptual patterns among groups, certain symbolic gestures from political leadership toward the disaffected groups may at least in part alleviate negative feelings, at least to the extent that those concerned do not feel impelled toward deviant behavior. Or perhaps mitigation involves material consideration (as in the case of the *samurai* in Meiji Japan). Tangible or intangible values involved in such mitigative measures must correspond to the safe minimal level of mitigation warranted by each particular case. For there is a danger of overcompensation and undercompensation. Overcompensation not only is uneconomical but also tends to strengthen the group concerned as well as cause it excessively to raise its expectations in the future, thus in the end undermining the ability and capability of government and political leadership. Undercompensation is more immediately dangerous because it leaves the level of hostility, alienation, and anomie of the group unabated, perhaps even aggravates it.

In the case of differential impact in the material sense, as in the hypothetical example of agricultural modernization above, again the type of mitigative policy employed must be geared to the nature of contingency of the situation. In order to prevent the initial negative effect of agricultural modernization on small and marginal farmers, government perhaps can provide some type of guarantee against loss so that those less well-off farmers may experiment and adopt modern methods without fear of failure.[25] Their obvious disadvantage in unit production cost vis-a-vis large farmers may be partly offset by some kind of pricing policy which will pay higher prices for the first so-many units of production (this policy suggestion assumes that the government controls the food market as it perhaps should), without destroying the profitability of increased production and higher productivity. Superfluous and unemployed, members of the agricultural labor force, who have little or no skill that is useful in the non-agricultural sector, should be given job training so that they, especially the young among them, may become employable in other areas. Depending upon the particular levels of situational assets of individual nations, there is a wide spectrum of mitigative measures that can be taken singly or in some combination, such as reclamation of new agricultural lands, enlistment into public-works projects, training and recruitment for expanding industrial activities. At the same time, a number of regulatory decisions may be made to prevent large landowners and traditional rural financial institutions from taking unfair advantage of hard-pressed farmers and peasants of small or marginal means and to control rates of urban migration in order to forestall the danger of high urban unemployment, congestion, and other serious social, political, and economic ills to which developing urban sectors are susceptible.

The basic relationship between differential impact and mitigative measures may be summarized as in Figure 3.

ON RATES AND STAGES OF DEVELOPMENT

Compensatory mobilization is a phenomenon most frequently necessitated in transitional societies. It is a strategy employed in a situation that is not conducive to developmental change. Its purpose is to engender the kind of condition that allows for the implementation of developmental policies and programs for concrete change. There is,

166 *The Dangers of Compensatory Mobilization*

	Mitigative Measures	
	Appropriate	Inappropriate or Absent
Differential Impact — Limited	development	deviant growth
Differential Impact — Extensive	development hampered	decay

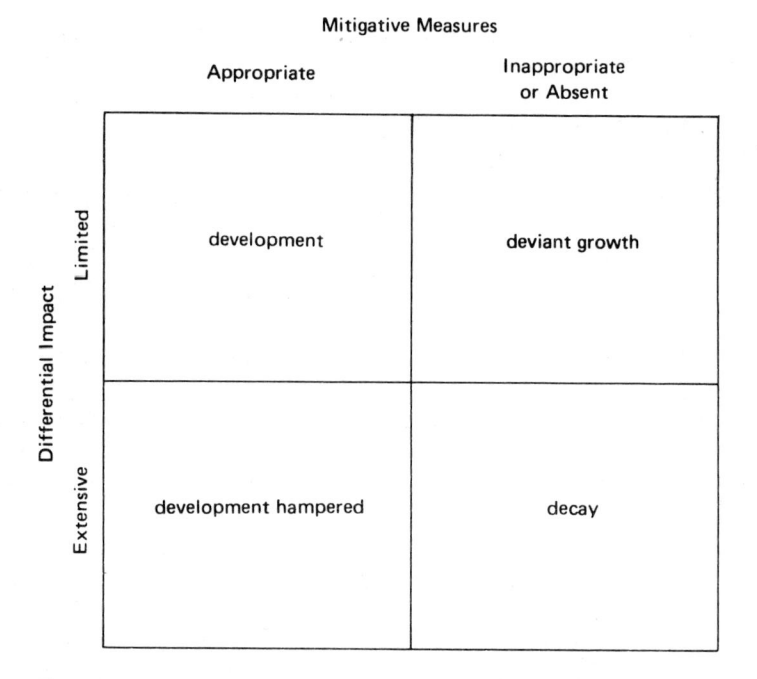

Figure 3. Relationship between differential impact and mitigative measures.

therefore, a positive correlation between compensatory mobilization and instability. Society suffers from instability when its government cannot govern well. Government cannot govern well because its capability is low. Since its capability is low, it cannot implement those policies and programs which will enable it to govern well and to promote national development. Hence, the need for compensatory mobilization to overcome this basic handicap. The more unstable the society, the more difficult it is to govern and to implement curative developmental measures, hence the more frequent recourse to compensatory mobilization. Compensatory mobilization may, therefore, be analogous to what Machiavelli called "extraordinary measures." A stable society, free from serious cleavages and division, is one that is generally characterized by the absence of repressive laws, charismatic leaders or organizations, emotionally intense political doctrines, a jingoistic international posture, and class or sectional favoritism. Such a society has little serious pain for which anesthesia is required. Therefore, the frequency and intensity of compensatory mozilization decline as society moves further along the road of development and modernization toward an integrated society with built-in capacity for continuous change and adaptation.

Compensatory mobilization becomes less frequently employed for several reasons. First, as society undergoes successive developmental changes without the emergence of serious instability and deviant growth, the general modal patterns of perception, values, and beliefs of members of society are slowly modified (for example, affective pluralism) whereupon change, progress, and developmental efforts come to be taken for granted (or, to put the same idea a bit differently, resistance against change or progress declines). In short, the idea as well as the fact of change and progress becomes institutionalized. Second, as the process of development and modernization continues without serious digressive occurrences, there will gradually emerge an increasingly built-in capacity for further growth, and subsequently the need for critical deprivation for purposes of development will gradually decline. This situation also suggests that the routinized level of governmental capability rises in proportion to the level of leadership increment to such capability. In short, total situational assets increase significantly. Third, because of the first two phenomena, the process of manifest socialization is likely to become more effective relative to costs involved, rendering increasing proportions of society more and more integratable; hence an expansion in meaningful political participation becomes increasingly feasible. All these, cumulatively, produce the effect of routinizing a rising level of governmental capability, institutionalizing the polity, and regularizing a new network of horizontal and vertical political relationships, thereby stabilizing society at large. Thus the need for compensatory mobilization declines. This is not to say, however, that compensatory mobilization as a political instrument altogether disappears. Politics being what it is, there will always be need for palliatives. As noted earlier, even highly developed modern nations occasionally resort to compensatory mobilization in order to implement certain policies that would otherwise be unpopular and therefore invite critical challenge and opposition. It is salient, nevertheless, that, as society develops, blatant and frequent uses of compensatory mobilization will decline.

By extension of this consideration, it is also suggested that there is a positive relationship between the pace of development and modernization desired and compensatory mobilization. Given a particular level of situational assets (or situational score, as discussed in Chapter III), the society is capable of, say, x rate of development and modernization in y period of time. If x is greater than y, that is, if political leadership pursues a faster rate of development of society than would otherwise be feasible, then the rate (that is, frequency and intensity) of compensatory mobilization will have to be increased proportionately.

A comparison of India with China may elicit some pertinent point in this regard. It has often been said, though fewer people still believe, that the developmental competition between "democratic" India and "Communist" China will determine the outcome of the struggle between democracy and Communism in Asia. Whether such an argument is meaningful is beside the point here. In terms of the uses of compensatory mobilization, however, these two nations present a very interesting contrast. China, apparently, is intent upon rapid national development, that is, far more rapid than her existing conditions would admit of. It is contended here that the frequency and intensity in her use of compensatory mobilization (personal charisma of Mao, organizational charisma of the CCP, use of Liu and his kind as scapegoats, repression of landlords and revisionists, aggressive foreign policy, books of quotations from Chairman Mao) are symptomatic of this desire and effort on the part of the Chinese leadership. The more impatient the CCP leadership, the more intense its resort to compensatory mobilization. Whether or not this stratagem will in fact succeed, however, is another question.

India, on the other hand, has demonstrated a rather remarkable (that is, considering its predicament) lack of compensatory mobilization, except, perhaps, the charisma of Jawaharlal Nehru. The Congress Party, dominant though it has been in Indian politics since before independence, is rather colorless and pedestrian in comparison to the emotional, ideological, and charismatic intensity of the CCP. The Indian government, perhaps because many of its top leaders have been deeply imbued with British humanism and evolutionary socialist doctrines, and were molded by the long experience of Gandhian passive resistance, has thus far refrained generally from recourse to compensatory mobilization.[26] There is reason to believe that Nehru's international posture of positive neutrality, though it may have had the effect of eliciting mass support for his government, was motivated primarily by his particular view of the East-West conflict, the Cold War, and the unique role his nation might be able to play in the world arena. Clearly, the Indian political leadership desires rapid national development, but its willingness to resort to extraordinary measures is significantly reduced by its past political experience and philosophical and ideological inhibitions. It is not certain whether and how fast, China is developing, but there seems to be little doubt that India has been stagnating, and there is reasonable suspicion that, despite its serious internal turmoil, China will develop much faster than India. India, in the words of Myrdal, has remained a "soft state."

Another point to be noted in the same context is that, as society develops along the line of the positive phenomena suggested in the preceding discussion, the level of differential impact will decline also. As particular patterns of modal perception, values, and beliefs relevant to modern society spread more widely throughout society, the type of differential impact arising out of perceptual disparity of early transitional stages will significantly decline. In this connection, Coser contributes a relevant point, although his concern is primarily with more advanced societies. He argues that there are two kinds of conflict: conflict that involves "the basic assumptions" upon which society is based or which constitute basic norms for society's modus operandi; and conflict that concerns "goals, values or interests that do not contradict the basic assumptions."[27] Conflict in the context of the early stages of national development—the incompatibility of the environment with developmental policies and programs that makes compensatory mobilization necessary—is the first type. It involves the question of nature of society, its goal, its structure, and man's role in it. It is the conflict that causes critical discontinuity, shatters tradition, pits forces toward modernity and tendencies toward tradition against each other, and thus renders the viability of society's future uncertain. It is precisely this type of conflict that seriously hinders, distorts, sometimes even prevents national development. Perceptual disparity and fragmentation that underscore this critical conflict cause serious kinds of differential impact. As the process of modernization and development continues without serious instances of digression and regression and as those positive major developmental phenomena which decrease the need for compensatory mobilization begin to spread, however, the conflict also begins to change in nature and gradually becomes Coser's second type of conflict.

This second type of conflict is the source of political dynamics, while the first is the source of disruption, discontinuity, even decay. Conflict customary in the political arena of a modern state is the second type and covers a wide range of issues and problems. These issues and problems, while causing some candidates and politicians to lose election or office, or to suffer political oblivion, do not call into critical question those basic assumptions or core values that Coser talks about. Those issues and problems certainly do cause public controversy and political dispute between their supporters and their opponents (for example, liberals versus conservatives) and thus generate tension in society in general and the political arena in particular. This kind of conflict, however, is a source of political dynamics, hence progress. It is the conflict that takes place within the political arena; it is, one might say, an intrapolity conflict rather than an antipolity conflict. This type of conflict is predicated upon a broad acceptance of the basic values and goals of society, that is, a widespread pattern of modal perceptions about the polity. Such fundamental consensus becomes possible only after the initial stages of development and modernization have been successfully experienced. And it is only then that the level of differential impact of developmental policies begins to decline significantly.

There is another reason for the decline in the level of differential impact: As the pattern of skill distribution (a function of education, training, exposure to modernity, and so on) relevant to modern methods, occupational diversity, and competence changes—whereby the earlier disparity in integratability and adaptability among various groups in society becomes narrower—differential material impact upon different groups will become less and less, so that there will be fewer and fewer instances of serious deprivation, alienation, and anomie and hostility. There is the same kind of relationship between differential impact and levels of national development as there is between compensatory mobilization and levels of national development. Both differential impact and compensatory mobilization, therefore, are related clearly to the issue of political instability.

NOTES

1. Gunner Myrdal, *Asian Drama: An Inquiry into the Poverty of Nations* (New York: Pantheon, 1968), Vol. I, p. 302.
2. Jean Lacouture, *The Demigods: Charismatic Leadership in the Third World* (New York: Knopf, 1970), p. 14.
3. See W. Howard Wriggins, *The Ruler's Imperative: Strategies for Political Survival in Asia and Africa* (New York: Columbia University Press, 1969), p. 106.
4. Manfred Halpern, *The Politics of Social Change in the Middle East and North Africa* (Princeton: Princeton University Press, 1963), p. 285.
5. See Wriggins, *The Ruler's Imperative*, pp. 243-244.
6. The danger emanating from the wide gap in prestige, status, and power between one charismatic leader and other members of leadership and political institutions is cogently discussed in Myrdal, *Asian Drama*, Vol. I, Chap. 8. See also Wriggins, *The Ruler's Imperative*, pp. 124-125.
7. For a highly suggestive description of the manner in which the danger inherent in charismatic leadership may be minimized and the value of charisma positively utilized for political development, see Seymour Martin

Lipset, *The First New Nation: The United States in Historical and Comparative Perspective* (New York: Basic Books, 1963), pp. 20–23.

8. Michel C. Oksenberg, "Policy Making Under Mao Tse-tung, 1949–1968," *Comparative Politics*, III (April 1971), 325.

9. Myrdal, *Asian Drama*, Vol. I, p. 301.

10. Lester G. Seligman, *Leadership in a New Nation* (New York: Atherton, 1964), p. 3.

11. On this point, see also James R. Townsend, *Political Participation in Communist China* (Berkeley and Los Angeles: University of California Press, 1969), p. 199.

12. John W. Lewis, "The Social Limits of Politically Induced Change," in Chandler Morse et al., *Modernization by Design: Social Change in the Twentieth Century* (Ithaca and London: Cornell University Press, 1969), p. 15.

13. *Ibid.* See also Wriggins, pp. 140–142.

14. Richard M. Merelman, "Learning and Legitimacy," *American Political Science Review*, LX (September 1966), 553.

15. *Ibid.*

16. Richard R. Fagen, *Politics and Communication* (Boston and Toronto: Little, Brown, 1966), p. 90. See also Warren F. Ilchman and Norman Thomas Uphoff, *The Political Economy of Change* (Berkeley and Los Angeles: University of California Press, 1969), p. 37.

17. See S. N. Eisenstadt, *Modernization: Protest and Change* (Englewood Cliffs, N.J.: Prentice-Hall, 1966), p. 81.

18. For danger of this actual and potential phenomenon accompanying the process of national development, see Gabriel Almond and G. Bingham Powell, Jr., *Comparative Politics: A Developmental Approach* (Boston and Toronto: Little, Brown, 1966), p. 355.

19. For the danger of military mentality and attitudes in this regard, see Alexander J. Groth, *Comparative Politics: A Distributive Approach* (New York: Macmillan, 1971), pp. 42–43.

20. The critical nature of differential impact was first brought to the author's attention by Professor John Montgomery of Harvard University at one of the sessions of the Harvard–M.I.T. Joint Faculty Seminar on Political Development in the spring of 1969.

21. Differential impact is relevant not only to "developmental policies" as such but also to "political formulae" as well. On this point, see the interesting discussion of "democracy" as a political formula in Latin America in Charles W. Anderson, *Politics and Economic Change in Latin America* (Princeton: Van Nostrand, 1967), Chap. 4.

22. See S. N. Eisenstadt, "Some Observations on the Dynamics of Transitions," *Comparative Studies in Society and History*, XI (October 1969), 458–460.

23. See C. S. Whitaker, "A Dysrhythmic Process of Political Change," *World Politics*, XIX (January 1967).

24. Thus, "A man must borrow to buy the new seed and the fertilizer it needs. Failure will mean not only hunger but also a cash debt." Guy Hunter, *Modernizing Peasant Societies* (New York and London: Oxford University Press, 1969), p. 34.

25. One suggestive work in this regard is Stephen A. Marglin, "Insurance for Innovation," in David Hapgood (ed.), *Policies for Promoting Agricultural Development: Report on a Conference on Productivity and Innovation in Agriculture in the Developing Countries*, (Massachusetts Institute of Technology Center for International Studies, January 1965). However, for the danger of continued governmental aid and assistance in this and other regards in the agrarian sector, see *1965 Report on the World Social Situation* (New York: United Nations, 1966), pp. 23-24.

26. Concerning political and philosophical factors that apparently inhibit the Indian political leadership in its efforts to govern and modernize the nation, see Satish Arora and Harold Lasswell, *Political Communication: The Public Language of Political Elites in India and the United States* (New York: Holt, Rinehart and Winston, 1969), Chaps. 2 and 3, but esp. pp. 21-25.

27. Lewis A. Coser, *The Functions of Social Conflict* (Glencoe, Ill.: Free Press, 1956), p. 80. See also David Easton, *A Systems Analysis of Political Life* (New York: Wiley, 1965), pp. 177-180.

VI

Conclusion: Political Leadership, Tradition, and Modernity

Political scientists as well as statesmen of modern nations have come grudgingly to accept that developing nations require strong, central, and unifying political leadership that may be variously called authoritarian, oligarchic, or even totalitarian. Gone, it seems, is the naive hope once entertained by Western statesmen and students of politics alike that, once given the right of self-determination, new nations would quickly develop democratic forms of government. Even leaders of developing nations themselves once held such a dream, as reflected in the vocabulary they employed for their political communication and rhetoric, though, undoubtedly, they had their own ideas and versions of democracy. Almost every nation, in the wave of independence following World War II, initially adopted a representative constitutional system patterned after one or another Western example.[1] And almost every new nation has since discarded it, in practice if not in theory, in favor of some kind of authoritarian rule. A typical view of the Western political system, held by political leaders of developing nations who have been deeply disillusioned by its failures and have since opted for an allegedly undemocratic form of government, is eloquently expressed by Sékou Touré, president of the Republic of Guinea:

... *parliamentary life was nothing more than a sum of disordered activities tending to satisfy selfish ambitions and interests.* Those elected behaved like feudal rulers, profiting both from the naiveté, lack of consciousness, and disorganization of the people and from colonial bribes. Scandalously, the parliamentary system snared political power for the benefit of the elected officials, whose behavior was marked by corruption, irresponsibility, and unpardonable indifference to the harsh living conditions of the people and the future of their country.

These anti-democratic, anti-popular trends of parliamentary life were the direct consequences of the importation into our countries of the bourgeois regime and of French political customs....[2]

Where the initial democratic practice still seems to linger on, which is rare indeed, society apparently has dissolved itself into seemingly perpetual stagnancy or into a "soft state," to borrow Myrdal's phrase, and the existence of a democratic form has little relevance either to the everyday life of its citizens or to the problem of resolving issues and problems afflicting the stagnating polity.

One intellectual phenomenon arising out of the apparent failure of democratic forms of government in new nations is the recognition that the traditional normative debate on democracy versus nondemocracy is empirically irrelevant to the process of national development.[3] While statesmen still piously spout the jargons of democratic faith and optimism, they are resigned to the notion that a military junta, for example, may perhaps be better than an ineffectual, corrupt constitutional government. Political scientists are more and more sanguine in admitting that democracy of the kind they once wanted to export lacks the necessary congruence with the soil and climate of new nations. As Huntington argues:

> The most important political distinction among countries concerns not their form of government but their degree of government. The differences between democracy and dictatorship are less than the differences between those countries whose politics embodies consensus, community, legitimacy, organization, effectiveness, stability, and those countries whose politics is deficient in these qualities.[4]

The aim of developing nations is no longer liberty as such, but rather order.

Since national development means continuous growth in governmental capability accompanied by a constantly rising level of institutionalization of the various organs of the polity and political process, and regularization of political relationships among various groups in society and between government and governed, the relative merits of different governments are to be evaluated in terms of the extent to which they are respectively able to engineer, regulate, and direct such increases in governmental capability and in levels of institutionalization and regularization. In this sense, there is no significant relationship between a particular normative form of government and the level of competence in governance. As indicated in Chapters I and III, the only meaningful determinant as to the ability to govern and to promote modernization and development is political leadership, and the types of political leadership to be identified are derived from a consideration of three general political criteria: commitment, intelligence and skill, and dominance over subnational elites. It is not possible to predict whether a given form of government (or so-called political system) is capable of governing and promoting national development. It is possible, however, to make a probabilistic assessment about the ability to govern and to promote development if the type of political leadership is identified.

The crux of the predicament of developing nations is that they are societies in crisis—crises of fragmentation, discontinuity, dissensus. They are societies characterized by instability, behavioral incongruence, perceptual disparity, and low governmental capability. The task of political leadership, therefore, is threefold: (1) to generate order and stability, (2) to institutionalize the polity and regularize the political process and relationships, and (3) to engineer, regulate, and direct the process of national development. Certain types of political leadership can, at least in the short run, achieve the first part of the task; certain other types may be able to accomplish both the first and the second parts of the task; but only one type of leadership is really capable of accomplishing all three dimensions of the task. And such effective modernizing leadership has, in itself, nothing to do with any special form of government or political system. It is the pacification engineer, the initiator of a new political order, and the creator of a new society. It engenders stability from the situation of instability; it contrives to institutionalize various organs of a modern polity, to regularize a new modus operandi in the political arena and a new modus vivendi among various politically relevant groups and strata in society, and to routinize a rising level of governmental capability; and it attempts to formulate and implement policies and corporate programs and enterprises that will bring about change and progress of society. In short, it reeducates and re-forms society. Its politics are the politics of forming new habits and outlooks, not of formed habits and outlooks, for the entire society, to achieve a new level of predictable behavior of man and government and thus to give the necessary quality of continuity and permanence to civil politics and civil societal life. Underlying this enormous task of the political leadership of a developing nation is the notion of discreet planning, careful social engineering, and judicious control. This feature, in turn, clearly suggests the centrality of the manipulative dimension of political leadership.

Yet there still remains a nagging question. If political leadership is the crucial determinant of the process of development and modernization, is the issue of forms of government, however they might be typologized, altogether irrelevant? Many political scientists and politicians are still concerned about forms of government and types of political system in developing nations. The suggestion here is that the question, as it has traditionally been phrased, is irrelevant, but that the question itself still remains seriously pertinent. The whole of the discussion in this volume, especially in Chapters III and V, indicates the vital importance of continuity in the fabric of any society. This consideration is germane in the use of such terms as "development," "growth," and "modernization"—all terms that connote not transfiguration or metamorphosis but rather the maturing, the unfolding of potentials, and the adaptiveness. Tradition and modernity need not and should not be rendered mutually exclusive. The process of national development is not a process of total re-creation, nor is it one of complete severance from one generic category of existence and headlong espousal of another, altogether novel one. What in fact takes place in the transitional period of development and modernization is that a society develops into a functionally and substantively superior, adaptationally and operationally more sophisticated society without at the same time losing its generic links and autochthonic characteristics. This is precisely the reason why political leadership should consider situational assets which necessarily include the inventory of cumulative societal knowledge and experience and of the peculiarities and characteristics unique to each society. This is precisely the reason why compensatory mobilization is a delicate and hazardous business.

Yet it is precisely for this reason that compensatory mobilization, especially the more manipulative kinds of it, becomes such an important consideration, for its function is, in an important sense, to bridge the gap between what is and what is to become, between developmental policies and the existing environment, between tradition and modernity. Its function is catalytic, for catalysis means causing or accelerating a desired reaction or generating a desired pattern of interaction and integration between two substantially alien or disharmonious factors for the purpose of producing a desired result or outcome. Catalysis produces an outcome that would not come about if the two disharmonious factors were left to interact indiscreetly according to their respective internal proclivities. It is also the process of engendering symbiosis, "reinforcing dualism,"[5] and affective pluralism, through which the society may be able to advance on the path of national development while preserving such autochthonic values as will constitute, together with necessary and desirable new values, the fabric of a new society. No society, however revolutionary it may appear, can be built upon a wholly new set of values and beliefs alone. The so-called civic culture that is the foundation of a stable yet dynamically evolving society draws its strength, as Almond and Verba suggest, from the indigenous basis of society and its nourishment from progressive ideas and values. It is only through such a merging of the traditional and the modern that a given society becomes dynamic and cosmopolitan but remains unique. It is the basic tradition that constitutes the essential psychic fabric of society by which its members are sewn together as a unique national, geographic, and cultural entity.[6]

It is thus that Aristotle two millenia ago counseled that "the sort of constitutional system which ought to be proposed is one which men can be easily induced and will be readily able to graft on to the system they already have."[7] During the height of flux and volatility of the Renaissance, Machiavelli warned would-be princes: "He who desires or attempts to reform the government of a state and wishes to have it accepted and capable of maintaining itself to the satisfaction of everybody, must at least retain the semblance of the old forms . . ."[8] The strikingly similar, essentially identical view of those two classic theorists were "rooted in a conviction that a viable polity could emerge only from its autochthonic foundation and that whatever new elements to be introduced should be rendered symbiotic with the existing condition and capability of society."[9] It is only through a proper and intelligent merger of certain basic tradition and modernity that political leadership of a new nation can hope to accomplish the difficult task of institutionalizing the new polity, engendering order and stability, regularizing necessary political processes and relationships, and at the same time promoting development and modernization. This, indeed, is the central task of the Aristotelian law-giver, the Machiavellian prince, and the twentieth-century nation-builder. The form of government in each society is appropriate, therefore, only if it conforms to this twin requirement. It should reflect both the cumulative experience, knowledge, and tradition of each particular society and the requirements of a modern state. No foreign nation can impose upon a developing society its own version of proper government, however normatively plausible, with the expectation of continuity and permanence.

The central hypothesis of this inquiry has been that the role of political leadership is most crucial—in fact, that political leadership is the arbiter of, rather than one participant or factor among many in, the process of national development. The extent to which this hypothesis has been discussed in the preceding pages may well be inadequate, however exploratory the inquiry may have been. Nevertheless, the kind of perspective that the hypothesis tends to elicit calls for some cautionary remark. Any approach that shuns, however implicitly, normative considerations and instead stresses the central importance of manipulative criteria is likely to invite two types of unwarranted attention. One is the attack from normative ideologues that the approach is amoral and devoid of any ethical consideration (especially on matters of compensatory mobilization, among others). The other is the curious interest of unscrupulous seekers of power who are in constant search of ways and means which may help them in their quest for naked power. In a way, Machiavelli is the most famous theorist who was first caught in the middle of these two types of unwarranted notice, precisely because his approach to the study of politics eschewed the normative orientations of metaphysics and theology so characteristic of classical theory and instead focused explicitly on the manipulative dimension of politics. At any rate, the perspective that derives from the central hypothesis of this inquiry neither excludes ethical considerations nor adheres to the notion that the end justifies the means.

Throughout, one major assumption which justified the effort was the need to create a politically, socially, and economically integrated society with built-in capabilities for further growth, change, and adaptation. Such a vision, however hazy, is predicated upon the notion that man and society always seek a higher level of existential universe, an antithesis of the Hobbesian state of nature, the meaning of which is clear without being couched in the language of ethical pretension. Another major assumption underlying the inquiry in general and the consideration of the requirements for political leadership in particular is that violence is ultimately the mark of leadership incompetence, whether perpetrated by leadership itself or against it. Violence is the sign of ultimate decay: A society in which violence prevails is a corrupt society; a political leadership that has no other means but violence to stay in power is corrupt. The corollary to this consideration is the concern about the idea of legitimacy as the basis of societal stability. And this consideration transcends differences in forms of government or so-called political systems. Plato was perhaps the first major theorist clearly to recognize the nature of legitimacy and stability. He perceived the positive and indispensable relationship between the two and at the same time wisely discounted any fixed relationship between a particular form of government and stability. To him, good society was stable society, whatever the form of its government. Unstable society was a sick society, again whatever its political system.[10] The classical orientation in this sense, from Plato on, was essentially and invariably concerned about the substance of societal life rather than about the forms and procedures of government. The rule by many, therefore, might be good or it might be bad, depending upon what it would and could do for society. Likewise with the rule of few or one.

In recent times, there has been a rather callous confusion of form and substance; or, to put it differently, substance has been regarded as naturally inherent in particular form. This, as has become increasingly apparent, is patently not the case. What Huntington calls "political decay" results precisely because of the excessive importance attached to forms and procedures of government and the corresponding lack of concern about the substance of governance—a phenomenon that pervades not only developing nations but some of the more modern states as well. Good government is one that can govern—in the sense of providing peace, security, and minimal levels of material and psychic satisfaction to citizens and of making progressive efforts to solve existing and emergent political, social, and economic problems so as to promote harmony, justice, and equity. Conversely, a government, however plausible its form and structure, is bad if it cannot govern. Huntington argues:

The primary problem is not liberty but the creation of a legitimate public order. Men may, of course, have order without liberty, but they cannot have liberty without order. Authority has to exist before it can be limited, and it is authority that is in scarce supply in those modernizing countries where government is at the mercy of alienated intellectuals, rambunctious colonels, and rioting students.[11]

Here are the two interrelated aspects of legitimacy: the ability to govern, and public acceptance. In neither of these two aspects does legitimacy inhere in any form of government as such. The ability to govern, at the outset of any polity, inheres in the quality of political leadership and grows out of it; public acceptance is the result of the meaningful symbiosis of positive values of both tradition and modernity. These two dimensions of legitimacy are mutually complementary and reinforcing. They are ultimately inseparable. It is for this reason that the truly stable society retains its autochthonic identity, for such identity is the basis for the mutuality of interest and trust between government and governed, hence the genuinely viable stability and legitimacy.

In the final analysis, therefore, politics becomes educative and reformative of society, and political leadership determines the content and direction of such societal education and reform. Aristotle long ago contended that the regime of a society is only as good as its citizenry.

Perhaps this sage contention can be turned around: society is only as good as its political leadership succeeds in educating and reforming it. Herein lies the essence of political leadership and statecraft.

NOTES

1. Karl Von Vorys, "Use and Misuse of Development Theory," in James C. Charlesworth (ed.), *Contemporary Political Analysis* (New York: Free Press of Glencoe, 1967), pp. 353-355.
2. From Sékou Touré, *Guinean Revolution and Social Progress*, as reprinted in Irving Leonard Markovitz (ed.), *African Politics and Society* (New York: Free Press, 1970), p. 218.
3. One of the earlier and more cogent authors in this regard is Karl de Schweinitz, "Economic Growth, Coercion and Freedom," *World Politics*, IX (January 1957), which he later expanded in *Industrialization and Democracy* (New York: Free Press of Glencoe, 1964).
4. Samuel P. Huntington, *Political Order in Changing Societies* (New Haven: Yale University Press, 1969), p. 1.
5. For the concept of "reinforcing dualism," see Robert E. Ward, "Political Modernization and Political Culture in Japan," *World Politics*, XV (July 1963), and "Conclusion" in Ward and Dankwart Rustow (eds.), *Political Modernization of Japan and Turkey* (Princeton: Princeton University Press, 1964).
6. Thus "a country is likely to attain democracy not by copying the constitutional laws or parliamentary practices of some previous democracy, but rather by honestly facing up to its particular conflicts and by devising or adapting effective procedures for their accommodation." Dankwart A. Rustow, "Transition to Democracy: Toward a Dynamic Model," *Comparative Politics*, II (April 1970), 354.
7. Aristotle, *Politics* (London: Oxford University Press, 1950, trans. by Ernest Barker), Bk. IV, Chap. i, p. 7. See also Gunnar Myrdal, *Asian Drama: An Inquiry into the Poverty of Nations* (New York: Pantheon, 1968), Vol. I, pp. 16-20.
8. Niccolò Machiavelli, *The Discourses*, in a Modern Library edition of *The Prince and the Discourses* (New York, 1950), Bk. I, Chap. XXV, p. 182.
9. Taketsugu Tsurutani, "Machiavelli and the Problem of Political Development," *Review of Politics*, XXX (July 1968), 323.
10. See Plato, *The Republic* (London: Oxford University Press, 1962, trans. by F. M. Cornford), esp. Part IV (Bks. VIII-IX).
11. Huntington, *Political Order in Changing Societies*, pp. 7-8.

Selected Bibliography

Ake, Claude. *A Theory of Political Integration.* Homewood, Ill.: Dorsey Press, 1967.

Almond, Gabriel. "Comparative Political Systems," *Journal of Politics,* XVIII (August 1956).

Almond, Gabriel. "Political Development: Analytical and Normative Perspectives," *Comparative Political Studies,* I (January 1969).

Almond, Gabriel, and G. Bingham Powell, Jr. *Comparative Politics: A Developmental Approach.* Boston and Toronto: Little, Brown, 1966.

Almond, Gabriel, and Sidney Verba. *The Civic Culture: Political Attitudes and Democracy in Five Nations.* Boston and Toronto: Little, Brown, 1965.

Anderson, Charles W. *Politics and Economic Change in Latin America.* Princeton: Van Nostrand, 1967.

Anderson, Charles W., Fred R. von der Mehden, and Crawford Young. *Issues of Political Development.* Englewood Cliffs, N.J.: Prentice-Hall, 1967.

Apter, David E. *The Politics of Modernization.* Chicago: University of Chicago Press, 1965.

Apter, David E., ed. *Ideology and Discontent.* New York: Free Press, 1964.

Arendt, Hannah. *On Revolution.* New York: Viking, 1965.

Aristotle. *Politics.* London: Oxford University Press, 1950. Trans. by Ernest Barker.

Arora, Satish, and Harold Lasswell. *Political Communication: The Public Language of Political Elites in India and the United States.* New York: Holt, Rinehart and Winston, 1969.

Bachrach, Peter. *The Theory of Democratic Elitism: A Critique.* Boston and Toronto: Little, Brown, 1967.

Banks, Arthur S., and Robert B. Textor. *A Cross-Polity Survey.* Cambridge, Mass.: M.I.T. Press, 1963.

Bayley, David H. "The Effects of Corruption in a Developing Nation," *Western Political Quarterly,* XIX (December 1966).

Bendix, Rinehard. *Nation-Building and Citizenship: Studies in Our Changing Social Order.* New York: Wiley, 1964.

Bendix, Reinhard, ed. *State and Society: A Reader in Comparative Political Sociology.* Boston: Little, Brown, 1968.

182 Selected Bibliography

Bienen, Henry. *Violence and Modernization.* Chicago: University of Chicago Press, 1968.
Black, C. E. *The Dynamics of Modernization: A Study in Comparative History.* New York: Harper & Row, 1966.
Black, C. E., and T. P. Thornton. *Communism and Revolution: The Strategic Use of Political Violence.* Princeton: Princeton University Press, 1964.
Cassirer, Ernst. *Language and Myth.* New York: Dover, 1946. Trans. by Susanne K. Langer.
Charlesworth, James C., ed. *Contemporary Political Analysis.* New York: Free Press of Glencoe, 1967.
Christenson, Reo M., et al. *Ideologies and Modern Politics.* New York: Dodd, Mead, 1971.
Coleman, James S. "Political Money," *American Political Science Review*, LXIV (December 1970).
Collingwood, Robin G. *The Idea of History.* New York: Oxford University Press, 1967.
Conquest. Robert. *The Great Terror.* New York: Macmillan, 1968.
Coser, Lewis A. *The Functions of Social Conflict.* Glencoe, Ill.: Free Press, 1956.
Crozier, Brian. *The Masters of Power.* Boston and Toronto: Little, Brown, 1969.

Dahrendorf, Ralf. *Class and Class Conflict in Industrial Society.* Stanford: Stanford University Press, 1959.
DeGrazia, Sebastian. *The Political Community: A Study in Anomie.* Chicago: University of Chicago Press, 1948.
Dennis, Jack, et al. "Political Socialization to Democratic Orientations in Four Western Systems," *Comparative Political Studies*, I (April 1968).
de Schweinitz, Karl. "Economic Growth, Coercion and Freedom," *World Politics*, IX (January 1957).
de Schweinitz, Karl. *Industrialization and Democracy.* New York: Free Press of Glencoe, 1964.
Deutsch, Karl W. *The Nerves of Government.* New York: Free Press of Glencoe, 1963.
Deutsch, Karl W. "Social Mobilization and Political Development," *American Political Science Review*, LV (September 1961).
Deutsch, Karl W., and Lewis Edinger. *Germany Rejoins the Powers.* Stanford: Stanford University Press, 1959.
Deutsch, Karl W., et al. *Political Community and the North Atlantic Area.* Princeton: Princeton University Press, 1957.
Dowse, Robert E. "A Functionalist's Logic," *World Politics*, XVIII (July 1966).
Drucker, Peter. *The Age of Discontinuity* New York: Harper & Row, 1969.
Duff, Ernest A., and John F. McCamant. "Measuring Social and Political Requirements for System Stability in Latin America," *American Political Science Review*, LXII (December 1968).
Duverger, Maurice. *Political Parties.* New York: Wiley, 1963.

Easton, David. *A Framework for Political Analysis.* Englewood Cliffs, N.J.: Prentice-Hall, 1965.

Easton, David. *A Systems Analysis of Political Life.* New York: Wiley, 1965.
Easton, David, ed. *Varieties of Political Theory.* Englewood Cliffs, N.J.: Prentice-Hall, 1966.
Eckstein, Harry, ed. *Internal War.* New York: Free Press, 1964.
Edelman, Murray. *The Symbolic Uses of Politics.* Urbana: University of Illinois Press, 1964.
Edinger, Lewis J., ed. *Political Leadership in Industrialized Societies.* New York, London, and Sidney: Wiley, 1967.
Eisenstadt, S. N. *Modernization: Protest and Change.* Englewood Cliffs, N.J.: Prentice-Hall, 1966.
Eisenstadt, S. N. "Some Observations on the Dynamics of Transitions," *Comparative Studies in Society and History,* XI (October 1969).
Ellul, Jacques. *The Political Illusion.* New York: Knopf, 1967.
Emerson, Rupert. *From Empire to Nation.* Cambridge, Mass.: Harvard University Press, 1962.
Emerson, Rupert. "The Problem of Identity, Selfhood, and Image in the New Nations," *Comparative Politics,* I (April 1969).

Fagen, Richard R. *Politics and Communication.* Boston and Toronto: Little, Brown, 1966.
Feierabend, Ivo K., and Rosalind L. Feierabend. "Aggressive Behaviors within Polities 1948–1962: A Cross-National Study," *Journal of Conflict Resolution,* X (September 1966).
Feierabend, Ivo K., *et al.* "Correlates of Political Stability," a paper presented at the annual meeting of the American Political Science Association, September 3–7, 1963.
Field, G. Lowell. *Comparative Political Development: The Precedent of the West.* Ithaca: Cornell University Press, 1967.
Finkle, Jason L., and Richard W. Gable, eds. *Political Development and Social Change.* New York, London and Sidney: Wiley, 1966.
Frey, Frederick W. *The Turkish Political Elite.* Cambridge, Mass.: M.I.T. Press, 1965.
Friedrich, Carl J. *Man and His Government: An Empirical Theory of Politics.* New York: McGraw-Hill, 1963.

Gregor, A. James. "Political Science and the Uses of Functional Analysis," *American Political Science Review,* LXII (June 1968).
Gross, Llewelyn, ed. *Symposium on Sociological Theory.* Evanston: Northwestern University Press, 1959.
Groth, Alexander J. *Comparative Politics: A Distributive Approach.* New York: Macmillan, 1971.
Gurr, Ted. "A Causal Model of Civil Strife: A Comparative Analysis Using New Indices," *American Political Science Review,* LXII (December 1968).
Gurr, Ted, and Charles Ruttenberg. *The Conditions of Civil Violence: First tests of a Causal Model.* Research Monograph No. 28, Princeton University Center for International Studies, April 1967.
Guttsman, W. L. *The British Political Elite.* London: MacGibbon and Kee, 1963.

Halpern, Manfred. *The Politics of Social Change in the Middle East and North Africa*. Princeton: Princeton University Press, 1963.

Hapgood, David, ed. *Policies for Promoting Agricultural Development: Report on a Conference on Productivity and Innovation in Agriculture in the Developing Countries*. Massachusetts Institute of Technology Center for International Studies, January 1965.

Heilbroner, Robert L. *The Making of Economic Society*. Englewood Cliffs, N.J.: Prentice-Hall, 1962.

Hobsbawm, E. J. *Primitive Rebels*. New York: Norton, 1959.

Holt, Robert T., and John E. Turner. *The Political Basis of Economic Development: An Exploration in Comparative political Analysis*. Princeton: Van Nostrand, 1966.

Horowitz, Irving Louis. *Three Worlds of Development: The Theory and Practice of International Stratification*. New York: Oxford University Press, 1966.

Hunter, Guy. *Modernizing Peasant Societies*. New York and London: Oxford University Press, 1969.

Huntington, Samuel P. "The Change to Change: Modernization, Development, and Politics," *Comparative Politics*, III (April 1971).

Huntington, Samuel P. "Political Development and Political Decay," *World Politics*, XVII (April 1965).

Huntington, Samuel P. *Political Order in Changing Societies*. New Haven: Yale University Press, 1969.

Ilchman, Warren F., and Norman Thomas Uphoff. *The Political Economy of Change*. Berkeley and Los Angeles: University of California Press, 1969.

Illich, Ivan. "Outwitting the Developed Countries," *New York Review of Books*, November 6, 1969.

Inkeles, Alex. "Participant Citizenship in Six Developing Countries," *American Political Science Review*, LXIII (December 1969).

Jennings, Eugene E. *An Anatomy of Leadership*, New York: Harper & Row, 1960.

Johnson, Chalmers. *Revolutionary Change*. Boston and Toronto: Little, Brown, 1966.

Johnson, John J., ed. *The Role of the Military in Underdeveloped Countries*. Princeton: Princeton University Press, 1963.

Jouvenel, Bertrand de. *Sovereignty: An Inquiry into the Political Good*. Chicago: University of Chicago Press, 1957.

Kaplan, Abraham. *The Conduct of Inquiry*. Scranton: Chandler, 1964.

Kautsky, John H., ed. *Political Change in Underdeveloped Countries*. New York and London: Wiley, 1962.

Klausner, Samuel Z., ed. *The Study of Total Societies*. Garden City, N.Y.: Doubleday, 1967.

Kuznets, Simon. "Quantitative Aspects of the Economic Growth of Nations: Distribution of Income by Size," *Economic Development and Cultural Change*, IX (January 1963).

Lacouture, Jean. *The Demigods: Charismatic Leadership in the Third World.* New York: Knopf, 1970.
Lane, Robert. *Political Life.* Glencoe, Ill.: Free Press, 1959.
Langton, Kenneth P. *Political Socialization.* New York: Oxford University Press, 1969.
LaPalombara, Joseph, ed. *Bureaucracy and Political Development.* Princeton: Princeton University Press, 1963.
Lasswell, Harold, and Abraham Kaplan. *Power and Society.* New Haven: Yale University Press, 1950.
Lasswell, Harold, Nathan Leites, and Associates. *Language of Politics.* New York: Steward, 1949.
Lasswell, Harold, Daniel Lerner, and Easton Rothwell. *The Comparative Study of Elites.* Standord: Stanford University Press, 1952.
Lasswell, Harold, and Daniel Lerner, eds. *World Revolutionary Elites: Studies in Coercive Ideological Movements.* Cambridge, Mass.: M.I.T. Press, 1965.
Leiden, Carl, and Karl Schmitt. *The Politics of Violence: Revolution in the Modern World.* Englewood Cliffs, N.J.: Prentice-Hall, 1968.
Lerner, Daniel. *The Passing of Traditional Society.* Glencoe, Ill.: Free Press, 1958.
Leys, Collin, ed. *Politics and Change in Developing Countries.* London: Cambridge University Press, 1969.
Lipset, Seymour Martin. *The First New Nation: The United States in Historical and Comparative Perspective.* New York: Basic Books, 1963.
Lipset, Seymour Martin. *Political Man: The Social Bases of Politics.* Garden City, N.Y.: Doubleday, 1963.
Lockwood, William W. "Japan's Response to the West: The Contrast with China." *World Politics,* IX (July 1959).

McClosky, Herbert A. "Consensus and Ideology in American Politics," *American Political Science Review,* LVIII (September 1964).
Machiavelli Niccolò. *The Prince and the Discourses.* New York: Modern Library, 1950.
McCord, William. *The Springtime of Freedom.* New York: Oxford University Press, 1964.
McKenzie, Robert T. *British Political Parties.* New York: Praeger, 1962.
Mannheim, Karl. *Ideology and Utopia.* New York: Harcourt Brace Jovanovich, 1954.
Markovitz, Irving Leonard, ed. *African Politics and Society.* New York: Free Press, 1970.
Marvick, Dwaine, ed. *Political Decision-Makers.* Glencoe, Ill.: Free Press, 1961.
Merelman, Richard M. "Learning and Legitimacy," *American Political Science Review,* LX (September 1966).
Merkl, Peter H. *Political Continuity and Change.* New York: Harper & Row, 1967.
Merriam, Charles E. *Systematic Politics.* Chicago: University of Chicago Press, 1945.
Millikan, Max F., and Donald L. M. Blackmer. *The Emerging Nations.* Boston and Toronto: Little, Brown, 1961.

Moore, Barrington, Jr. *Political Power and Social Theory.* New York: Harper & Row, 1965.
Morse, Chandler, et al. *Modernization by Design: Social Change in the Twentieth Century.* Ithaca and London: Cornell University Press, 1969.
Mosca, Gaetano. *The Ruling Class.* New York: McGraw-Hill, 1939.
Myrdal, Gunnar. *Asian Drama: An Inquiry into the Poverty of Nations.* New York: Pantheon, 1968. 3 vols.

Needler, Martin. *Political Development in Latin America: Instability, Violence, and Evolutionary Change.* New York: Random House, 1968.
Needler, Martin. "Political Development and Socioeconomic Development: The Case of Latin America," *American Political Science Review,* LXII (September 1968).
Nesvold, Betty A. "Scalogram Analysis of Political Violence," *Comparative Political Studies,* II (July 1969).
Nettl, J. P. *Political Mobilization: A Sociological Analysis of Methods and Concepts.* New York: Basic Books, 1967.
Nettl, J. P., and Roland Robertson. *International Systems and the Modernization of Societies: The Formation of National Goals and Attitudes.* New York: Basic Books, 1968.
Nieburg, H. L. *Political Violence: The Behavioral Process.* New York: St. Martin's, 1969.
Nisbet, Robert A. *Social Change and History.* London and New York: Oxford University Press, 1969.
Nordlinger, Eric A. "Political Development: Time Sequences and Rates of Change," *World Politics,* XX (April 1968).
Nordlinger, Eric A. "Soldiers in Mufti: The Impact of Military Rule Upon Economic and Social Change in the Non-Western States," *American Political Science Review,* LXIV (December 1970).
North, Robert C. *Kuomintang and Chinese Communist Elites.* Stanford: Stanford University Press, 1952.
Nove, Alec. *An Economic History of the U.S.S.R.* London: Penguin, 1969.
Nye, J. S. "Corruption and Political Development: A Cost-Benefit Analysis," *American Political Science Review* LXI (June 1967).

Ojha, P. D., and V. V. Bhatt, "Patterns of Income Distribution in an Underdeveloped Economy: A Case Study of India," *American Economic Review,* LIV (September 1964).
Oksenberg, Michel C. "Policy Making Under Mao Tse-tung, 1949–1968," *Comparative Politics,* III (April 1971).
Olson, Mancur, Jr. *The Logic of Collective Action: Public Goods and the Theory of Groups.* Cambridge Mass.: Harvard University Press, 1965.
Organski, A. F. K. *The Stages of Political Development.* New York: Knopf, 1965.
Oshima, Harry T. "The International Comparison of Size Distribution of Family Incomes with Special Reference to Asia," *Review of Economics and Statistics,* XLIV (November 1962).

Park, Richard L., and Irene Tinker. *Leadership and Political Institutions in India.* Princeton University Press, 1959.
Parsons, Talcott. *The Social System.* New York: Free Press of Glencoe, 1963.
Pennock, J. Roland. "Political Development, Political Systems, and Political Goods," *World Politics,* XVIII (April 1966).
Pennock, J. Roland, ed. *Self-Government in the Modernizing Nations.* Englewood Cliffs, N.J.: Prentice-Hall, 1964.
Perlmutter, Amos. "The Praetorian State and the Praetorian Army," *Comparative Politics,* I (April 1969).
Plato. *The Republic.* London: Oxford University Press, 1962. Trans. by F. M. Cornford.
Pye, Lucian W. *Aspects of Political Development.* Boston and Toronto: Little, Brown, 1966.
Pye, Lucian W. *Politics, Personality, and Nation Building.* New Haven: Yale University Press, 1962.
Pye, Lucian W., ed. *Communication and Political Development.* Princeton: Princeton University Press, 1963.
Pye, Lucian W., and Sidney Verba, eds. *Political Culture and Political Development.* Princeton: Princeton University Press, 1965.

Quandt, William B. *The Comparative Study of Political Elites.* A Sage Professional Paper, Comparative Politics Series No. 01-004, Vol. I, 1970.

Riggs, Fred. "The Dialectics of Developmental Conflict," *Comparative Political Studies,* I (July 1968).
Rokkan, Stein. *Citizens, Elections and Parties.* New York: McKay, 1970.
Rostow, W. W. *The Stages of Economic Growth: A Non-Communist Manifesto* London: Cambridge University Press, 1963.
Rousseau, Jean-Jacques. *The Social Contract.* Edition used is New York: Hafner, 1965.
Rudner, Richard. *Philosophy of Social Science.* Englewood Cliffs, N.J.: Prentice-Hall, 1966.
Rudolph, Lloyd I., and Suzanne H. Rudolph. *The Modernity of Tradition.* Chicago: University of Chicago Press, 1967.
Russett, Bruce, *et al. World Handbook of Political and Social Indicators.* New Haven and London: Yale University Press, 1964.
Rustow, Dankwart A. "Transition to Democracy: Toward a Dynamic Model," *Comparative Politics,* II (April 1970).
Rustow, Dankwart A. *A World of Nations.* Washington: Brookings Institution, 1967.

Sartori, Giovanni. "Politics, Ideology, and Belief Systems," *American Political Science Review,* LXIII (June 1969).
Scalapino, Robert A., and Junnosuke Masumi. *Parties and Politics in Contemporary Japan.* Berkeley and Los Angeles: University of California Press, 1962.
Scott, Roger, ed. *The Politics of New States.* London: George Allen & Unwin, 1970.
Seligman, Lester G. *Leadership in a New Nation.* New York: Atherton, 1964.
Sereno, Renzo. *The Rulers.* New York: Praeger, 1962.

Sigmund, Paul, Jr. *The Ideologies of the Developing Nations.* New York and London: Praeger, 1963.
Silberman, Bernard. *Ministers of Modernization.* Tucson: University of Arizona Press, 1964.
Silvert, K. H., ed. *Expectant People: Nationalism and Development.* New York: Vintage Books, 1967.
Simon, Herbert. *Administrative Behavior.* New York: Macmillan, 1947.
Singer, Marshall R. *The Emerging Elite: A Study of Political Leadership in Ceylon.* Cambridge, Mass. M.I.T. Press, 1964.
Smelser, Neil, and S. M. Lipset, eds. *Social Structure and Mobility in Economic Development.* Chicago: Aldine, 1966.

Townsend, James R. *Political Participation in Communist China.* Berkeley and Los Angeles: University of California Press, 1969.
Tsurutani, Taketsugu. "Machiavelli and the Problem of Political Development," *Review of Politics,* XXX (July 1968).
Tsurutani, Taketsugu. "Stability and Instability: A Note in Comparative Political Analysis," *Journal of Politics,* XXX (November 1968).

Ward, Robert E. "Political Modernization and Political Culture in Japan," *World Politics,* XV (July 1963).
Ward, Robert E., ed. *Political Development in Modern Japan.* Princeton: Princeton University Press, 1968.
Ward, Robert E., and Dankwart Rustow, eds. *Political Modernization of Japan and Turkey.* Princeton: Princeton University Press, 1964.
Weldon, T. D. *The Vocabulary of Politics.* Baltimore: Penguin Books, 1960.
Whitaker, C. S. "A Dysrhythmic Process of Political Change," *World Politics,* XIX (January 1967).
Willhoite, Fred H., Jr. "Political Order and Consensus: A Continuing Problem," *Western Political Quarterly,* XVII (June 1963).
Willner, Ann Ruth. *Charismatic Political Leadership: A Theory.* Research Monograph No. 32, Princeton University Center for International Studies, 1968.
Wolf, Eric R. *Peasant Wars of the Twentieth Century.* New York, Evanston, and London: Harper & Row, 1969.
Wolin, Sheldon. *Politics and Vision.* Boston: Little, Brown, 1961.
Wriggins, W. Howard. *The Ruler's Imperative: Strategies for Political Survival in Asia and Africa.* New York: Columbia University Press, 1969.

Index

A

Ability to govern, 179
Adaptability, 18f., 25
  of social classes, 163, 170
Adaptation, 117
Affect, 40ff., 77, 132, 141
  disruption in, 134
  modernity in, 132f.
  pluralistic development of, 120, 131–140, 141ff., 176
  traditional orientation of, 133f.
Affective pluralism, *see* Affect, pluralistic development of
Afghanistan, 126
Agricultural modernization, 162f., 165
Algeria, 126
Almond, Gabriel, 34, 37, 38ff., 46, 136, 176
Apter, David, 118
Aramburu, Gen. Pedro, 88
Arendt, Hannah, 94
Argentina, 87–91
Aristotle, 74, 141, 177, 179
Attenuated modernizing leadership, 96f.
Ayub Khan, Mohammed, 97f., 119

B

Banks, Arthur, and Robert Textor, 47ff.
Behavior, group, human, and institutional, 14ff., 44f., 76

Brazil, 98
Brzezinski, Zbygniew, 8

C

Canada, 57
Catalysis, 176
Categories of analysis, 37ff.
Change, 6, 8, 32, 35f., 77, 94, 116f., 148
  anticipation and manipulation of, 109ff.
  control of, 15ff., 21f., 107ff., 112
  in values and behavior patterns, 14ff., 45, 131f.
Charisma, 42, 118
  dangers of, 149f., 155, 158f.
  function of, 133ff., 148
  organizational, 118ff., 135f.
  personal, 118ff., 133ff.
  use of, 118ff., 133ff., 148
China, 96, 119f., 121ff., 126, 135f., 139, 168f.
Choice, xii, 8, 20
Churchill, Winston, xii
Commitment to modernization, as leadership requirement, 92f.
  measurement of, 101ff.
Compensatory mobilization, 113
  dangers of, 148–170
  meaning of, 115, 117f., 130
  and national development, 157ff.
  need for, 165–170, 176
  short-run versus long-run problems of, 154ff., 159

Compensatory mobilization contd.
  strategy of, 115-143
  types of, 118-130
Conflict, 1, 5ff., 16f.
  two kinds of, 169f.
Congo (Kinshasa), 97, 100
Control, 8, 11, 26f., 175
  of behavior, 40-52
  of change, *see* Change, control of
Coser, Lewis, 169
Crisis, 118
  dangers in use of, 150f.
  external, 120f.
  internal, 121f.
  as predicament of developing nations, 175
Crude modernizing leadership, 97f.
Cuba, 72, 96, 99, 126
Curative policies, 116f., 118, 166
  meaning of, 117
  negative impact of, *see* Differential impact

D

Demand, 45, 62, 71, 74, 109ff., 123
Democracy, 9f., 137f., 173f.
Denmark, 57
Dennis, Jack, 46
Deutsch, Karl, 44, 116
Developmental decision-making, areas of, 103
Developmental dimension and developmental spectrum, 131
Differential impact, 160-165
  mediation of, 164f., 169f.
Distribution, 61ff. (*see also* Governmental capability, distributive)
  direct versus indirect, 61
  material versus nonmaterial, 61f.
  ultimate capability of, 63
Dominance, as leadership requirement, 94ff., 125ff.
  measurement of, 105f.
  ways to achieve, 95
Dominican Republic, 99f.
Duff, Ernest and John McCamant, 73

E

Easton, David, 135
Education, 58ff.
  distribution of, 60f.
Effective modernizing leadership, 96, 175
Egypt, 26, 99f., 126
Ethics, consideration of, 175-180
Ethiopia, 75, 99
Expectations, 3ff., 73f., 77, 109ff., 123f.
Extortionist leadership, 99f.

F

Fagen, Richard, 159
France, 100, 125f., 135
Frondizi, Arturo, 88ff.
Functionalist approach, comments on, 34ff.

G

Gandhi, Indira, 119
Germany, 122, 135
Ghana, 156
Golding, William, 136
Goulart, Joao, 98
Governance, form versus substance of, 178f.
Governmental capability, 17, 37-44, 73f., 76f., 83, 87, 118f., 130, 166
  demonstrated level versus routinized level of, 82-87, 100f., 110f.
  distributive, 38, 61-70, 71ff. (*see also* Distribution)
    measurement of, 62-70
  extractive, 37ff., 52-61, 70
    measurement of, 55-61
  fluctuation in, 82f., 85ff.
  internal relationship of, 70-75
  responsive, 37ff., 110
  routinization of, 75ff., 87
  substitutability of, 74f.
Governmental revenue, 55ff.
Great Britain, 26

Great Proletarian Cultural Revolution, 120
Guatemala, 97
Guinea, 173

H

Haiti, 75, 99
Halpern, Manfred, 149
Holt, Robert, and John Turner, 35
Horowitz, Irving L., 20
Hukbalahap, 50
Humanization, 4
Hungary, 50
Huntington, Samuel P., 6, 174, 179

I

Ideology, 8f., 118
  danger of, 152, 155f.
  function of, 123f.
  and myth, 123ff.
Illia, Arturo, 91
Income distribution, 64f., 74
India, 97, 119, 149, 168f.
Indonesia, 121f., 156
Inkeles, Alex, 46
Institutionalization, 5f., 18f., 22, 25, 75ff., 82f., 93f., 111, 148ff., 167, 174, 177
  meaning of, 82, 94
Integrability of social classes, 164, 170
Integration of the traditional ruling class, 126ff.
Intelligence and skill, as leadership requirement, 93f., 95
  measurement of, 103ff.
Iran, 96f., 100f.
Italy, 100

J

Japan, xiiif., 91f., 96, 99, 127f., 130, 142f., 152f., 157ff.
Jennings, Eugene, 110
Jouvenel, Bertrand de, 22

K

Kautsky, John, 6f.

L

Lacouture, Jean, 136, 149
Land distribution, 71f.
Language in politics, 137f.
Leadership, *see* Political leadership
Leadership increment, 83ff., 119, 130
  meaning of, 83
Legitimacy, 27, 112f., 129, 138–144, 179
Lerner, Daniel, 132
Lewis, John W., 139
Liberia, 49, 99
Libya, 99
Lipset, S. M., 62, 135, 138f.
Liu Shao-ch'i, 168

M

McClosky, Herbert, 46
Machiavelli, 3, 11f., 75f., 94, 148, 166, 177f.
Mao Tse-tung, 120, 139, 168
Matossian, Mary, 22
Menderes, Adnan, 98
Merelman, Richard, 153
Mexico, 96, 136
Mobility, 117
Mobilizability of social classes, 164
Modernization (*see also* National development), commitment to, 102
  pace of, 107
Modernization index, 107, 109
Morocco, 100
Mutuality of interest, 140ff.
Myrdal, Gunnar, 92, 97, 149, 169, 174

N

National development, xiiif.
  conditions for, 115f., 117f.
  goal of, 5f., 9ff., 12, 178

National development contd.
  meaning of, 3ff., 17–21, 32, 131, 174, 176
  measurement of, 106ff.
  pace of, 101, 107, 110, 165–170
  politics of, 2f., 5–9, 11f., 22
  process of, 6, 12–19, 76f., 115f., 157ff., 174f.
  requirements of, 13–16
  resistance to, 9–17, 20
Needler, Martin, 77
Nehru, Jawaharlal, 119, 149, 168
Nicaragua, 100
Nigeria, 99
Nkrumah, Kwame, 98, 156

O

Oksenberg, Michel, 139
Olson, Mancur, 9

P

Pakistan, 97f., 119
Palliative policies, 117f.
  purpose of, 117
  types of, 118
Panama, 57
Paraguay, 49, 72, 75, 99
Parsons, Talcott, 77
Perlmutter, Amos, 74
Peron, Juan, 88f.
Peronistas, 88ff.
Philippines, 50, 97, 99
Plato, 178f.
Pluralistic development of affect, 120, 131–140, 141f., 176
Political beliefs, 131
Political culture, 40f., 131f.
Political leadership, 6, 10f., 13, 19, 21–27, 32f., 41f., 70, 72ff., 82–113, 123ff., 130, 155ff., 163f., 173–180
  concept of, 24ff.
  goals of, 9ff.
  measurement of, 101–107
  requirements of, 91–96
  role of. xiiff., 26f., 33, 62f., 84, 93f., 110, 174f., 177

structure of, 26
studies of, 22ff.
typology of, 96–100
Politics, xii, 1f., 5ff., 39
  as leadership control, 21f.
  of national development, 2, 21ff., 17
  views of, 1f., 175
Portugal, 57, 72, 75
Poverty, 2ff.
  politicization of, 7
Powell, G. Bingham, 34, 37ff.
Predictability of behavior, 53, 76f., 111
Public health and education, expenditures on, 66–72

R

Rational behavior, 141
Regularization, *see* Institutionalization
Religion, 3
Renaissance, 3
Revolving-door leadership, 100
Rhee, Syngman, 98
Rhodesia, 99
Routinization, *see* Institutionalization
Rules and procedures, 6f.

S

Saudi Arabia, 26, 49, 99
Scapegoat and repression, 118
  use of, 122f.
  dangers in, 151f.
Selective bribery, 118, 125–129
  dangers of, 152f.
Seligman, Lester, 151
Sigmund, Paul, 123
Simon, Herbert, 25
Situational assets, 106, 167f., 176
Situational score, 106ff.
Situations, incompatibilities of, xii
Skill distribution, 161, 170
Sociocultural values, 14ff.
South Africa, the Union of, 99
South Vietnam, 100

Stability and instability, 32, 40, 51f., 62, 71–77, 83, 118f., 124, 129, 139, 148, 150, 163f., 167, 175, 178f.
Stable conservative leadership, 98f.
Stagnating leadership, 99
Sukarno, 121f., 156
Sun Yat-sen, 98
Symboisis of tradition and modernity, 176f., 179
Symbols, manipulation of, 42
Syria, 126

T

Taxation, 52, 56f., 70
Teacher-population ratio, 58
Teacher-pupil ratio, 59
Tension, 2ff., 16f.
Thailand, 99f.
Touré, Sékou, 173
Traditional ruling class, integration of, 126f.
 liquidation of, 125f.
Traditional symbols and values, 118
 dangers in use of, 153f.
 function of, 140
 use of, 129f., 136–140
Turkey, 48ff.

U

U.S.A., 75, 122, 128
U.S.S.R., 96, 104f., 122, 126
Unwarranted attention, two types of, 178

V

Venezuela, 57, 100f.
Verba, Sidney, 46, 136, 176
Violence, 47–52, 178
 group, 47ff.
 and instability, 51f.
 as sign of leadership failure, 105, 178
Visionary modernizing leadership, 98